DATA STRUCTURES THE FUN WAY

An Amusing Adventure with Coffee-Filled Examples

Jeremy Kubica

no starch press®

San Francisco

DATA STRUCTURES THE FUN WAY. Copyright © 2023 by Jeremy Kubica.

All rights reserved. No part of this work may be reproduced or transmitted in any form or by any means, electronic or mechanical, including photocopying, recording, or by any information storage or retrieval system, without the prior written permission of the copyright owner and the publisher.

Printed in the United States of America

Second printing

27 26 25 24 23   2 3 4 5 6

ISBN-13: 978-1-7185-0260-4 (print)
ISBN-13: 978-1-7185-0261-1 (ebook)

Publisher: William Pollock
Managing Editor: Jill Franklin
Production Manager: Rachel Monaghan
Production Editor: Katrina Horlbeck Olsen
Developmental Editors: Liz Chadwick and Abigail Schott-Rosenfield
Cover Illustrator: Gina Redman
Interior Design: Octopod Studios
Technical Reviewer: Daniel Zingaro
Copyeditor: Paula L. Fleming
Compositor: Jeff Wilson, Happenstance Type-O-Rama
Proofreader: Liz Wheeler

For information on distribution, bulk sales, corporate sales, or translations, please contact No Starch Press® directly at info@nostarch.com or:

No Starch Press, Inc.
245 8th Street, San Francisco, CA 94103
phone: 1.415.863.9900
www.nostarch.com

Library of Congress Control Number: 2022020565

No Starch Press and the No Starch Press logo are registered trademarks of No Starch Press, Inc. Other product and company names mentioned herein may be the trademarks of their respective owners. Rather than use a trademark symbol with every occurrence of a trademarked name, we are using the names only in an editorial fashion and to the benefit of the trademark owner, with no intention of infringement of the trademark.

The information in this book is distributed on an "As Is" basis, without warranty. While every precaution has been taken in the preparation of this work, neither the author nor No Starch Press, Inc. shall have any liability to any person or entity with respect to any loss or damage caused or alleged to be caused directly or indirectly by the information contained in it.

To Edith and Anthony

About the Author

Jeremy Kubica is an engineering director specializing in artificial intelligence and machine learning. He received a PhD in robotics from Carnegie Mellon University and a BS in computer science from Cornell University. He spent his graduate school years creating algorithms to detect killer asteroids (actually stopping them was, of course, left as "future work"). He is the author of multiple books designed to introduce people to computer science, including *Computational Fairy Tales* and *The CS Detective* (No Starch Press, 2016), as well as the Computational Fairy Tales blog.

About the Technical Reviewer

Dr. Daniel Zingaro is an associate teaching professor of computer science and award-winning teacher at the University of Toronto. His research focuses on understanding and enhancing student learning of computer science. He is the author of *Algorithmic Thinking* (No Starch Press, 2020), a no-nonsense, no-math guide to algorithms and data structures, and *Learn to Code by Solving Problems* (No Starch Press, 2021), a primer for learning Python and computational thinking.

BRIEF CONTENTS

CONTENTS IN DETAIL

4
STACKS AND QUEUES 43

5
BINARY SEARCH TREES 55

6
TRIES AND ADAPTING DATA STRUCTURES 75

7
PRIORITY QUEUES AND HEAPS 93

ACKNOWLEDGMENTS

I would like to start by thanking the whole team at No Starch Press who helped make this book a reality. A huge thank-you to Bill Pollock for starting this entire journey by suggesting I do a more technical follow-up to *The CS Detective*. Thank you to my amazing editors, Abigail Schott-Rosenfield and Liz Chadwick, for their excellent help, guidance, and suggestions. I would also like to thank Carlos Bueno, who originally pointed me to the team at No Starch.

Thank you to Daniel Zingaro for his thorough and insightful technical review. His work was vital in improving both the accuracy and understandability of the material.

A tremendous thanks goes out to all the people who provided valuable comments on earlier versions of this book: Bambi Brewer, Andrew Moore, Eleanor Rieffel, and Kit Stubbs, PhD. Their suggestions helped guide my approach and the direction of the book.

A deep thank-you to my family for their support. Thank you to Regan, Nathan, and Julie for their encouragement and patience.

INTRODUCTION

This is a book about computational thinking through the lens of *data structures*, constructs for organizing and storing data. It is more than a cookbook of handy data structures. Rather, it explores the thinking behind these structures and their fundamental impact on solving complex problems, using real-world analogies to make abstract computational concepts intuitive. The goal of this book is to provide new insights into how you can use preexisting structure within the data to your advantage or create new structures to efficiently solve problems.

Among other things, I discuss the differences between arrays and linked lists, the complexity and power of pointers, the effect of data structures on algorithmic behavior, the branching of tree-based data structures, mathematical mappings in hash tables, and the usefulness of randomization. In short, you'll learn to think about algorithms by investigating different ways to organize the data they process. You'll also apply these computational approaches to real-world problems, a surprising number of which focus on procuring a decent cup of coffee.

Understanding how data structures function is critical to using them effectively. Just as an experienced carpenter wouldn't pound screws into wood with a hammer or use sandpaper to cut a two-by-four in half, an experienced programmer needs to choose the right tools for every job. As we'll see repeatedly throughout the following chapters, every data structure comes with tradeoffs. Saws cut through wood more effectively than sandpaper but create coarse edges. There is no single data structure that is perfect for every possible use case, but this is what makes computer science and the development of algorithms so interesting. A good computer scientist must understand how different data structures behave in order to determine where they can be best used.

This book focuses on a few canonical data structures and uses them to explore fundamental themes in computational thinking. Each of these data structures is a useful exemplar of a more general class of data structures and of a conceptual approach. For example, B-trees demonstrate one approach to the problems of keeping search trees balanced and optimizing for expensive memory accesses. I discuss the tradeoffs between memory usage and accuracy with Bloom filters; the use of randomization with skip lists; and how to capture multidimensional structure with grids, quadtrees, or k-d trees. As such, this book is neither an introduction to programming, a comprehensive anthology of data structures, nor a full analysis of brewing coffee (although we will touch repeatedly on this important topic). Our goals are different—to develop mental tools that apply across a range of specific problems and programming languages.

Intended Audience

This book is for anyone who wants to learn more about the thinking behind the data structures that lie at the heart of computer science. I assume such basic familiarity with programming as can be expected after taking an introductory course, participating in a boot camp, or working through a beginners' programming book. Readers should be familiar with fundamental programming concepts such as variables, loops, and conditional statements. Some more adventurous readers might even have coded up some of the data structures or algorithms in this book already or might do so as they read through it. However, you won't need to know the specific details of particular programming languages or algorithms.

I hope this book appeals to a wide range of audiences. Practitioners who have learned basic programming from an introductory course will find an introduction to computational thinking that can provide a foundation for future investigation. Students will find a new way to understand particularly difficult or tricky topics. Mathematicians will learn new names and jargon for ideas they've used since well before computer science existed. And experienced computer scientists will find amusing new analogies to explain concepts they use every day.

Language-Agnostic

This book is designed to apply to a wide range of programming languages. While this might come as a disappointment to the more opinionated readers who want to either (a) see their favorite language featured throughout these pages or (b) argue about the author's terrible language preferences and how they must reflect suboptimal life choices (since programming languages, like sports teams, are always a topic for heated debate), the concepts presented in the book are generally applicable across a range of languages. You can implement a binary search tree in almost any language, for instance. In fact, most programming languages already include many of these basic data structures as part of their core language or a standard library.

The book uses pseudocode examples that are largely based on Python's general syntax, since Python is a widely used and easily readable programming language. I denote code blocks via indentation, use standard equality notation (== for equal and != for not equal), use True and False to indicate Boolean values, denote comments with lines starting with the # symbol, and pass composite data structures as references. Arrays are zero indexed, and the value at index i is referenced as arr[i].

However, I also deviate from the Python syntax wherever this aids readability. I specify all variables as Type: Name to make the types explicit, and I use the value null to indicate a null pointer. I often use WHILE loops over FOR loops or other compact forms to clearly show how the loop is iterating and its termination condition.

I've intentionally kept the examples in this book simple in order to focus on the computational ideas behind them. This means that individual implementations may not be fully optimized and will often be more verbose than strictly necessary. Throughout the text, I break out different conditions to illustrate the thought process behind the approach. At times the implementations vary from programming best practices in order to structure the code in a way that matches the explanation. In addition, to keep the examples simple, I often leave out the basic validity checks that are vital to include in production programs, such as checking that our array access is inbounds. Needless to say, treat these examples only as illustrations of the concepts at hand, rather than using them verbatim in your own projects. This is a good rule in general: never treat pseudocode as a full implementation. Always incorporate the relevant testing, validity checks, and other best practices when implementing algorithms yourself.

On Analogies and Brewing Coffee

This book makes extensive use of metaphor and analogy, illustrating complex technical concepts by comparison to (sometimes absurd) real-world scenarios. Similes are scattered through this book like blueberries through a muffin. Each chapter explains the intricate working of data structures and algorithms with examples ranging from organizing your kitchen to determining whether you've ever tried a specific brew of coffee, inviting you to consider how these computational concepts work in a different way from computer code.

The examples will often bend the rules of reality, be oversimplified, or border on the ridiculous. For example, we repeatedly consider the question of storing and sorting extensive coffee collections, ignoring the tragic fact that coffee does go stale. While that means this book is not a strictly realistic guide to making the ultimate cup of coffee, the absurd analogies keep things fun and should encourage you to think outside your normal approaches. Simplifying the analogies allows us to focus on just those aspects that are critical to the computational concept. For example, when discussing the use of nearest-neighbor search to find a close cup of coffee, I focus on distances (the core computational concept) and neglect such complicating factors as fences or rivers. My goal is to tailor the analogy to the core of the problem.

I use analogies to augment formal descriptions and precise code. Personally, I find it easier to break free from technicalities and minutiae when viewing a data structure's operation in an active, narrative context with people (or even overcaffeinated squirrels) interacting with physical objects, rather than sticking to the vocabulary of FOR loops and variable counters. Visualizing a frantic chase through a maze of alleyways provides a different perspective of a graph algorithm from the formal context of iterating over abstract nodes and edges. I encourage readers to map these analogies to their own broad range of concepts, whether part of their daily life or fancies of the absurd.

How to Use This Book

The book is structured progressively. That is, while each chapter focuses on a different computational concept—either a data structure or motivating problem—each also builds upon the previous chapters. Most of the later chapters, for example, rely on the discussion of memory-linked data structures and the use of pointers introduced in Chapter 3. We return to the basic binary search tree structure introduced in Chapter 5 again and again as we examine variations of branching data structures. Thus, I recommend that you approach the chapters in order.

As we explore different data structures and how they apply to various problems, we will see consistent themes appear, including:

- The impact of the data's structure on algorithms accessing it
- How to think about performance in the worst case
- The importance of allowing for dynamic changes in your data set and how to efficiently enable these changes
- Tradeoffs among memory, runtime, code complexity, and accuracy
- How we may need to tune data structures for the problem and what tradeoffs to consider
- How we can adapt data structures to tackle new problems

These themes provide both a framework for thinking about the data structures and a set of questions to ask when facing a new problem. A critical aspect of choosing the data structure is understanding why it performs the way it does and how it will apply to new data.

Most of all, the two questions that you should keep in mind throughout the book are "How?" and "Why?" *How* does a given data structure enable a computation? *How* do we structure the data to maximize efficiency in a given context? *Why* does a given structure enable these computations? *How* does this data structure break down in a different context? *Why* is the author using that ridiculous analogy? *Why* is the author so obsessed with coffee? Understanding the answers to these questions (other than the last one) will provide the foundation you need to effectively use already-existing data structures and develop novel techniques in the future.

1

INFORMATION IN MEMORY

Any remotely interesting computer program needs to be able to store and access data from memory. This data might be the text in a document, the information on a web page, or the details of every variety of coffee we've ever sampled stored within a database. In each case, the data is fundamental to the program performing its intended function.

These examples only represent the data that users see and think about. The program must also track numerous pieces of data behind the scenes, such as how many times we have passed through a loop, the current location of our character in a game, or the current system time. Without this data, a program can't represent changes to its internal state.

In this chapter, we examine the very basics of storing data in memory. We'll look at how the simplest data structures—plain old variables, composite data structures, and arrays—store their data. We'll also introduce the book's pseudocode conventions. For readers who have experience programming, this chapter's key concepts might already be familiar. Even so, they're a critical starting point for our journey and worth a review since they provide the foundations to build more powerful and exciting data structures.

Variables

Individual pieces of data are often stored in *variables*, which are essentially names representing the location (or *address*) of a piece of data in the computer's memory. Readers with even a passing exposure to programming will already be familiar with variables: they are a foundational concept in computer science, necessary for even the simplest programs. Variables enable programs to track information that changes throughout the course of the program. Need to count how many times you have passed through a FOR loop? Track the player's score in a game? Count how many spelling errors you've made while writing an introductory chapter about variables? Use a variable.

Without variables, a programmer can't track, evaluate, or update the program's internal state. When you create a variable, the system allocates and assigns it a location behind the scenes. You are then free to write data to that location using a variable name of your choice and look it up using the same name. As long as you know the variable's name, you don't need to know the memory location of the data. We can visualize the computer's memory as a long column of bins. Each variable occupies one or more contiguous bins, depending on the size of the variable, as shown in Figure 1-1 for three variables: Level, Score, and AveScore. In this illustration, the average score (AveScore) is a floating-point number (a number with a decimal) that uses two bins of memory.

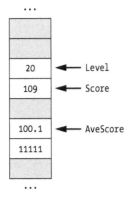

Figure 1-1: Computer memory
depicted as a column of bins

In some ways, variables are like the little paper labels on file folders, like the ones in Figure 1-2: once we have attached the label, we don't need to remember the folders' order or exactly how we stored them. We just look up the folder by its label—but this means that it's important to use informative names. The author's own filing cabinet is crammed full of overloaded folders with names such as *Stuff*, *Misc*, *Important*, and *Other Stuff*, making it difficult to know what is stored inside. Likewise, vague variable names make it hard to guess what values they represent.

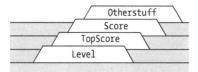

Figure 1-2: Variables, like the labels on file folders, provide a convenient way to find and access your stored values.

In many programming languages, variables have an associated type that denotes exactly what type of data they store, such as integers, "floats" for floating-point values, or Booleans for true or false values. These types tell the program how much memory the variable occupies and how to use it. A Boolean variable, for example, stores a limited range of values and often requires only a small amount of memory. A double-precision floating-point number might store a much larger and more precise number and so would use multiple bins. The syntax of defining types, and even whether types need to be explicitly defined, varies among programming languages.

Throughout this book, we will use the language-independent <type>: <name> pseudocode format to specify our variables in examples. For example:

```
Integer: coffee_count = 5
Float: percentage_words_spelled_correctly = 21.0
Boolean: had_enough_coffee = False
```

Sometimes a variable will be of the general type Type to indicate that it could take on a range of types depending on the implementation. We'll operate on the variables using syntax typical of most programming languages, including the use of = for assignment:

```
coffee_count = coffee_count + 1
```

For numeric types, including integers and floats, we'll use standard arithmetic operations, such as +, -, *, and /. For Boolean data types, we'll use Boolean operations, such as AND, OR, and NOT. The syntax you'll need to use in your programs will vary depending on your programming language (and is a common focal point in fights over the relative merits of different languages).

Composite Data Structures

Many programming languages provide the ability to create *composite data structures*, such as a struct or an object, which gather multiple individual variables into a single group. Composite data structures provide an easy way to gather related pieces of data and pass them around together. For example, we might define a CoffeeRecord to track some information about the kinds of coffees we have sampled:

```
CoffeeRecord {
    String: Name
    String: Brand
    Integer: Rating
    Float: Cost_Per_Pound
    Boolean: Is_Dark_Roast
    String: Other_Notes
}
```

Instead of maintaining six individual variables to track a coffee's properties, we store all of that information in a single composite data structure, CoffeeRecord. Of course, a true coffee connoisseur would likely track a few hundred additional properties, as well as exact information about the date, time, location, and weather conditions related to the coffee consumption. Coffee is, after all, a complex subject and deserves thorough documentation. Each additional property further underscores the importance of using a composite data structure: the alternative of passing around hundreds of related variables not only is tedious but also increases the probability that the programmer will make a mistake, such as passing variables to a function in the wrong order.

Business cards provide a real-world example of composite data structures. Each individual card is a packet of data containing multiple pieces of information such as your name, phone number, and email address. Bundling this information into a single card increases the efficiency of tracking it and passing it around. Imagine the mess and confusion of handing a colleague five different scraps of paper, each containing a single datapoint.

In many programming languages, including Java and Python, data composites can take the form of *objects*, which contain both the data and functions for operating on their own data. The object's functions use special syntax to access that object's data, such as the self reference in Python. An object can also provide different visibility rules that specify whether its internal data is publicly accessible outside the object's own functions or only privately accessible.

In an attempt to be general, we will treat composite data structures in their most general form: as a collection of data. While example code snippets in this book and elsewhere may implement the composite data structures as objects, the algorithms can be adapted to use non-object representations as well. In code that uses composite data structures or objects, we use the syntax of *composite.field* to indicate accessing a particular field of a composite data structure. For example, using the following:

```
latest_record.name = "Sublime Blend"
```

we set the name field of the record latest_record in our coffee log to have the value Sublime Blend.

Arrays

An *array* is generally used to store multiple related values. For example, we might want to track the amount of coffee consumed daily over a year. We could brute-force the storage by creating 365 individual variables, such as AmountDay1, AmountDay2, AmountDay3, and so forth, but this is tedious to type and doesn't allow us to use any structure for the data. AmountDay2 is only a textual tag, so the program doesn't know that AmountDay1 stores information for the day before and AmountDay3 for the day after; only the programmer knows this.

Arrays provide a simple mechanism for storing multiple values in adjacent and indexable bins. An array is effectively a row of variables—a contiguous block of equal-sized bins in the computer's memory, as in Figure 1-3. Like individual variables, arrays occupy a chunk of memory and can sit adjacent to arbitrary other information. Each of the array's bins can store a value of the given type, such as a number, a character, pointer, or even other (fixed-size) data structures.

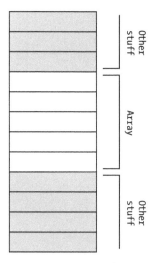

Figure 1-3: Arrays as bins in the computer's memory

Arrays appear throughout our real-world daily lives as well. The row of lockers lining a high school hallway, for example, is a physical array for storing students' coats and books. We can access any individual storage container by just opening the corresponding locker.

The structure of an array allows you to access any value, also known as an *element*, within the array by specifying its location, or *index*. The bins occupy adjacent locations in the computer's memory, so we can access individual bins by computing their offset from the first element and reading the memory in that location. This requires just a single addition and memory lookup regardless of which bin we access. This structure makes arrays especially convenient for storing items that have an ordered relationship, such as our daily coffee intake tracker.

Formally, we reference the value at index i of array A as A[i]. In our locker example, the index would be the number displayed on the front of the locker. Most programming languages use *zero-indexed arrays*, which means the first value of the array resides at index 0, the second at index 1, and so forth, as shown in Figure 1-4.

Value:	3	14	1	5	9	26	5	3	5
Index:	0	1	2	3	4	5	6	7	8

Figure 1-4: A zero-indexed array

We will use zero-indexed arrays throughout this book, to stick to general computing convention. Figure 1-5 represents how zero-indexed arrays appear in the computer's memory, where the white spaces are the elements of the array.

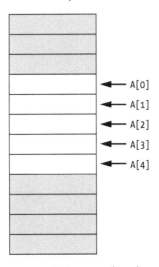

Figure 1-5: A zero-indexed array arranged in computer memory

Zero-indexing conveniently allows us to compute an element's location in memory as an offset from where the array starts in memory. The location of the *i*th item in the array can be computed by:

$$Location(item\ i) = Location(start\ of\ array) + Size\ of\ each\ element \times i$$

The location of the element at index zero is the start of the array. For example, the fifth element of the example array A in Figure 1-5 would be A[4], and, going by the values indexed in Figure 1-4, contain the value 9.

NOTE *It's possible to start an index at 1, too, and some programming languages do use that convention. The equation for a bin's address in a one-indexed array would be* Location(start of array) + Size of each element × (*i* −1).

In most programming languages, we get and set values in an array using a combination of the array's name and the index. For example, we might set the value of the bin with index 5 equal to 16:

```
A[5] = 16
```

For our coffee-tracking example, we could define an array Amount to store the number of cups consumed in a day and store the corresponding counts in Amount[0] through Amount[364]. The single array allows us to access 365 distinct values, in order, through a single variable name. We have transitioned from a series of similarly named, but independent, variables to a mathematical offset of a single location. To understand the power of this, consider our school lockers. Naming individual lockers "Jeremy's Locker" or "Locker for the third student with a last name starting with K" would make them nearly impossible to find quickly. Rather than simply accessing a specific index, students would have to check a large number of lockers, comparing textual tags until they found the correct match. With array indexing, the students can just use its offset to determine where the locker is and access it directly.

Although we often visualize and discuss arrays as the whole data structure, it is important to remember that each bin behaves like an individual variable. When we want to make a global change to the array, such as shifting the elements forward one position, we need to apply the change individually to each bin as shown in Figure 1-6.

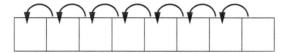

Figure 1-6: Shifting elements in an array forward, bin by bin

Arrays aren't like books on a bookshelf. We can't shove the entire collection over at once to make room for the newest edition of *Coffee Lover's Guide to the Best Free-Trade Coffees*. Arrays are more like a row of storefronts. We can't just squeeze a new coffee shop between our favorite neighborhood bookseller and barbershop. To make space, we'd need to shift the storefronts down one by one, by emptying each store and moving its contents into the adjacent building.

In fact, we have to juggle values simply to swap two values in an array. To swap the values at some indices i and j, for instance, we need to first assign one of them to a temporary variable:

```
Temp = A[i]
A[i] = A[j]
A[j] = Temp
```

Otherwise, we would overwrite the value in one of the bins and the two bins would end up with the same value. Similarly, if we are swapping the locations of the coffee shop and bookseller, we first need to move the contents of the bookstore into an empty third location in order to make space for the contents of the coffee shop. Only after we've moved the coffee shop can we move the bookstore's contents from the temporary third location into the coffee shop's former location.

Insertion Sort

The best way to understand the impact an array's structure has on how it can be used is to examine it in the context of an actual algorithm. *Insertion sort* is an algorithm to sort the values in an array. It works on any type of value that can be ordered. We could sort integers, strings, or even the coffees in our pantry by expiration date.

Insertion sort works by sorting a subset of the array and expanding this sorted range until the entire array is in order. The algorithm iterates through each element in the unsorted array and moves it down into the correct location of the sorted section. At the start of iteration i, the items in bins 0 through i – 1 are all in sorted order. The algorithm then takes the item at index i, finds the correct location in the sorted prefix, and inserts it, shifting the necessary items down to make room. The sorted prefix has now grown by one—bins 0 through i are in sorted order. We can start at i = 1 by declaring the first element to be our initial sorted prefix.

Say we want to sort our coffee collection in order of freshness—after all, it would be tragic to leave a bag of premium coffee languishing at the back of the pantry until it was stale. We need to move the earliest best-by dates to the left side of the shelf where they can be readily accessible.

We begin our coffee insertion sort by proclaiming a single bag at the front to be *sorted* and using this range as our sorted prefix. We then look at the second bag on the shelf and compare dates to determine whether it should go before the first one. After we swap the order, or determine that a swap isn't necessary, we can confidently proclaim that the first two elements are sorted. We have a subset that's fully sorted. We then progress to the third bag and determine where it should sit relative to the first two, perhaps making a few swaps in the process. This process continues down the shelf until we've achieved perfect coffee organization.

We can implement insertion sort with a pair of nested loops, as shown in Listing 1-1.

```
InsertionSort(array: A):
    Integer: N = length(A)
    Integer: i = 1
 ❶ WHILE i < N:
        Type: current = A[i]
        Integer: j = i - 1
     ❷ WHILE j >= 0 AND A[j] > current:
            A[j + 1] = A[j]
            j = j - 1
        A[j + 1] = current
        i = i + 1
```

Listing 1-1: Implementing insertion sort with nested loops

The outer loop with iterator i starts at the first unsorted element, i = 1 and progresses through each value in the unsorted range ❶. The inner loop with iterator j shifts the current value down into the sorted prefix ❷. At each step, we check the position within the sorted prefix by comparing the current value to the preceding location in the prefix, index j. If the element at j is larger, the two values are in the wrong order and must be swapped. Since we are storing the current value in a separate variable current, we copy the data from the preceding bin directly. There is no need to do a full swap. The inner loop continues until it shifts the current value to the front of the array or it finds a preceding value that is smaller, which indicates the current value is in the correct location of the sorted prefix. We only need to write the current value at the end of the loop when it is in the correct location. The outer loop then proceeds to the next unsorted value.

We can visualize the behavior of the algorithm as shown in Figure 1-7. Each row shows the state of the array at the beginning of the iteration. The shaded box represents the current item being shifted into position, and the arrows represent the corresponding shifts.

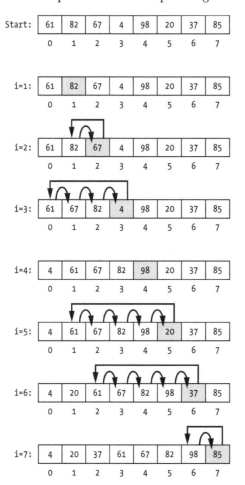

Figure 1-7: Visualization of an insertion sort algorithm

Insertion sort isn't particularly efficient. When inserting elements into the array, we could end up shifting around significant portions of the array. In the worst case, the cost of the algorithm scales proportionally with the square of the number of items—for every item in the list, we shift all the items in front of it. If we double the size of the array, we increase the worst-case cost by a factor of four. While this may not be a huge cost in our coffee pantry, where we are likely to keep only a small number of coffees that we can consume before they go stale, the quadratic cost of the algorithm skyrockets in many applications.

Yet insertion sort provides an important insight into how arrays function. Within this simple algorithm we illustrate several attributes of the array, including the power of being able to access items by their index, the ability to swap values when inserting new elements, and the valuable ability to iterate over entries.

Strings

Strings are ordered lists of characters that can often be thought of as a special kind of arrays. Each bin in the string holds a single character, be that a letter, number, symbol, space, or one of a limited set of special indicators. A special character is often used to indicate the end of the string, as represented by the / in the last bin in Figure 1-8. Characters in strings can often be accessed directly using their index.

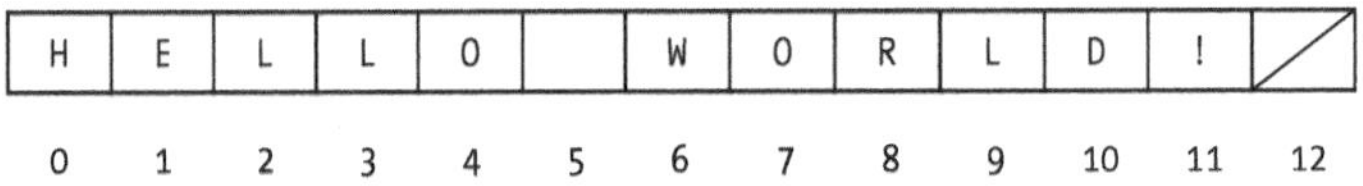

H	E	L	L	O		W	O	R	L	D	!	⧄
0	1	2	3	4	5	6	7	8	9	10	11	12

Figure 1-8: A string spelling "Hello world!"

In some programming languages, strings are directly implemented as simple arrays of characters. In others, strings may be objects, and the string class serves as a wrapper around an array or other data structure holding the characters. The wrapper class for a string provides additional functionality, such as the ability to dynamically resize the string or search for a substring. In either case, it is useful to think about how the general array-like structure impacts operations on the string. When we display a string on the computer screen, we are effectively iterating through each of its characters and displaying them one at a time.

The common test of equality is more interesting to consider. Unlike integers, which can be directly compared with a single operation, strings must be compared by iterating through each character. The program compares it individually to its counterpart and returns whether it finds a mismatch.

Listing 1-2 shows the algorithm for checking the equality of two strings. The algorithm starts by comparing the strings' size. If they are not the same length, the algorithm stops there. If they are the same length, the algorithm iterates through each position and compares the respective letters of each string. We can terminate the loop as soon as we find a single mismatch. Only if we make it all the way to the end of the strings without a mismatch can we declare the strings equal.

```
StringEqual(String: str1, String: str2):
    IF length(str1) != length(str2):
        return False
    Integer: N = length(str1)
    Integer: i = 0
    WHILE i < N AND str1[i] == str2[i]:
        i = i + 1
    return i == N
```

Listing 1-2: The algorithm for checking the equality of two strings

Figure 1-9 demonstrates how this algorithm operates on two strings. The equality sign indicates which pairs of characters matched when compared. The X represents the first mismatched pair, where the test terminates.

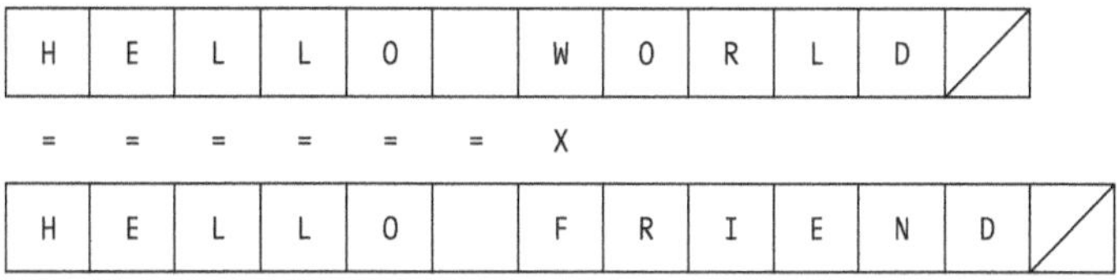

Figure 1-9: A comparison of two strings

The worst-case computational cost of string comparison grows proportionally with the length of the strings. While the work required to compare two small strings can be negligible, the same operation on two long strings can be time-consuming. For comparison, imagine the tedium of scanning through two editions of the same book, letter by letter, looking for each difference in the arrangement of text from one book to the next. In the best case, we find a mismatch early. In the worst case, we need to examine the majority of the book.

Many programming languages, such as Python, provide a string class that allows direct comparisons, so we never need to implement the comparison code in Listing 1-2 directly. Still, underneath the simple comparison function lies a loop that iterates over all the letters. Without understanding this vital detail, it is possible to vastly underestimate the cost of string comparisons.

Why This Matters

Variables and arrays are staples of introductory programming classes and thus might seem less than exciting, but they are important to examine because they provide the very foundations for computer programming and data structures. These concepts also provide the baseline against which to evaluate dynamic data structures and their impact on algorithms. In later chapters, we will see how dynamic data structures can offer different trade-offs among efficiency, flexibility, and complexity.

2

BINARY SEARCH

Binary search is an algorithm for efficiently searching a sorted list. It checks the sorted list for a target value by repeatedly dividing the list in half, determining which of the two halves could contain the target value, and discarding the other half. This algorithm's simplicity of logic and implementation make it a perfect introductory topic for computer science, so binary search algorithms are nearly universal throughout computer science courses and textbooks.

The skeptical reader might wonder, "How often will I really need to search a sorted list?" or, more accurately, "How often will I need to implement a function to search my sorted list? Haven't a few million people done this? Isn't it in a library somewhere?" While you shouldn't reject the possibility of one day needing to implement your own binary search, its true importance goes well beyond its implementation.

Binary search illustrates how clever algorithms can use the structure in which data is stored to achieve significant computational savings, even when this structure is as simple as sorted data. Binary search is easily analyzed for correctness and efficiency, provides guarantees of both speed and correctness, and demonstrates the fundamental interaction between data and algorithms. It's an excellent lens with which to examine difference in data storage techniques, such as the difference between linked lists and arrays, or the motivation behind many tree-based algorithms. It can even be used to create a better cup of coffee.

The Problem

Before defining any new algorithm, we must define the problem the algorithm will try to solve. In this chapter, our aim is to find a single item in a list that matches the given target value; we need an algorithm that can efficiently perform such a search. Formally we can define this search as:

> Given a set of N data points $X = \{x_1, x_2, \ldots, x_N\}$ and a target value x', find a point $x_i \in X$ such that $x' = x_i$, or indicate that no such point exists.

In our everyday lives, we would likely describe the task as "Find me this particular thing." This search problem is one that we all face numerous times a day. We might be hunting for a word in a dictionary, a name in our contacts list, a specific date in a list of historical of events, or our preferred brand of coffee in a densely packed supermarket shelf. All we need is a list of candidates and a way to check whether we've found a match.

Linear Scan

To appreciate the advantages of binary search, we start with a simpler algorithm, *linear scan*, to provide a baseline for comparison. Linear scan searches for a target value by testing each value in our list, one after the other, against the target value, until the target is found or we reach the end of our list. This is how the author normally searches supermarket shelves—running his finger along the brightly colored packages of coffee, one by one, while mumbling to himself about the need for better indexing schemes.

Imagine that we are looking to find the target value in an array A of numbers. In this case, let's use `target = 21`. We iterate through each bin in the array and check whether that value equals 21, as illustrated in Figure 2-1.

Listing 2-1 shows the code for linear scan. The code returns the index of the matching element if one is found and returns an index of `-1` if the search fails and the item is not in our array.

```
LinearScan(Array: A, Integer: target):
    Integer: i = 0
    WHILE i < length(A):
        IF A[i] == target:
            return i
        i = i + 1
    return -1
```

Listing 2-1: The code for linear scan

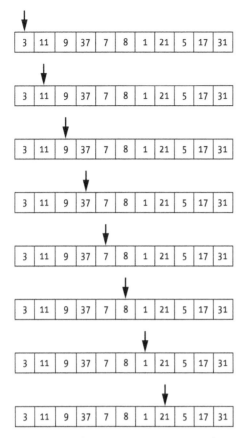

Figure 2-1: A linear scan over an array of integers

A single WHILE loop iterates over each element of the array, and the internal IF statement compares that element to the target. As soon as we come across an element matching the target, we return the corresponding index. If we make it to the end of the array, we return -1.

Linear scan isn't fancy or clever. It's a *brute-force* test guaranteed to find the item of interest (if the item is in the data) because it checks every possible item until it finds a match or confirms the item is missing. This is thorough but inefficient, especially for large lists. If we know nothing about the structure of the data in A, there is nothing we can do to streamline the process. The target value could be in any bin, so we may need to check them all.

To illustrate linear scan's limitations, imagine performing such a scan on a physical row of items, like a line of introductory computer science students standing outside a classroom. The teacher, looking to return a specific student's assignment, walks down the line asking each student "Is your name Jeremy?" before potentially moving onto the next. The search stops when the teacher finds the correct student or makes it to the end of the line. The students (correctly) roll their eyes and mutter about their inefficient instructor.

Sometimes there are ways to make linear search faster *per comparison*. For example, we might optimize the comparison time for more complex data by stopping at the first mismatched letter when comparing strings, as described in Chapter 1. Likewise, in the supermarket case, we could consume massive amounts of coffee ahead of time, so our shaky finger zips faster along the shelf. However, this only helps to a point. We are still limited to checking every item, one by one.

In the next section, we'll see how a small amount of structure in the data changes everything.

Binary Search Algorithm

Binary search is an algorithm to find a target value v in a *sorted* list and only works on sorted data. The algorithm can be written to work with data sorted in either increasing or decreasing order, but, for now, let's consider the case of data sorted in increasing order—lowest to highest. The algorithm operates by partitioning the list in half and determining in which half v must reside. It then discards the half that v is not in and repeats the process with only the half that can possibly still contain v until only one value remains. For example, if we were searching the sorted list in Figure 2-2 for the value 7, we would find 5 at the midpoint and could rule out the first half of the list. Anything before the middle element cannot be greater than 5, and, since 5 is less than 7, everything before 5 is also less than 7.

Figure 2-2: A sorted list of integers from 1 to 9, where 5 is the midpoint

The key to efficient algorithms is using information or structure within the data. In the case of binary search, we use the fact that the array is sorted in increasing order. More formally, consider a sorted array A:

$A[i] \leq A[j]$ for any pair of indexes i and j such that $i < j$

While this might not seem like a lot of information, it's enough to allow us to rule out entire sections of the array. It's similar to the logic we use to avoid the ice cream aisle when searching for coffee. Once we know an item won't be in a given area, we can rule out that entire set of items in that area without individually checking them.

Binary search tracks the current search space with two bounds: the upper bound IndexHigh marks the highest index of the array that is part of the active search space, and the lower bound IndexLow marks the lowest. Throughout the algorithm, if the target value is in the array, we guarantee the following:

```
A[IndexLow] ≤ v ≤ A[IndexHigh]
```

Binary search starts each iteration by choosing the midpoint of the current search space:

```
IndexMid = Floor((IndexHigh + IndexLow) / 2)
```

where `Floor` is a mathematical function that rounds a number down to an integer. We then compare the value at the middle location, `A[IndexMid]`, with the target value v. If the middle point is less than the target value, `A[IndexMid] < v`, we know the target value must lie after the middle index. This allows us to chop the search space in half by making `IndexLow = IndexMid + 1`. Alternately, if the middle point is greater than the target value, `A[IndexMid] > v`, we know the target value must lie before the middle index, which allows us to chop the search space in half by making `IndexHigh = IndexMid - 1`. Of course, if we find `A[IndexMid] == v`, we immediately conclude the search: we've found the target. Boisterous celebration is optional.

Each row in Figure 2-3 represents a step in the binary search process on a sorted array. We're searching the array at row (a) for the value 15. At the start, our search bounds include the entire array: `IndexLow = 0` and `IndexHigh = 11`.

In row (b), we compute the midpoint (rounding down) to be `IndexMid = 5`. Comparing the midpoint's value to the target value, we see that `A[5] = 11`, which is less than our target value of 15. Therefore, in row (c), we rule out every element in the array up to and including index 5—that is, all the shaded elements—by adjusting the lower bounds: `IndexLow = 6`. We've eliminated almost half our search space with a single comparison! The algorithm repeats this process on the remaining range, computing the new midpoint as `IndexMid = 8`, comparing to the target value (`A[8] = 30`, which is greater than `v = 15`), and refining our bounds to `IndexHigh = 7`. In row (d), we once again eliminate half of the remaining search in the same way. In row (e), we again compute the midpoint as `IndexMid = 6` and compare it to the target value (`A[6] == v`). We've found the target!

Note that even though the lower bound's index pointed to the target value (v = 15) for several iterations, we continued the search until the *midpoint* pointed to the target value. This is because our search checks only the value at the midpoint against the target and not the values at the lower or upper indexes.

Returning to our line of introductory computer science students, we can imagine that by the end of the semester, the teacher asks the students to line up in alphabetical order. The teacher then starts a binary search by asking the middle student "What is your name?" and uses the responses to prune out half the line. The professor then mentally revises the bounds, moves to the new midpoint, and repeats the process. Thus, the professor can turn the exercise of returning an assignment into a demonstration of binary search—while also covering up the fact that they never managed to learn the students' names.

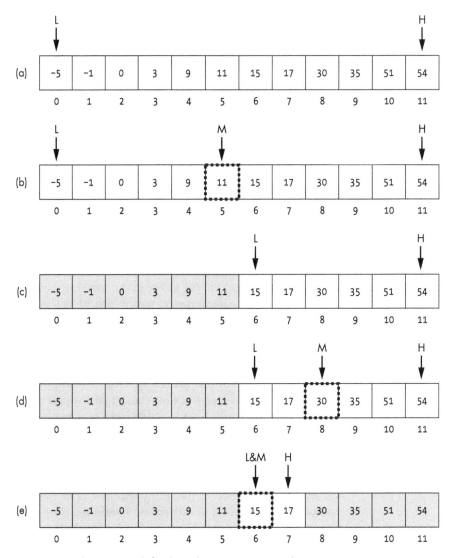

Figure 2-3: A binary search for the value 15 over a sorted array

Absent Values

Next, we need to consider what happens if the target value is not in the list
and how the binary search confirms the value's absence. In the linear scan
case, we know that an element is not in the list as soon as we hit the end of
the list. For binary search, we can conclude that our target item does not exist
by testing the bounds themselves. As the search progresses, the upper and
lower bounds move closer and closer until there are no unexplored values
between them. Since we are always moving one of the bounds *past* the midpoint index, we can stop the search when IndexHigh < IndexLow. At that point,
we can guarantee the target value is not in the list. Figure 2-4 shows an example search for v = 10 on a sorted array, where 10 does not appear in the array.

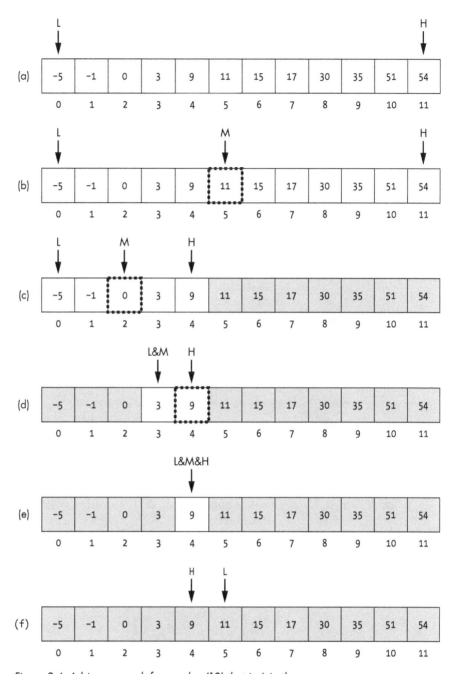

Figure 2-4: A binary search for a value (10) that isn't in the array

We could theoretically have stopped the search earlier than row (f): once the value at our high bound is less than the target value (IndexHigh = 4) we know that the target can't be in the array. However, as with our search in Figure 2-3, the algorithm only checks the value at the midpoint against the target. It tracks the indices of the high and low bounds, but does not check the values at these locations explicitly. While we could add logic to capture this case, as well as the corresponding case of the lower bound being greater than the target value, we will keep the logic simple for now.

Implementing Binary Search

We can implement a binary search in code with a single WHILE loop, as shown in Listing 2-2. Like the code for linear search in Listing 2-1, the binary search algorithm returns the index of the target element if it is in the array. If there is no matching element in the array, the algorithm returns -1.

```
BinarySearch(Array: A, Integer: target):
    Integer: IndexHigh = length(A) - 1
    Integer: IndexLow = 0
❶ WHILE IndexLow <= IndexHigh:
    ❷ Integer: IndexMid = Floor((IndexHigh+IndexLow) / 2)

        IF A[IndexMid] == target:
            return IndexMid
        IF A[IndexMid] < target:
          ❸ IndexLow = IndexMid + 1
        ELSE:
          ❹ IndexHigh = IndexMid - 1
    return -1
```

Listing 2-2: Implementing binary search with a single loop

While the high and low indices have not crossed, we continue the search ❶. During each iteration, we compute a new midpoint ❷ and check the midpoint value against the target. If it's an exact match, we've found our target and can directly return the corresponding index. If the value at the midpoint is too small, we adjust the lower bounds ❸. If the value is too high, we adjust the upper bounds ❹. If IndexHigh < IndexLow, the element is not in the array, so we return -1.

Depending on the programming language, we could use approaches other than returning -1 to indicate failure, such as throwing an exception. Regardless of the actual mechanism, your code and documentation should always be absolutely clear about what happens if the element is not in the array so that callers of the function can use it correctly.

Adapting Binary Search

So far, we have considered binary search in the context of lists and arrays— fixed sets of discrete items. It is easy to see how we could bring this algorithm into the real world by applying it to a shelf of sorted books, names in a telephone book, or a clothing rack ordered by size. But we can adapt this same approach to continuous data, where we don't start with a set of individual items or indices, as well. Instead, we use high and low bounds on the values themselves.

Imagine you aim to craft the perfect cup of coffee. After months of laborious research, you've confirmed the optimal temperature and quantity of water. Yet one mystery remains: What quantity of coffee grounds should you use? Here the sources diverge. The Strong Coffee camp recommends a tremendous 5 tablespoons of coffee grounds, while the Watery Coffee camp recommends a paltry 0.5 tablespoons.

The problem of determining your own optimal scoop of coffee grounds lends itself perfectly to a binary search, as shown in Figure 2-5. We start with reasonable upper and lower bounds as illustrated in Figure 2-5(a).

LowerBound = 0 tablespoons   The "coffee" was a cup of warm water.

UpperBound = 5 tablespoons   The coffee was too strong.

The true value must be somewhere in between. Note that our bounds are now the values themselves instead of item indices.

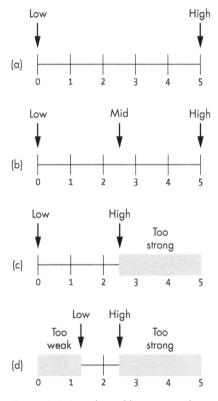

Figure 2-5: An adapted binary search can be used to search a range of real numbers.

As with a binary search on an array of values, we can define the mid-point at 2.5 tablespoons and test that (Figure 2-5(b)). Again, 2.5 tablespoons is just a value. It doesn't correspond to an element in an array or item on the shelf. We do not have an array of predetermined values, but rather the infinite range of all real numbers between 0.0 and 5.0, and any individual measurement effectively corresponds to an index into that range.

We find the coffee made from 2.5 tablespoons is a little too strong for our taste, allowing us to refine the bounds. Our optimal amount of coffee is now constrained to lie between 0 tablespoons and 2.5 tablespoons (c). Our search continues with a new midpoint of 1.25 tablespoons, an amount that produces a weak brew. We need to refine our lower bound (d).

The search for morning bliss continues this way until we've sufficiently narrowed down our range. Unlike with a discrete array of values, we may never find the exact point that satisfies our search. After all, there is an infinite number of real values. If our optimal amount of coffee is 2.0 tablespoons, we might try values of 2.50, 1.25, 1.875, 2.1875, and 2.03125 before concluding that we are close enough. Therefore, we terminate the search when our range is sufficiently small:

```
UpperBound - LowerBound < threshold
```

Contrast this search with a linear scan through the options. In the name of science, we may resolve to try every possible increment of 0.05 tablespoons until we find the optimal brew. After all, this is coffee, and we must be thorough. Starting at our low index (0.0 tablespoons—alternately known as a cup of warm water), we continually increment the amount by 0.05 and retest. We run through 0.05, 0.10, 0.15, . . . , 1.00 before we start to get to a reasonable strength. We would need many trials to get to the correct point, at least 20 of which would be too weak to even to count as coffee. That's a lot of wasted effort and coffee beans.

The use of binary search also allows for better precision. By sampling only 0.05 increments during our linear scan, we are limited to how close to the target value we can get. Binary search keeps homing in on a smaller range until we stop. We choose what value of UpperBound - LowerBound is sufficient to halt the search, allowing us to narrow it down to within 0.0001 tablespoons or closer.

This adaptation of the binary search approach forms the basis of important mathematical techniques, such as bisection search. *Bisection search* uses it to find the zero of a function, or the value of x such that $f(x) = 0$. Instead of evaluating whether coffee is too strong or too weak, bisection search tracks bounds where the function is above zero and below zero. By repeatedly dividing the interval in half at the midpoint, the algorithm zooms in on the value of x where the function is exactly zero.

Runtime

Intuitively, we can see that binary search is often faster than a linear scan of the data. Let's find out how much faster binary search can be to determine whether it's worth the additional code complexity.

Of course, the relative speed of the two algorithms depends on the data itself. If we are searching for values that always occur at the start of the list, linear scan will win. Similarly, binary search might be unnecessary for tiny lists. We don't need to partition a list in half if it has only two elements. We can just look at those elements directly.

We often analyze the runtime of an algorithm in terms of its average and worst-case performance as the size of the data N grows. Computer scientists often use measures such as Big-O notation to more formally capture those concepts. We won't formally analyze algorithms in this book or use Big-O notation, but we will consider the same two aspects throughout for each algorithm:

- The average-case runtime of an algorithm as the size of the data grows
- The worst-case runtime of an algorithm as the size of the data grows

For now, let's compare worst-case performance for linear scan and binary search. For linear scan, the worst case occurs when the target value is at the end of the list or not in the list at all. In these cases, the algorithm has to check every single value. If the array has N values, it will require N comparisons. Its worst-case running time is *linear* with the size of the data.

In contrast, even the worst-case binary search will discard half the data at each step, so the number of comparisons is *logarithmic* with the size of the data set. It scales proportional to $\log_2 N$, which is the base-2 logarithm of N. Admittedly there is more work per step: instead of checking a single value, we have to move our bounds and compute a new midpoint. However, for large enough lists, the benefit of needing only a logarithmic number of comparisons will far outweigh additional per-step costs.

Why This Matters

This fixation on binary search in introductory computer science classes isn't the result of binary-search advocacy campaigns, fan clubs, or secret societies (although those would all be understandable). Rather, it's binary search's simplicity that makes it a perfect introductory topic. It is a clean and effective example of one of the most fundamental concepts of computational thinking: that designing algorithms by using the structure in the problems themselves helps us construct efficient solutions. By taking advantage of the sorted nature of the data, we are able to cut the worst-case runtime from linear with the number of values to logarithmic—a difference that becomes more significant as the data grows.

Throughout the rest of the book, we will continue to look at the tight relationship between problem structure (including within the data) and how we can create efficient solutions.

3

DYNAMIC DATA STRUCTURES

This chapter introduces *dynamic data structures*, which alter their structure as the data changes. These structural adaptations may include growing the size of the data structure on demand, creating dynamic, mutable linkings between different values, and more. Dynamic data structures lie at the heart of almost every computer program in the world and are the foundation of some of the most exciting, interesting, and powerful algorithms in computer science.

The basic data structures introduced in the previous chapters are like parking lots—they give us a place to store information, but don't provide much in the way of adaptation. Sure, we can sort the values in an array (or cars in our parking lot) and use that structure to make binary search efficient. But we're just changing the ordering of the data within the array. The data structure itself is neither changing nor responding to changes in the data. If we later change the data in a sorted array, say by modifying the value of an element, we need to re-sort the array. Worse yet, when we need to change the data structure itself—by growing or shrinking the array, for example—simple static data structures don't provide any help.

This chapter compares the static data structure introduced in Chapter 1, the array, with a simple dynamic data structure, the linked list, to demonstrate the advantages of the latter. In some respects, these two data structures are similar: they both allow programmers to store and access multiple values through a single reference, either the array or the head of the linked list. However, arrays have a structure fixed at time of creation, like rows of parking spaces. In contrast, linked lists can grow throughout the program's memory. They behave more like a lengthening or shrinking line of people, allowing for additions and removals. Understanding these differences provides a foundation for understanding the more advanced data structures that we will visit in the rest of this book.

The Limitations of Arrays

While arrays are excellent data structures for storing multiple values, they suffer from one important limitation: their size and layout in memory are fixed at the time of creation. If we want to store more values than can fit in our array, we need to create a new, larger array and copy over the data from the older array. This fixed-size memory is acceptable for when we have an unmoving upper bound on the number of items we need to store. If we have sufficient bins to fit our data, we can set individual entries all day long without worrying about the array's static layout in memory. However, many applications require dynamic data structures that can grow and change with our program.

To meet this need for dynamic data structures, many modern programming languages offer dynamic "arrays" that grow and shrink as you add elements. However, these are actually wrappers around static arrays or other data structures that hide the complexities and costs associated with their dynamic nature. While this is convenient for the programmer, it can lead to hidden inefficiencies. When we add elements past the end of the array, the program still needs to increase the memory used. It just does so behind the scenes. To understand why dynamic data structures are so important, we need to discuss the limitations of static data structures. In this book, we'll use the term *array* to refer to a simple static array.

To illustrate the array's restrictions, imagine that you spend an entire week mastering the latest retro video game phenomenon, Space Frogger 2000. You smile with glee every time the main screen displays your five top scores. These monumental achievements represent hours of sweat, tears, shouting, and more tears. However, the very next day, your (soon to be former) best friend visits and goes on to beat your highest score five times in a row. Once you kick the traitorous ex-friend out of the house, you return to your game and gaze at the new top scores, shown in Figure 3-1, and cry out, "Why couldn't the game store more scores? Would it really be so hard to keep a top ten list, or at least add one more to the very end?"

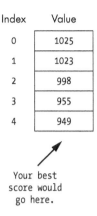

Index	Value
0	1025
1	1023
2	998
3	955
4	949

Your best
score would
go here.

*Figure 3-1: A five-element
array holding high scores
for a video game. None,
alas, are yours.*

This is one of the fundamental limitations of any fixed-size data structure and its fixed layout in memory—it can't grow with the data. As we see
below, this restriction makes some common operations expensive. More
practically, imagine the limitations of a word processor with space for only
a fixed number of characters, a spreadsheet with a fixed number of rows,
a photo storage program that can store a limited number of pictures, or a
coffee journal limited to only a thousand entries.

Since the size of an array is fixed at the time of creation, if we want to
extend the array to store more data, we must create a new, larger block of
memory. Consider the simplest case of adding a single element to the end
of an array. Because an array is a single, fixed-size block of memory, we
can't just shove another value into the end. There might be another variable
already occupying that space in the memory. Rather than risk overwriting
that variable's value, we have to allocate a new (bigger) block of memory,
copy all the values of the original array into the new block, and write the
new value at the end. That's a lot of overhead for a single addition, as illustrated in Figure 3-2.

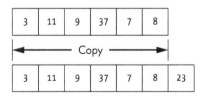

*Figure 3-2: Adding an element to the
end of a full array.*

Think of an array as one of those heated hotel buffet counters with
a fixed number of slots. It's easy to pop out the empty tray of scrambled
eggs and add a new one in its place. But you can't just stick a new tray onto

the end. There's no room for it. If the chef decides to add pancakes to the menu, something else has to go.

If you know you'll need to insert a lot of new values, you might spread the cost out over multiple updates, *amortizing* the cost. You might adopt a strategy like *array doubling*, in which the size of an array doubles whenever it is expanded. For example, if we try to add a 129th element to our array of size 128, we first allocate a new array of size 256 and copy over the original 128 elements. This allows us to continue growing the array for a while before we next need to worry about allocating new space. However, the cost is potentially wasted space. If we only need 129 elements total, we have over-allocated by 127.

Array doubling provides a reasonable balance between expensive array copies and wasted memory. As the array grows, the doublings become less and less frequent. At the same time, by doubling the array when it is full, we are guaranteed to waste less than half the space. However, even with this balanced approach, we can clearly see the cost of using a fixed-size array in terms of both copying cost and memory usage.

```
ArrayDouble(Array: old_array):
    Integer: length = length of old_array
    Array: new_array = empty array of size length * 2

    Integer: j = 0
    WHILE j < length:
        new_array[j] = old_array[j]
        j = j + 1
    return new_array
```

The code for array doubling starts by allocating a new array twice the size of the current array. A single WHILE loop iterates over the elements in the current array, copying their values into the new array. The new array is returned.

Imagine applying this strategy to shelf space. We establish a bookstore, Data Structures and More, in a location and install a humble five shelves. Opening day sees surprising demand and requests for more variety: we need to expand our inventory. Panicked, we move to a new location with 10 shelves and migrate the books. The demand has temporarily been met. Since the lack of a comprehensive data structure store is a clear gap in the retail books market, our store is a runaway success, and demand continues to grow and grow. We might upgrade the store a few more times to locations with 20, 40, then 80 shelves. Each time we pay a cost to secure a new location and migrate the books.

The fixed location of the array's values in memory provides another limitation. We cannot easily insert additional items in the middle of an array. Even if there are enough empty spaces at the end of our original array to accommodate a new element, and therefore we don't need to move the whole array to a new memory block, we still need to shift each existing element over one by one to make a space for the new value in the middle. Unlike a shelf of books, we can't just shove all the elements over at once with a single good push. If we had 10,000 elements and wanted to add something in the second position, we'd need to move 9,999 elements over. That's a lot of effort to insert a single element.

The problems compound when we try to insert new values into the middle of an array that is already full. Not only do we have to allocate a new block and copy the old values, but we need to shift the values after the new value down one position to clear a space for our new value. For example, suppose we wanted to insert the value 23 as the fourth element of an existing array of six elements, as illustrated in Figure 3-3.

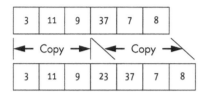

Figure 3-3: Adding an element to the middle of a full array

To address the shortfalls of arrays, we need to move to more flexible data structures that can grow as new data is added: dynamic data structures. Before we jump into the details, let's introduce pointers, the variable type that's key to reconfiguring and growing data structures.

Pointers and References

One variable type stands above its peers in terms of both its sheer power and its ability to confuse new programmers: *pointers*. A pointer is a variable that stores only the addresses in the computer's memory. The pointer therefore points to a second location in memory where the actual data is stored, as shown in Figure 3-4.

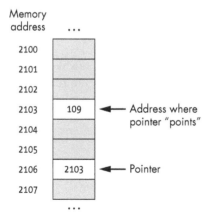

Figure 3-4: A pointer indicating an address in the computer's memory

The astute reader may ask, "What is the purpose of a variable that simply points to another location in memory? I thought the variable's name already served this function. Why not store your data in the variable like a normal person? Why do you always have to make things so complicated?" Don't listen to the skeptics. Pointers are the essential ingredient in dynamic data structures, as we'll see shortly.

Suppose we are working on a major architectural project at the office and have assembled a folder of example drawings to share with our team. Soon the project folder contains numerous floorplans, cost estimates, and artistic renderings. Rather than make a copy of the hefty file and leave it out in the open, we leave a note telling our collaborators to find the file in the third-floor records room, filing cabinet #3, the second drawer down, fifth folder. This note plays the role of a pointer. It doesn't detail all the information that's in the file, but rather allows our colleagues to find and retrieve the information. More importantly, we can share this single "address" with each of our coworkers without making a full copy of the file for them. They can each use this information to look up and modify the folder when needed. We could even leave an individual sticky note on each team member's desk, providing 10 variables pointing to the same information.

In addition to storing the location of a block of memory, pointers can take on a null value (denoted as None, Nil, or 0 in some programming languages). The null value simply denotes that the pointer isn't currently pointing to a valid memory location. In other words, it indicates that the pointer doesn't actually point to anything yet.

Different programming languages provide different mechanisms to accomplish the task of pointers, and not all of them provide the raw memory address to the programmer. Lower-level languages like C and C++ give you raw pointers and allow you to directly access the memory location they store. Other programming languages, such as Python, use references, which use syntax like that of a normal variable while still allowing you to reference another variable. These different variations come with different behaviors and usages (dereferencing, pointer math, the form of null values, and so forth). For the sake of simplicity, throughout this book we will use the term *pointer* to cover all variables implemented by pointers, references, or indices into preallocated blocks of memory. We won't worry about the complicated syntax needed to access the blocks of memory (which has caused more than a few programming enthusiasts to break down in tears). We will also use the final data's type (instead of the more generic type pointer) when defining a pointer variable in pseudocode. The key concept for our purposes is that pointers provide a mechanism for linking to a block of memory as featured in our first dynamic data structure: the linked list.

Linked Lists

Linked lists are the simplest example of a dynamic data structure and are a close cousin to arrays. Like arrays, they are a data structure for storing multiple values. Unlike arrays, linked lists are composed of a chain of nodes linked together by pointers. A basic *node* in a linked list is a composite data structure containing two parts: a value (of any type) and a pointer to the next node in the list:

```
LinkedListNode {
    Type: value
    LinkedListNode: next
}
```

We can picture a linked list as a series of linked bins, as in Figure 3-5. Each bin stores a single value and contains a pointer to the next bin in the series.

Figure 3-5: A linked list shown as a series of nodes linked by pointers

The slash at the end of the list represents a null value and indicates the end of the list. Effectively we are saying that the last node's next pointer does not point to a valid node.

A linked list is like a long line of people waiting at our favorite coffee shop. People rarely know their absolute position in the line—"I'm on the fifty-third floor tile back from the counter." They pay attention to their relative order, namely the single person before them, which we store in a pointer. Even if the line winds throughout the store (and its parking lot) in complex loops, we can still reconstruct the order by asking each person who is immediately in front of them. We can traverse the line toward the counter by asking each person who is before them.

Because they include pointers as well as values, linked lists require more memory than arrays to store the same items. If we have an array of size K, storing values of N bytes each, we only need $K \times N$ bytes. In contrast, if each pointer requires another M bytes, our data structure now has a cost of $K \times (M + N)$ bytes. Unless the size of the pointers is much smaller than the size of our values, the overhead is significant. However, the increased memory usage is often worth it for the increased flexibility the pointers provide.

While textbooks often represent linked lists as neat, orderly structures (as shown in Figure 3-5 or implied in our line-of-humans example), our list can actually be scattered throughout the program's memory. As illustrated in Figure 3-6, the list's nodes are linked only via their pointers.

This is the real power of pointers and dynamic data structures. We aren't constrained to keep the entire list in a single contiguous block of memory. We're free to grab space for new nodes wherever space happens to exist.

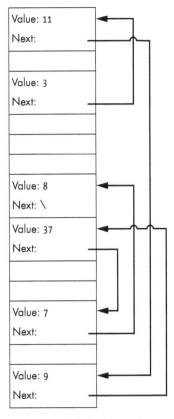

Figure 3-6: A linked list in the computer's memory. Nodes are not necessarily adjacent to each other.

Programs typically store linked lists by keeping a single pointer to the front, or *head*, of the linked list. The program can then access any element in the list by starting at the head and iterating through the nodes via the pointers:

```
LinkedListLookUp(LinkedListNode: head, Integer: element_number):
  ❶ LinkedListNode: current = head
     Integer: count = 0

  ❷ WHILE count < element_number AND current != null:
        current = current.next
        count = count + 1
     return current
```

The code starts at the head of the list ❶. We maintain a second variable count to track the index of the current node. The WHILE loop then iterates through each node in the list until it has found the correct number, count == element_number, or run off the end of the list, current == null ❷. In either case, the code can return current. If the loop terminates due to running off the edge of the list, then the index is not in the list and the code returns null.

For example, if we wanted to access the fourth element of a linked list, the program would access first the head, then the second, third, and fourth elements in order to find the correct memory location. Figure 3-7 shows this process, where the node with value 3 is the head of the list.

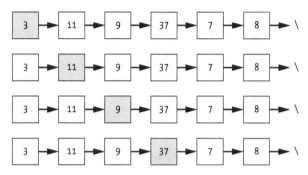

Figure 3-7: Traversing a linked list requires moving from one node to the next along the chain of pointers.

It's worth noting, however, that there's a tradeoff: linked lists have a higher computing overhead than arrays. When accessing an element in an array, we just compute a single offset and look up the correct address of memory. The array access only takes one mathematical computation and one memory lookup regardless of which index we choose. Linked lists require us to iterate from the beginning of the list until we get to the element of interest. For longer lists, the lack of direct access can add significant overhead.

At first glance, this restricted access pattern is a strike against the linked list. We've dramatically increased the cost of looking up an arbitrary element! Consider what this means for binary search. A single lookup requires iterating over many of the elements, removing the advantage of a sorted list.

Yet despite these costs, linked lists can become real assets in practical programs. Data structures almost always involve tradeoffs among complexity, efficiency, and usage patterns. The very behaviors that disqualify a data structure for one use might make it the perfect choice to support other algorithms. Understanding these tradeoffs is the key to effectively combining algorithms and data structures. In the case of linked lists, the tradeoff for increased overhead in accessing elements is a significant increase in the flexibility of the overall data structure, as we will see in the next section.

Operations on Linked Lists

While some lament the chaotic sprawl of the linked list compared to the aesthetic beauty of the compact array, it is exactly this ability to link across different blocks of memory that makes the data structure so powerful, allowing us to *dynamically* rearrange the data structure. Let's compare inserting a new value to an array with adding a value to a linked list.

Inserting into a Linked List

As we've seen, inserting a new element into an array may require us to allocate a new (bigger) block of memory and copy all the values of the original array into the new block. Further, the insertion itself may require us to traverse the array and shift elements over.

The linked list, on the other hand, doesn't need to stay in a single contiguous block—it probably isn't in a single block to begin with. We only need to know the location of the new node, update the previous node's next pointer to point to our new node, and point the new node's next pointer at the correct node. If we want to add a node with value 23 to the front of the linked list in Figure 3-5, we simply set the new node's next pointer to the previous start of the list (value = 3). This procedure is shown in Figure 3-8. Any variables previously pointing to the start of the list (the first node) also need to be updated to point to the new first node.

Figure 3-8: Extending a linked list by adding a new node to the front

Similarly, we can add a node to the end of the list, as shown in Figure 3-9, by traversing the list to the end, updating the next pointer from the final node (value = 8) to point to the new node, and setting the new node's next pointer to null. Done naively, this approach requires traversing the entire array to reach the end, but, as we will see in the next chapter, there are ways to avoid this additional cost.

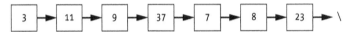

Figure 3-9: Extending a linked list by appending an additional node to the end

If we want to insert a value in the middle, we update two pointers: the previous node and the inserted node. For example, to add node N between nodes X and Y, we have two steps:

1. Set N's next pointer to point at Y (the same place X's next pointer currently points).
2. Set X's next pointer to point at N.

The order of these two steps is important. Pointers, like all other variables, can hold only a single value—in this case a single address in memory. If we set X's next pointer first, we would lose the data on where Y resides.

Once we've finished, X points to N and N points to Y. Figure 3-10 illustrates this process.

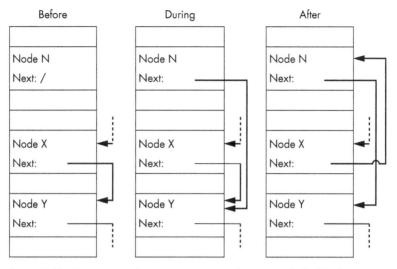

Figure 3-10: The process of inserting a new node N into a linked list between nodes X and Y

Despite the shuffling of pointers, the code for this kind of operation is relatively simple:

```
LinkedListInsertAfter(LinkedListNode: previous,
                      LinkedListNode: new_node):
    new_node.next = previous.next
    previous.next = new_node
```

Say we instead wanted to insert a node with value 23 between the nodes 9 and 37 in our current linked list. The resulting chain of pointers would appear as shown in Figure 3-11.

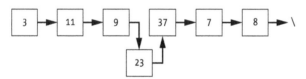

Figure 3-11: Inserting the node 23 into a linked list requires updating pointers from the previous node (9) and to the following node (37).

Likewise, when a customer lets their friend step in front of them to join the middle of the line, two pointers change. Recall that in this analogy, each person "points" to, or keeps track of, the person in front of them. The overly generous customer now points to their line-jumping friend who stands right in front of them. Meanwhile the happy line jumper points to the person who was previously in front of their enabling friend. Everyone behind them in line gives dirty looks and mumbles unkind things.

Again, the diagrams and the café line analogy hide the insertion process's true messiness. While we aren't inserting the new node in a memory location adjacent to the last node, we are logically inserting it next in line. The node itself could be on the other end of the computer's memory next to the variable counting our spelling errors or daily cups of coffee. As long as we keep the list's pointers up-to-date, we can treat them and the nodes to which they point as a single list.

Of course, we must take extra care when inserting a node in front of the head node (index == 0) or at an index *past* the end of the list. If we are inserting a node before the head node, we need to update the head pointer itself; otherwise, it will continue to point to the old front of the list, and we will lose the ability to access the new first element. If we are trying to insert a node into an index past the end of the list, there is no valid previous node at index - 1. In this case, we could fail the insertion, return an error, or append the element to the end of the list (at a smaller index). Whichever approach you choose, it is critical that you clearly document your code. We can bundle this extra logic into a helper function that combines our linear lookup code to insert a new node at a given position:

```
LinkedListInsert(LinkedListNode: head, Integer: index,
                 Type: value):
    # Special case inserting a new head node.
❶ IF index == 0:
       LinkedListNode: new_head = LinkedListNode(value)
       new_head.next = head
       return new_head

   LinkedListNode: current = head
   LinkedListNode: previous = null
   Integer: count = 0
❷ WHILE count < index AND current != null:
       previous = current
       current = current.next
       count = count + 1

   # Check if we've run off the end of the list before
   # getting to the necessary index.
❸ IF count < index:
       Produce an invalid index error.

❹ LinkedListNode: new_node = LinkedListNode(value)
   new_node.next = previous.next
   previous.next = new_node

❺ return head
```

The code for insertion starts with the special case of inserting a new node at index = 0, the beginning of the list ❶. It creates a new head node, sets the new head node's next pointer to the previous head of the list, and returns the new head of the list. Since there isn't a node before the new head node, we do not need to update a previous node's next pointer in this case.

For elements in the middle of the list, the code needs to traverse the list to find the correct location ❷. This is similar to the LinkedListLookUp search: the code follows each node's next pointer, while tracking the current node and the count seen, until it hits the end of the list or the correct location. The code also tracks an additional piece of information, previous, a pointer to the node *before* the current node. Tracking previous allows us to update the pointer into the inserted node.

The code then checks whether it has arrived at the desired index of insertion ❸. By making the check count < index, we still allow insertion at the very end of the list. We only fail with an error in cases where we try to insert at least one additional spot *past* the end of the list.

If the code has found the correct location to insert the node, it splices it in between previous and current. The code performs the insertion by creating a new node, setting that node's next pointer to the address indicated by previous.next, and then setting previous.next to point to the new node ❹. This logic also works for the case where we are appending the new node immediately after the last node in the list. Since previous.next == null in that case, the new node's next pointer is assigned to null and correctly indicates the new end of the list.

By returning the head of the list ❺, we can account for insertions before the head node. Alternatively, we could wrap the head node in a LinkedList composite data structure and operate on that directly. We will use this alternate approach later in the book to handle binary search trees.

Deleting from a Linked List

To delete an element anywhere in a linked list, all we need to do is delete that node and adjust the previous node's pointer, as shown in Figure 3-12.

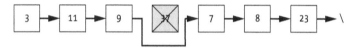

Figure 3-12: Removing a node (37) from a linked list requires updating the pointer in the previous node (9) to skip ahead to the following node (7).

This corresponds to someone making the questionable decision that coffee isn't worth the wait in line. They look at their watch, mutter something about having instant at home, and leave. As long as the person behind the newly departed customer knows who they are now behind, the line's integrity is maintained.

In the case of an array, we would have to pay a significantly higher cost to delete an element, shifting everything following the node containing 37 by one bin toward the front of the array in order to close up the gap. This could require us to walk the entire array.

Again, we must take special care when deleting the first element in a linked list or deleting past the end of the list. When deleting the first node, we update the list's head pointer to the address of the new head node, effectively making that node the new head of the list. When deleting past the end of the list, we have options similar to those for insertion: we can skip the deletion or return an error. The following code does the latter:

```
LinkedListDelete(LinkedListNode: head, Integer: index):
❶ IF head == null:
      return null

❷ IF index == 0:
      new_head = head.next
      head.next = null
      return new_head

   LinkedListNode: current = head
   LinkedListNode: previous = null
   Integer: count = 0
❸ WHILE count < index AND current != null:
      previous = current
      current = current.next
      count = count + 1

❹ IF current != null:
   ❺ previous.next = current.next
   ❻ current.next = null
   ELSE:
      Produce an invalid index error.
❼ return head
```

This code follows the same approach as insertion. This time we start with an additional check ❶. If the list is empty, there is nothing to delete, and we can return the value null to indicate the list is still empty. Otherwise, we check whether we are deleting the first node ❷ and, if so, remove the previous first node from the list and return the address of the new head node.

To remove any later nodes (index > 0), the code must travel to the correct location in the list. Using the same logic as for insertion, the code tracks current, count, and previous while iterating through the nodes until it either finds the correct location or hits the end of the list ❸. If the code finds a node at the correct index ❹, it splices out the node to be removed by setting previous.next to point at one node past the current node ❺. However, if the WHILE loop ran off the end of the list and current is null, there is nothing to delete, so the code throws an error. The function also sets the removed node's next pointer to null both to ensure consistency (it no longer has a next node in the list) and to allow programming languages with memory management to correctly free memory that is no longer used ❻. The function completes by returning the address of the list's head node ❼.

We can adapt this code to use information other than the node's index for deletion. If we have the value of the node to delete, we could update the loop conditions ❸ to remove the first node with that value:

```
WHILE current != null AND current.value != value:
```

In this case, we need to reverse the order of comparison and check if current is null before accessing its value. Similarly, if we need to delete a node given a pointer to it, we could compare the address stored in that pointer to the address of the current node.

The strength of linked lists is that they allow us to insert or remove elements without shifting those elements around in the computer's memory. We can leave the nodes where they are and just update the pointers to indicate their movement.

Doubly Linked Lists

There are many additional ways we can add structure with pointers, many of which we'll examine in later chapters. For now, we'll discuss just one simple extension of the linked list: the *doubly linked list*, which includes backward as well as forward pointers, as shown in Figure 3-13.

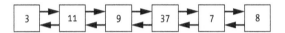

Figure 3-13: A doubly linked list contains pointers to both the next and previous entries.

For algorithms that need to iterate lists in both directions, or just for adventurous programmers looking to expand the number of pointers in their data structures, it is easy to adapt a linked list to a doubly linked one:

```
DoublyLinkedListNode {
    Type: Value
    DoublyLinkedListNode: next
    DoublyLinkedListNode: previous
}
```

The code for operating on doubly linked lists is similar to the code for singly linked lists. Lookups, insertions, and deletions often require traversing the list to find the correct element. Updating the appropriate nodes' previous pointers in addition to their next pointers requires additional logic. Yet this small amount of additional information can enable shortcuts to some of the operations. Given the pointer to any node in a doubly linked list, we can also access the node before it without having to traverse the entire list from the beginning, as we would have to do for a singly linked list.

Arrays and Linked Lists of Items

So far, we have primarily used arrays to store individual (numeric) values. We might be storing a list of top scores, a list of reminder times for a smart alarm clock, or a log of how much coffee we consume each day. This is useful in a variety of applications but is only the most basic way to use an array. We can use the concept of pointers to store more complex and differently sized items.

Suppose you're planning a party. We will make the generous assumption that, unlike many parties thrown by the author, your gathering is popular enough to require an RSVP list. As you begin to receive responses to your invitations, you write a new program using an array to keep track of the guests. You'd like to store at least a single string in each entry, indicating the name of the person who has responded. However, you immediately run into the problem that strings might not be fixed size, so you can't guarantee they will fit in the array's fixed-size bin. You could expand the bin size to fit all possible strings. But how much is enough? Can you reliably say all your invitees will have fewer than 1,000 characters in their name? And if we allow for 1,000 characters, what about the waste? If we are reserving space for 1,000 characters per invitee, then entries for "John Smith" are using only a tiny fraction of their bins. What if we want to include even more dynamic data with each record, such as a list of each guest's music preferences or nicknames?

The natural solution is to combine arrays and pointers, as shown in Figure 3-14. Each bin in the array stores a single pointer to the data of interest. In this case, each bin stores a pointer to a string located somewhere else in memory. This allows the data for each entry to vary in size. We can allocate as much space as we need for each string and point to those strings from the array. We could even create a detailed composite data structure for our RSVP records and link those from the array.

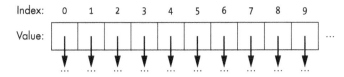

Figure 3-14: Arrays can store a series of pointers, allowing them to link to larger data structures.

The RSVP records don't need to fit into the array bins, because their data lives somewhere else in memory. The array bins only hold (fixed-size) pointers. Similarly, a linked list's nodes can contain pointers to other data. Unlike the next pointers in a linked list, which are pointing to other nodes, these pointers can point to arbitrary other blocks of data.

The rest of the book includes many cases where individual "values" are actually pointers to complex and even dynamic data structures.

Why This Matters

Linked lists and arrays are only the simplest example of how we can trade off among complexity, efficiency, and flexibility in our data structures. By using a pointer, a variable that stores addresses in memory, we can link across blocks of memory. A single fixed-size array bin can point to complex data records or strings of different lengths. Further, we can use pointers to create dynamically linked structures through the computer's memory. By changing a pointer's value to point to a new address, we can change this structure as needed at any time.

Over the remaining chapters, we will see numerous examples of how dynamic data structures can be used to both improve organization of the data and make certain computations more efficient. However, it is important to keep the relative tradeoffs in mind. As we saw with arrays and linked lists, each data structure comes with its own advantages and disadvantages in terms of flexibility, space requirements, efficiency of operations, and complexity. In the next chapter, we will show how can build on these fundamental concepts to create two data structures, stacks and queues, that enable different behavior.

4

STACKS AND QUEUES

This chapter introduces stacks and queues, two data structures that retrieve stored data based on the order in which it was inserted. Stacks and queues are very similar and require only minor implementation differences. However, the simple fact that stacks return the most recently inserted data first, while queues return the oldest, completely changes the behavior of algorithms and the efficiency with which we can access data.

Stacks form the core of depth-first search, which searches deeper and deeper along an individual path until it hits a dead end. Queues enable breadth-first search, which shallowly explores adjacent paths before digging deeper. As we will see later, this one change can dramatically impact real-world behavior, such as how we surf web pages or conduct coffee research.

Stacks

A *stack* is a *last-in, first-out (LIFO)* data structure that operates much like a pile of papers: we add new elements to the top of the stack and remove elements starting with the top of the stack. Formally, a stack supports two operations:

Push   Add a new element to the top of the stack.

Pop   Remove the element from the top of the stack and return it.

Since items are extracted from the top of the stack, the next item removed will always be the one most recently added. If we insert the elements 1, 2, 3, 4, and 5 into a stack, we retrieve them in the order 5, 4, 3, 2, 1.

You can visualize stacks as lettuce bins in a suboptimally run salad bar where the bins are cleaned out every few years. The waiters continually dump new lettuce on the top of the bin, paying no attention to the increasingly squishy mass of lettuce accumulating underneath. Diners see the new lettuce on top and scoop it onto their plates, oblivious to the horrors a few layers below.

We can implement stacks with either arrays or linked lists.

Stacks as Arrays

When implementing a stack as an array, we use the array to hold the values in the stack and use an extra variable to track the index corresponding to the top of the stack—the last element in our array:

```
Stack {
    Integer: array_size
    Integer: top
    Array of values: array
}
```

Initially we set the top index to –1, indicating that there is nothing in the stack.

When we push a new element onto the stack, we increment the top index to the next space and add the new value to that index. We thus order the array from bottom to top, as shown in Figure 4-1. If the last item of the array is fresh, crispy lettuce, the first element of the array represents the items languishing at the bottom of the stack.

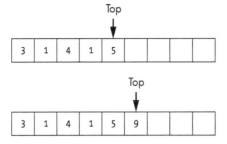

Figure 4-1: Pushing an element on top of a stack represented as an array

When adding elements to an array of fixed size, we must be careful to avoid adding more elements than space allows. If we run out of space, we might expand the array with a technique such as array doubling (see Chapter 3), as shown in the following code. This allows our stack to grow as we add data, though be aware that it introduces additional cost for some insertions.

```
Push(Stack: s, Type: value):
    IF s.top == s.array_size - 1:
        Expand the size of the array
    s.top = s.top + 1
    s.array[s.top] = value
```

This code for pushing an element onto a stack implemented as an array starts by checking that we have room to insert the new element. If not, the code expands the array. The code then increments the index of the top element and inserts the value at that new index.

When we pop an item off the stack, we again use the top index to find the correct element. We remove this element from the array and decrement the top index, as shown in Figure 4-2. In other words, we scoop the newest lettuce from the bin and move one level closer to the lower, older layers.

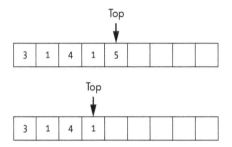

Figure 4-2: Popping an element from a stack represented as an array

The code for popping an element from a stack implemented as an array is simpler than the code for insertion:

```
Pop(Stack: s):
    Type: value = null
    IF s.top > -1:
        value = s.array[s.top]
        s.top = s.top - 1
    return value
```

The code starts by checking that the stack is not empty. If it isn't, the code copies the last element of the array into value, then decrements the pointer to the last element. The code returns the value of the top element or null if the stack was empty. Since we are only adding or removing items from the end of the array, we don't need to shift around any other elements.

As long as our stack has sufficient room, we can perform both additions and removals at a constant cost. Whether we have 10 elements or 10,000, adding or removing an element requires the same number of operations. However, we do pay additional cost when expanding the size of an array during an insertion, so it helps to preallocate a stack that is large enough for the use case.

Stacks as Linked Lists

Alternately, we could implement a stack as either a linked list or doubly linked list, as shown in Figure 4-3. Here the list is drawn left to right, the reverse order of lists in previous chapters, to show the same order as the array representation. Our standard pointer to the head of the list also serves as the pointer to the top of the stack.

```
Stack {
    LinkedListNode: head
}
```

Instead of filling in new array bins and updating indices, the linked list implementation requires us to create and remove nodes in the linked list, update the respective node pointers, and update the pointer to the top of the stack.

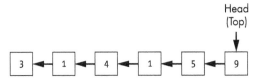

Figure 4-3: A stack implemented as a linked list

We push items on to the stack by adding them to the front of our linked list:

```
Push(Stack: s, Type: value):
    LinkedListNode: node = LinkedListNode(value)
    node.next = s.head
    s.head = node
```

The code for pushing starts by creating a new linked list node. Then it inserts this node into the front of the list by updating the new node's next pointer and the stack's head pointer.

Similarly, when we pop an item from the stack, we return the value in the head node and move the head node pointer to the next item in our list:

```
Pop(Stack: s):
    Type: value = null
```

```
IF s.head != null:
    value = s.head.value
    s.head = s.head.next
return value
```

The code starts with a default return value of null. If the stack is not empty (s.head != null), the code updates the return value to be the head node's value and then updates the head pointer to the next node on the stack. Finally, it returns value.

Along with the memory cost of storing additional pointers, the pointer assignments add a small, constant cost to both the push and pop operations. We're no longer setting a single array value and increment- ing an index. However, as with all dynamic data structures, the tradeoff is increased flexibility: a linked list can grow and shrink with the data. We no longer have to worry about filling up our array or paying the additional costs to increase the array's size.

Queues

A *queue* is a *first-in, first-out (FIFO)* data structure that operates like the line at your favorite coffee bar: we add new elements at the back of the queue and remove old elements from the front. Formally a queue supports two operations:

Enqueue   Add a new element to the back of the queue.

Dequeue   Remove the element from the front of the queue and return it.

If we enqueue five elements in the order 1, 2, 3, 4, 5, we would retrieve them in the same order: 1, 2, 3, 4, 5.

Queues preserve the order in which elements are added, allowing such useful behavior as processing items in the order they arrive. For example, the FIFO property allows our favorite café to serve its custom- ers in an organized fashion. Due to its amazing menu, this shop always has a line of excited customers waiting for their morning brew. New cus- tomers enter the store and enqueue at the back of the line. The next cus- tomer to be served is the person at the front of the line. They place their order, dequeue from the front of the line, and eagerly await the perfect start to their morning.

Like stacks, queues can take the form of both arrays and linked lists.

Queues as Arrays

To implement queues with arrays, we track two indices: the first and last element in the queue. When we enqueue a new element, we add it behind the current last element and increment the back index, as shown in Figure 4-4.

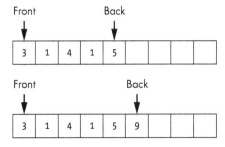

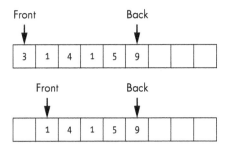

Figure 4-4: Enqueuing an element in a
queue represented as an array

When we dequeue an element, we remove the front element and increment the front index accordingly, as shown in Figure 4-5.

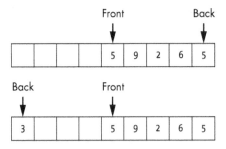

Figure 4-5: Dequeuing an element in a
queue represented as an array

When dequeuing from a fixed array, we quickly run into a drawback: a
block of empty space will accumulate at the front of the array. To solve this
problem, we can either wrap the queue around the end of the array or shift
items down to fill up the space. As we saw in Chapter 1, shifting elements
is expensive, since we have to move all the remaining elements with each
dequeue operation. Wrapping is a better solution, though it does require
us to carefully handle indices being incremented past the end of the array
during both enqueuing and dequeuing, as shown in Figure 4-6.

Figure 4-6: Using an array to represent
queues can result in the elements wrapping
around.

While wrapping adds some complexity to our implementation, it avoids the high cost of shifting elements.

Queues as Linked Lists

It's a better idea to implement the queue as a linked list or a doubly linked list. In addition to maintaining a special pointer to the head of the list (the front of the queue), we maintain one to the last element in the list, the tail or back:

```
Queue {
    LinkedListNode: front
    LinkedListNode: back
}
```

This list, shown in Figure 4-7, is similar to the linked list we used for the stack in Figure 4-3. Each element in the queue links to the element immediately behind it, allowing us to traverse the next pointers from the front of the queue to the back.

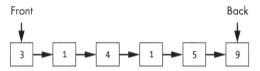

Figure 4-7: A queue represented as a linked list with additional pointers for the front and back elements

Once again, insertions and deletions require us to update both the nodes in the list and our special pointer nodes:

```
Enqueue(Queue: q, Type: value):
    LinkedListNode: node = LinkedListNode(value)
 ❶ IF q.back == null:
        q.front = node
        q.back = node
    ELSE:
      ❷ q.back.next = node
      ❸ q.back = node
```

When we add new element to the queue, we use the queue's back pointer to find the correct location for the insertion. The code starts by creating a new node for the inserted value, then checks whether the queue is empty ❶. If it is, the code adds the new node by setting the queue's front and back pointers to point to the new node. Both pointers need to be updated because otherwise they wouldn't be pointing to valid nodes.

If the queue is not empty, the code appends the new node to the end of the list by modifying the current last node's next pointer to point to our new node ❷. Finally, the code updates the queue's back pointer to point to our new node, indicating it is the new last node in the queue ❸. The front pointer doesn't change unless the queue was previously empty.

Deletions update primarily the pointer to the front of the queue:

```
Dequeue(Queue: q):
 ❶ IF q.front == null:
        return null

 ❷ Type: value = q.front.value
 ❸ q.front = q.front.next
    IF q.front == null:
        q.back = null
    return value
```

The code first checks whether there is anything in the queue by testing whether the queue's front pointer actually points to anything or is null ❶. If the queue is empty (q.front == null), the code immediately returns null. If there is at least one element in the queue, the code saves that value to return later ❷. Then the code updates q.front to point to the next element in the queue ❸. We must take care to update the back pointer as well when dequeuing the last element. If the front item is no longer pointing to a valid element, then the queue is empty, and we set the back pointer to null as well.

Both the enqueue and dequeue operations require a constant number of operations, regardless of the size of the queue. Each operation requires us to adjust a few pointers. We don't care what else is in the data structure; we could be appending elements at the end of a list snaking through the entirety of the computer's memory.

The Importance of Order

The order in which we insert or remove elements can have a staggering impact on the behavior of algorithms (and, in the case of the salad bar, the health of our diners). Queues work best when we need our storage to preserve the ordering of insertions. When processing incoming network requests, for example, we want to process earlier requests first. In contrast, we use stacks when we want to process the most recent item first. For instance, programming languages may use stacks to process function calls. When a new function is called, the current state is pushed onto a stack and execution jumps into the new function. When a function completes, the last state is popped off the stack and the program returns to where that function was called.

We can shift the entire behavior of a search algorithm depending on which data structure we choose. Imagine we are exploring our favorite online encyclopedia to research coffee-grinding methods. As we scan down the page on burr grinders, we see links to other fascinating options. If we were to follow one of those links, we'd reach another page of information along with branches of new potential topics to explore. Whether we use a stack or queue to track the topics we want to pursue later will impact the nature of our coffee exploration, as we'll see in the next two sections.

Depth-First Search

Depth-first search is an algorithm that continues exploring, deeper and deeper, along a single path until it hits a dead end. The algorithm then backs up to the last branching point and checks other options. It maintains a list of future states to explore using a stack, always choosing the most recently inserted option to try next.

In the coffee research example, suppose we start a depth-first search at the page on burr grinders and quickly find three additional topics to pursue. We push these onto the stack, as shown in Figure 4-8(1). Most searches will add options in the order in which they are encountered. For consistency in this example, we add elements in reverse alphabetical order, so that we begin our research at A and continue to Z (or whatever letter is the final topic).

For simplicity's sake, Figure 4-8 shows each of the topics (web pages) as an individual letter. The lines drawn between them represent the web links. This structure is known as a *graph*, which we'll discuss in detail in Chapter 15. Shaded nodes indicate topics we have explored, and the circled topic indicates the topic we're examining on that iteration of the search. The stack data, storing the future options to explore, is represented as the Next array to the graph's right.

Once we've finished reading everything we can about burr grinders (A), we move on to the next topic: blade grinders (B). At this point, our search is waiting to explore topics B, F, and H. We take topic B from the top of the stack, open that page, start reading, and find even more topics of interest (C). Coffee is clearly a deep and complex topic; we could spend a lifetime researching the finest details. We push the new topic C onto the top of the stack for future investigation, as shown in Figure 4-8(2). Newer topics are thus primed to be the next areas of exploration.

The search continues in this way, prioritizing recently added topics, making this search ideal for someone who always wants to explore the most recent topic they've seen. We explore deeper and deeper into each topic thread until we hit a dead end and return to earlier items on the stack. For this example, visited nodes are never revisited or added to the stack, but the stack may contain duplicates. The remaining subfigures in Figure 4-8 illustrate this process.

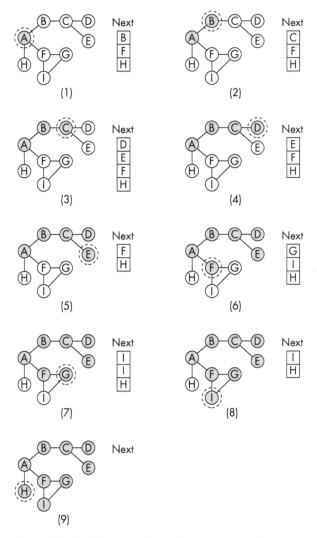

Figure 4-8: Depth-first search: exploring a graph of topics using a stack to track the next topic to explore

Breadth-First Search

Breadth-first search uses logic similar to that of a depth-first search to explore topics, but stores future states with a queue. At each step, the search explores the option that has been waiting the longest, effectively branching out over different directions before going deeper. Figure 4-9 shows a breadth-first search of the coffee grinder–related website from the last section. Again, the circles represent topics, and lines are the links between them. Shaded topics have been explored, and the circled topic is the topic we are researching during that iteration.

In Figure 4-9(1), we read a page about burr grinders (A) and note down three future topics of interest (B, F, and H) in reverse alphabetical order.

The first topic in the queue is the same as the last in the stack—this is the key ordering difference between the two data structures.

We continue our research, taking the item at the front of the queue (H), reading the page, and adding any new items of interest to the back of the queue. In Figure 4-9(2), we explore the next page, only to hit an immediate dead end.

In Figure 4-9(3), the search progresses to the next topic in the queue (F). Here we find new topics (I and G) and add the new links to the queue.

Instead of following those topics further, we take the next item (B) from the front of the queue, as shown in Figure 4-9(4), and explore the final link from the initial page. Again, the search only adds unexplored nodes that are not already in the queue.

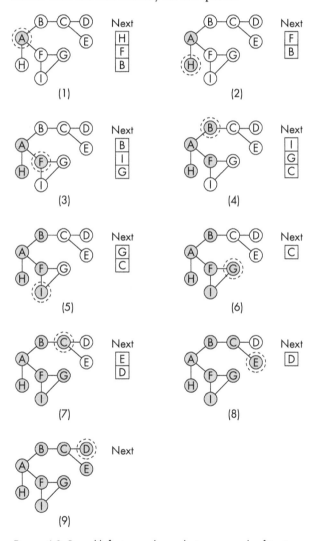

Figure 4-9: Breadth-first search: exploring a graph of topics using a queue to track the next topic to explore

As the search progresses, its advantages become clear: instead of deeply exploring each thread before returning to previous ones, we explore along a frontier of topics, prioritizing breadth over depth. We might survey five different types of grinders before diving into the histories of each grinding mechanism and their respective inventors. This search is ideal for people who don't want to let old topics linger and prefer to cross them off before moving onto new topics.

Since both depth-first search and breadth-first search only explore one option at a time, both work at the same rate: depth-first search deeply explores a few paths in the time it takes breadth-first search to shallowly explore many paths. However, the actual behavior of the search is radically different.

Why This Matters

Different data structures both allow the programmer to use data in different ways and strongly impact the behavior of the algorithms working with that data. Both stacks and queues store objects, both can be implemented with either arrays or linked lists, and both can handle insertions and removals efficiently. From the perspective of simply storing bits, either will suffice. However, the way they handle the data, and specifically the order in which they return their items, gives these similar data structures radically different behavior. Stacks return the newest data they've stored, making them ideal for prioritizing the most recent items. Queues, in contrast, always return the oldest data they've stored, making them ideal for cases where we need to handle items in the order in which they arrive.

As we work to use data structures effectively, efficiency isn't our only consideration. When designing or choosing a data structure for a specific algorithm, we must ask how that data structure's properties will impact the behavior of the algorithm. As the search examples in this chapter show, we can change from breadth-first to depth-first behavior by simply swapping out the data structure. Later chapters give more detail on this logic, using it to design other data structures that aid both the behavior and performance of our algorithms.

5

BINARY SEARCH TREES

Binary search trees use the concepts underpinning the binary search algorithm to create a dynamic data structure. The key word here is *dynamic.* Unlike sorted arrays, binary search trees support the efficient addition and removal of elements in addition to searches, making them the perfect blend of the algorithmic efficiency of binary search and the adaptability of dynamic data structures. They also make for wonderful decorative mobiles for any room.

In addition to introducing binary search trees, this chapter discusses algorithms for searching for values, adding new values, and deleting values. It shows how to use pointers to create branching structures more powerful than the list-based structures in previous chapters. You'll learn how, by carefully structuring the relationships among the values, we can encode the approach used for binary search into the very structure of the data itself.

Binary Search Tree Structure

Trees are hierarchical data structures composed of branching chains of nodes. They are a natural extension of linked lists, where each tree node is permitted two next pointers that point to subsequent nodes in disjoint lists. Figure 5-1 shows a sample binary search tree.

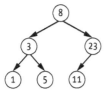

Figure 5-1: An example binary search tree

A node contains a value (of a given type) and up to two pointers to lower nodes in the tree, as shown in Figure 5-2. We call nodes with at least one child *internal nodes* and nodes without any children *leaf nodes.*

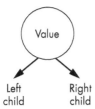

Figure 5-2: The required components of a binary search tree node

Tree nodes may contain other information, depending on their use. We often store a pointer back to the node's parent, for instance. This single piece of additional information allows us to traverse the tree from the bottom up as well as from the top down, which comes in handy when we consider removing nodes.

Formally, we specify a *binary search tree node* as a data structure with this minimal information: a value (or key), pointers to two child nodes (either of which can be set to null if no corresponding child exists), and an optional pointer to the parent node.

```
TreeNode {
    Type: value
    TreeNode: left
    TreeNode: right
    TreeNode: parent
}
```

We might also want to store auxiliary data. Storing and searching for individual values are useful, but using these values as keys for looking up more detailed information greatly extends the power of the data structure. For example, we could use the names of our favorite coffees as the node's values, allowing us to efficiently look up records for any coffee. In this case, our auxiliary data would be a detailed record of everything we know about that coffee. Or our values could be timestamps, and the nodes could contain indications of which coffee we brewed at that time, allowing us to efficiently search our historical coffee consumption. The tree node data structure can either store this auxiliary data directly or include a pointer to a composite data structure located somewhere else in memory.

Binary search trees start at a single *root* node at the top of the tree and branch into multiple paths as they descend, as shown in Figure 5-3. This structure allows programs to access the binary search tree through a single pointer—the location of its root node.

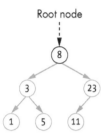

Figure 5-3: The root node indicates the top of the binary search tree and is the starting location for operations.

Botanical purists may draw trees with the root node at the bottom of the tree and nodes branching upward, instead of starting from the top as in Figure 5-3. However, the representations are equivalent. In truth, both the top-down and bottom-up illustrations hide the actual complexity of the binary search tree. Like a linked list, a search tree's individual nodes can be scattered throughout the computer's memory. Each node is only linked to its children and parents through the power and flexibility of pointers.

The power of the binary search tree stems from how values are organized within the tree. The *binary search tree property* states:

> For any node *N*, the value of any node in *N*'s left subtree is less than *N*'s value, and the value of any node in *N*'s right subtree is greater than *N*'s value.

In other words, the tree is organized by the values at each node, as shown in Figure 5-4. The values of the data in the left node and all nodes below it are less than the value of the current node. Similarly, the values of the data in the right node and all nodes below it are greater than the value of the current node. The values thus serve two roles. First, and most obviously, they indicate the value stored at that node. Second, they define the tree's structure below that node by partitioning the subtree into two subsets.

The above definition implicitly restricts the binary search tree to contain unique values. It is possible to define binary search trees that allow duplicate values by modifying the binary search tree property accordingly. Other references may vary in whether they allow duplicate values and thus how they handle equality in the binary search tree property. This chapter focuses on the case of non-duplicate values to stay consistent with other indexing data structures we will explore in the book, such as skiplists and hash tables, though the algorithms presented can be adapted to handle duplicates.

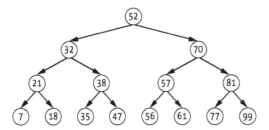

Figure 5-4: The values of the nodes in a binary search tree are ordered by the binary search tree property.

We could compare a binary search tree's structure to a public relations department that is organized by level of humor. Each employee measures their humor level with a single numerical value, the number of funny illustrations in a 30-minute presentation. A score of 0 represents the serious presenter who includes only technical diagrams. A score of 100 or above represents the aspiring comedian who adds multiple jokes to every slide. The entire department structures itself around this one metric. Internal nodes represent managers with either one or two direct reports. Each manager considers their own humor level and partitions their suborganization accordingly. Team members who include more jokes (a *larger* humor level) go in the right subteam. Those who include fewer jokes (a *smaller* humor level) go in the left subteam. Each manager thus provides both a partitioning function and a middle ground between the two subteams.

Although this ordering of nodes might not seem like a lot of structure, keep in mind the amount of power we got from using a similar property within binary search. The binary search tree property is effectively keeping the data within the tree sorted with respect to its position in the tree. As we will see, this allows us to not only efficiently find values in the tree but also efficiently add and remove nodes.

Searching Binary Search Trees

We search a binary search tree by walking down from the root node. At each step, we determine whether to explore the left or right subtree by comparing the value at the current node with the target value. If the target value is less than the current value, the search progresses to the left. If the target value is greater than the current value, the search progresses to the right. The node's value thus serves the same function as those helpful signs in hotels that tell us rooms 500–519 are to the left and rooms 520–590 are to the right. With one quick check, we can make the appropriate turn and ignore the rooms in the other direction. The search ends when either the target value is found or it reaches a node with no children in the correct direction. In the latter case, we can definitively say that the target value is not in the tree.

Iterative and Recursive Searches

We implement this search with either an iterative or recursive approach. The following code uses a recursive approach, where the search function calls itself using the next node in the tree, initially called on the root node of the tree. The code returns a pointer to the node containing the value, allowing us to retrieve any auxiliary information from the node.

```
FindValue(TreeNode: current, Type: target):
❶ IF current == null:
      return null
❷ IF current.value == target:
      return current
❸ IF target < current.value AND current.left != null:
      return FindValue(current.left, target)
❹ IF target > current.value AND current.right != null:
      return FindValue(current.right, target)
❺ return null
```

This algorithm performs only a few tests at each node; if any of the tests pass, we end the function by returning a value. First, the code checks that the current node is not null, which can happen when searching an empty tree. If it is null, the tree is empty and, by definition, does not contain the value of interest ❶. Second, if the current node's value equals our target value, the code has found the value of interest and returns the node ❷. Third, the code checks whether it should explore the left subtree and, if so, returns whatever it finds from that exploration ❸. Fourth, the code checks whether it should explore the right subtree and, if so, return whatever it finds from that exploration ❹. Note that in both the left and right cases, the code also checks that the corresponding child exists. If none of the tests trigger, the code has made it to a node that doesn't match our target value and does not have a child in the correct direction. It has reached a dead end and is forced to admit defeat by returning a failure value such as null ❺. A dead end occurs whenever there is no child in the correct direction, so it is possible for an internal node with a single child to still be a dead end for a search.

Suppose we used this strategy to search Figure 5-5 for the value 63. We start at the root node and compare its value (50) to that of our target. Since 50 is less than 63, we know that the target value is not in the left-hand branch, where every node has a value less than 50. This simple fact allows us to *prune* the entire left-hand subtree from our search. We can avoid checking 11 of the 22 nodes in our tree with a single comparison. This test is effectively the same as the pruning we did within the binary search algorithm from Chapter 2: we test a single element against our target value and use that to prune out a large section of our search space.

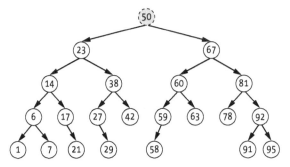

Figure 5-5: The first step in the search of a binary search tree. The search begins at the root node.

Our search progresses down the right-hand subtree to the node with value 67, as shown in Figure 5-6. We again employ the binary search tree property to rule out half the remaining search space. In this case 63 is less than 67, so we choose the left subtree. Anything in node 67's right-hand subtree must be larger than 67, and thus it cannot contain 63. We've pruned another 5 nodes.

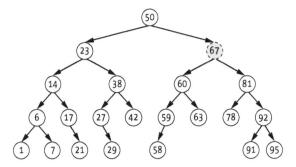

Figure 5-6: The second step in the search of a binary search tree

At this point, we can make definitive statements about the remaining search space underneath the current node. Since we branched right at 50 and left at 67, we know that all nodes in the new subtree will have values greater than 50 and less than 67. In fact, each time we take a right-hand branch, we're tightening the lower bound of the remaining search space. Whenever we take a left-hand branch, we're tightening the upper bound.

The search continues down the tree, traversing each of the shaded nodes as shown in Figure 5-7. The search passes through 4 of the 22 nodes before finding the target value.

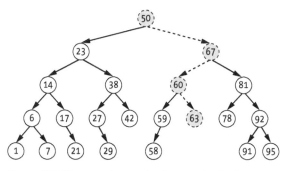

Figure 5-7: The complete path of a search of a binary search tree for value 63

Consider this search in the context of the public relations department organized by humor metric. Suppose the department head needs to find a speaker for an informal presentation at an industry conference. After some consideration, they determine a humor level of 63 jokes per 30 minutes will be optimal for this audience. The department head (root node) considers their own humor level, realizes they are too serious, and therefore asks their right-hand report to find someone within the report's organization. Everyone in the right-hand subtree is more comedic than the department head. That manager repeats the same steps of comparing their own humor level (67) with the target value and delegating to their appropriate report.

Of course, the search does not need to progress all the way down to a leaf node. As shown in Figure 5-8, the node in question might sit in the middle of the tree. If we search the same tree for the value of 14, we take two left branches and end at the appropriate internal node. The manager at this intermediate level perfectly fits our humor criterion and can give the talk. Thus, as we descend the tree, we need to check whether the current node is equal to our target value and terminate the search early if we find a match.

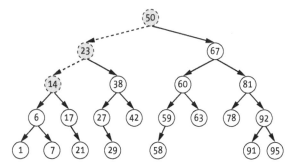

Figure 5-8: The search of a binary search tree can conclude at an internal node where the value matches our target value.

The iterative approach to searching a binary search tree replaces the recursion with a WHILE loop that iterates down the tree. The search again starts at the tree's root.

```
FindValueItr(TreeNode: root, Type: target):
❶ TreeNode: current = root
❷ WHILE current != null AND current.value != target:
    ❸ IF target < current.value:
          current = current.left
      ELSE:
          current = current.right
❹ return current
```

The code starts by creating a local variable current to point to the current node in the search ❶. Initially, this will be the root node, which may be null in an empty tree. Then a WHILE loop keeps iterating down the tree until it either hits a dead end (current == null) or finds the correct value (current.value == target) ❷. Within the loop, the code checks whether the next child should be to the left or right ❸ and reassigns current to point to the corresponding child. The function concludes by returning current, which is either the found node or, if the tree is empty or the value is not found, null ❹.

The computational cost of both the recursive and iterative searches is proportional to the depth of the target value in the tree. We start at the top of the tree and proceed down a single path. The deeper the tree, the more comparisons we need to perform. Structuring the tree to minimize its depth thus increases search efficiency.

Searching Trees vs. Searching Sorted Arrays

The skeptical reader might protest, "Chapter 2 already taught us how to do an efficient search on sorted data. Binary search scales logarithmically with the size of the data. You had illustrations and everything. Why bother putting the data in a tree rather than a sorted array? Are we adding unnecessary complexity and overhead with all these pointers?"

These concerns are reasonable. However, it's important to consider how the data structure and search will be used in a wider context. If our data is already in a sorted array and we want to search through it a single time, building a tree rather than simply performing a binary search does not help. In fact, building the tree itself is more expensive than a single linear scan. Similarly, if the data does not change, then sorting it once and using the sorted array may be preferable. We avoid the memory overhead of the tree structure itself. The tradeoffs change as our data becomes more dynamic.

Imagine the case where employees join or leave the PR department. In addition to the normal paperwork, the department needs to update its data structure of humor levels. Each new employee represents an addition to the list of humor levels. Each departure represents a deletion. Instead of using the reporting hierarchy, the department could use the office assignments to sort employees by humor level. The least humorous person is in office 1 and the most humorous in office 100. The manager can still efficiently search for the correct speaker. However, they now need to fix the office assignments with each new addition or departure. For a large department or a high number of changes, the overhead increases. In highly dynamic environments, such as a list of pending restaurant orders, the costs can become significant.

The power of binary search trees, and dynamic data structures in general, arises in cases where the data is *changing*. As we will see in the next sections, binary search trees allow us to efficiently add and remove data points. In a sorted array, we would need to constantly update the array as we add and remove data, which can be expensive. In contrast, the binary search tree keeps the data in an easily searchable structure as the data itself changes. If we are doing many searches over a dynamic data set, this combination of efficiencies becomes critical.

Modifying Binary Search Trees

The root node always deserves special care when using or modifying a binary search tree. When searching for a node in the tree, we always start at the root node. When inserting the first node into the tree, such as the first person joining our PR department, we make that node our new root. And, as we will see later in the chapter, when removing a node from a binary tree, we must treat the root node as a special case.

We can simplify the logic for using binary search trees by wrapping the entire tree in a thin data structure that contains the root node:

```
BinarySearchTree {
    TreeNode: root
}
```

While this might seem like a waste (more complexity and an extra data structure), it provides an easy-to-use interface for the tree and greatly simplifies our handling of the root node. When using a wrapper data structure (or class) for our binary search tree, we also need to provide top-level functions to add or find nodes. These are relatively thin wrappers with a special case for handling a tree without any nodes.

To search a tree, the code again starts by checking whether the tree is empty (tree.root == null):

```
FindTreeNode(BinarySearchTree: tree, Type: target):
    IF tree.root == null:
        return null
    return FindValue(tree.root, target)
```

If the tree is empty, it immediately returns null to indicate the search failed to find a match. Otherwise, the code recursively searches the tree using FindValue. Performing the null check here can even take the place of the check at the start of FindValue, requiring us to perform it only once for the entire tree instead of at each node.

Adding Nodes

We use the same basic algorithm to add values to a binary search tree as we do to search it. We start at the root node, progress down the tree as if searching for the new value, and terminate once we hit a dead end: either a leaf node or an internal node with a single child in the wrong direction. The primary difference between our search and insertion algorithms comes after we hit the dead end, when the insertion algorithm creates a new node as a child of the current node: a left-hand child if the new value is less than that of the current node or a right-hand child otherwise.

Here we can see a clear difference in behavior between trees that allow duplicates and ones that do not. If our tree allows duplicate values, we keep going until we hit a dead end and then insert a new copy of that value into our tree. If the tree doesn't allow duplicates, we might replace or augment the data stored at the matching node. For example, one simple piece of auxiliary data we could track is a counter—the number of times the value has been added to the tree. Below we focus on the case of overwriting data to stay consistent with other indexing data structures we will explore in the book.

As with our search function, we start with a wrapper function for addition that handles the case of empty trees:

```
InsertTreeNode(BinarySearchTree: tree, Type: new_value):
    IF tree.root == null:
        tree.root = TreeNode(new_value)
    ELSE:
        InsertNode(tree.root, new_value)
```

First, the code checks whether the tree is empty (tree.root == null). If so, it creates a new root node with that value. Otherwise, it calls InsertNode on the root node, kicking off the recursive process from below. Thus, we can ensure that InsertNode is called with a valid (non-null) node.

Here is the InsertNode code:

```
InsertNode(TreeNode: current, Type: new_value):
❶ IF new_value == current.value:
        Update node as needed
        return
❷ IF new_value < current.value:
    ❸ IF current.left != null:
            InsertNode(current.left, new_value)
        ELSE:
            current.left = TreeNode(new_value)
            current.left.parent = current
    ELSE:
    ❹ IF current.right != null:
            InsertNode(current.right, new_value)
        ELSE:
            current.right = TreeNode(new_value)
            current.right.parent = current
```

The `InsertNode` code starts by checking whether it is at a node with a matching value and, if so, updating the node's data as needed ❶. Otherwise, the code searches for the correct location to insert the new value by following either the left- or right-hand paths, based on the comparison of the new value and the current node's value ❷. In either case, the code then checks that the next node along that path exists ❸ ❹. If the next node exists, the code follows the path, progressing deeper into the tree. Otherwise, the code has found a dead end, indicating the correct location to insert the new node. The algorithm inserts nodes by creating a new node, linking the parent's corresponding child pointer (`left` or `right`), and setting the `parent` link.

For example, if we want to add the number 77 to the binary search tree in Figure 5-9, we progress down through nodes 50, 67, 81, and 78 until we hit a dead end at the node with value of 78. At this point, we find ourselves without a valid child in the correct direction. Our search is at a dead end. We create a new node with the value of 77 and make it the node 78's left child.

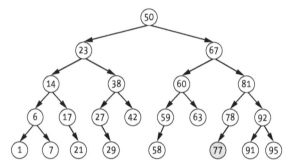

Figure 5-9: Inserting the value 77 into our binary search tree

The cost of inserting a new node into the tree is again proportional to the depth of the branch along which we insert the new node. We perform a single comparison for each node along the path until we hit a dead end, and, as with the search operation, we ignore all the nodes in other branches. Therefore, the worst-case cost of an insertion will scale linearly with the depth of the tree.

Removing Nodes

Removing nodes from a binary search tree is a more complicated process than adding them. There are three cases of node removal to consider: removing a leaf node (with no children), removing an internal node with a single child, and removing an internal node with two children. As you'd expect, the job becomes more complex as the number of children increases.

To remove a leaf node, we just delete that node and update its parent's child pointer to reflect the fact it no longer exists. This might make the parent node into a leaf. For example, to remove node 58 in Figure 5-10, we would just delete node 58 and set its parent's left child pointer to `null`.

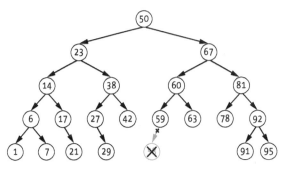

Figure 5-10: Remove a leaf node from a binary search tree by deleting it and updating the pointer from its parent node.

Removing leaf nodes shows the value of storing a pointer to the parent node: it allows us to search for the node to delete, follow the parent pointer back to that node's parent, and set the corresponding child pointer to null. Storing this single piece of additional data makes the deletion operation much simpler.

In the example of our public relations department, a leaf node that gets deleted corresponds to an employee with no direct reports leaving the company. After the farewell party and cake, the rest of the organization returns to work. The only change in the hierarchy is that the former employee's boss has one less person on their team. In fact, they might have no one reporting to them now.

If the target node has a single child, we remove it by promoting that single child to be the child of the deleted node's parent. This is like removing a manager from our reporting hierarchy without shuffling anyone else around. When the manager leaves, their boss assumes management of the former employee's single direct report. For example, if we wanted to remove node 17 from our example tree, we could simply shift node 21 up to take its place as shown in Figure 5-11. Node 14 now links directly to node 21.

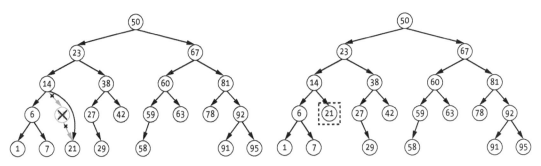

Figure 5-11: Remove an internal node with a single child by changing the pointers (left) and shifting that child up (right).

This way of removing a single-child node works even if the node we are shifting up has its own subtree. Since the node being moved up was already in the parent's subtree, all of its descendants will continue to respect the binary search tree property.

The complexity ramps up substantially when we try to remove an internal node with two children. It is no longer sufficient to just delete the node or shift a single child up. In our public relations department, a node's two children represent two distinct employees with different humor levels. We can't just choose one to promote and let the other accidentally disappear from the hierarchy, no longer anchored to the root node through the fragile chain of pointers. We must preserve the integrity of the rest of the tree and ensure it continues to follow the binary search tree property.

To remove a node with two children, we swap that node out for another node in the tree that will preserve the binary search tree property. We do this by finding the *successor* of the node to be deleted—the next node we would encounter if we traversed the nodes in sorted order. We swap the successor into the location of the deleted node. This swapped node might also have a child node that needs to be handled when it is removed from its old location. In order to remove the successor node from the binary tree without breaking any of its pointers, we reuse the delete procedure on the node to be swapped. We find the successor, save a pointer to that node, and then remove it from the tree.

For example, if we wanted to delete value 81 in Figure 5-12, we need to first swap in the node with a value of 91. We do this by saving pointers to the node to delete and the successor node (Figure 5-12(1)). Then we set the successor node to be the child of the deleted node's parent (Figure 5-12(2)). Finally, we update the successor node's children to those of the recently deleted node, effectively swapping it into place (Figure 5-12(3)).

In order to perform the deletion, we need to be able to efficiently find a node's successor. While this might seem like a daunting task, we have one critical advantage. Since we are only considering cases where the node in question has two children, we can always find the successor in the node's right-hand subtree. Specifically, the successor will be the minimum (or leftmost) node in the right-hand subtree. As a bonus, the successor node is guaranteed to have at most one (right-hand) child. If the candidate successor node had a child to the left, then that child (or a node down its own left-hand subtree) would be the true successor.

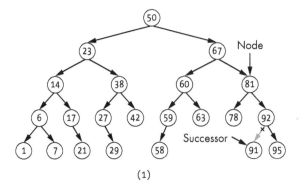

(1)

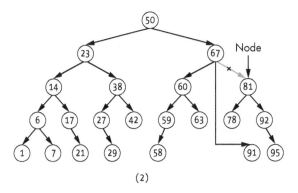

(2)

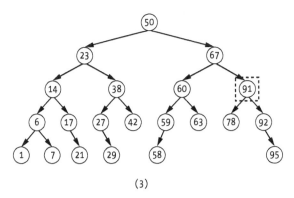

(3)

Figure 5-12: To remove an internal node with two children,
we first swap the node's successor into that position.

Listing 5-1 provides (admittedly verbose) pseudocode to demonstrate removing the three types of nodes we've just discussed from a binary search tree. Shorter implementations are possible. However, breaking the cases out explicitly helps to illustrate the complexities involved. Also note that we delete a node using its pointer instead of its value. Thus, in order to delete the node with a given value, we would first find a pointer to the node using FindTreeNode and then call delete with that pointer.

```
RemoveTreeNode(BinarySearchTree: tree, TreeNode: node):
❶ IF tree.root == null OR node == null:
      return

   # Case A: Deleting a leaf node.
❷ IF node.left == null AND node.right == null:
      IF node.parent == null:
          tree.root = null
      ELSE IF node.parent.left == node:
          node.parent.left = null
      ELSE:
          node.parent.right = null
      return

   # Case B: Deleting a node with one child.
❸ IF node.left == null OR node.right == null:
      ❹ TreeNode: child = node.left
      IF node.left == null:
          child = node.right

      ❺ child.parent = node.parent
      IF node.parent == null:
          tree.root = child
      ELSE IF node.parent.left == node:
          node.parent.left = child
      ELSE:
          node.parent.right = child
      return

   # Case C: Deleting a node with two children.
   # Find the successor and splice it out of the tree.
❻ TreeNode: successor = node.right
   WHILE successor.left != null:
      successor = successor.left
   RemoveTreeNode(tree, successor)

   # Insert the successor in the deleted node's place.
❼ IF node.parent == null:
      tree.root = successor
   ELSE IF node.parent.left == node:
      node.parent.left = successor
   ELSE:
      node.parent.right = successor
❽ successor.parent = node.parent

❾ successor.left = node.left
   node.left.parent = successor

   successor.right = node.right
   IF node.right != null:
      node.right.parent = successor
```

Listing 5-1: Removal of a node from a binary search tree

As with the wrapper functions for insertion and search, the code starts by checking whether the tree is empty ❶ and, if so, returning null. It also checks whether there is a valid node to delete (node != null), which is useful in cases where we want to combine the search and deletion into a single line:

```
RemoveTreeNode(tree, FindTreeNode(tree, target))
```

Since FindTreeNode returns null if the node is not found, we handle this case explicitly.

The code then considers the three cases in order. In case A, where it is removing a leaf node ❷, the code only needs to change the correct child pointer of the removed node's parent. First, it checks whether the node to be deleted has a parent node. If not, the code is removing the root itself and modifies the root node pointer to null, effectively removing the root. If the removed node was the parent's left-hand child, the code sets that pointer to null. Likewise, if the removed node was the parent's right-hand child, the code sets that pointer to null. The code can then return, having successfully removed the target leaf node from the tree.

In case B, removing a node with a single child ❸, the code starts by identifying which of the node's two child pointers links to the child by checking which of the two pointers is not null ❹. The code stores a pointer to that child node for later use. Next, it fixes the pointers between the newly promoted node and its new parent ❺. The code sets the child's parent pointer to its previous grandparent, splicing the removed node out of the tree in the upward direction. Finally, the code fixes the correct child pointer within the removed node's parent, including handling changes to the root node as a special case. The code takes the pointer that previously pointed to the removed node and redirects it to point to that node's single child. If the removed node doesn't have a parent, the code is dealing with the root node and needs to modify that pointer accordingly. Once the code has spliced out the correct node, it returns.

In case C, where the node to be removed has two children, the code starts by identifying the successor node and removing that from the tree ❻. Note that, as described above, the recursive call to RemoveTreeNode cannot itself trigger case C because the successor will have at most a single (right-hand) child. The code maintains a pointer to this successor even after removing it from the tree because it will use this node to replace the deleted node. The code then replaces the deleted node with the successor through the following series of steps:

1. Modifying the deleted node's parent to set the correct child pointer to the successor ❼.

2. Modifying the successor's parent pointer to point to its new parent ❽.

3. Setting the links to and from the left and right children of the successor ❾. The code takes extra care when dealing with the right child, as it is possible that it has already deleted that child with the RemoveTreeNode operation above (in the case where the successor was the immediate right child of node). It therefore needs to check whether the right-hand child is null before trying to assign the right child's parent pointer.

Depending on the programming language and how the code will be used, we might also want to set node's outgoing pointers to null as part of the deletion. This will clean up references from the deleted node to other nodes in the tree. We can do this by including the following lines at the end of each of the three cases (before the return statements in cases A and B and before the end of the function for case C):

```
node.parent = null
node.right = null
node.left = null
```

As with both search and insertion, the deletion operation involves at most traversing the tree from top to bottom along one path. In cases A and B, this trip happens before the RemoveTreeNode function (as part of the earlier call to FindTreeNode to get the pointer to the node itself). Case C adds an additional traversal from the internal node to be removed to its successor. Thus, the worst-case runtime of deletion is still proportional to the depth of the tree.

The Danger of Unbalanced Trees

The time it takes to perform searches, additions, and deletions on a *perfectly balanced* binary search tree is, in the worst case, proportional to the depth of the tree, making these operations highly efficient in trees that are not too deep. A perfectly balanced tree is one in which, at every node, the right subtree contains the same number of nodes as the left subtree. In this case, the depth of the tree grows by 1 each time we double the number of nodes in the tree. Thus, in balanced trees, the worst-case performance of all three operations grows proportionally to $\log_2(N)$, the logarithm of the number of elements N.

Binary search trees are still efficient as long as the trees are mostly, if not perfectly, balanced. But if the tree becomes highly unbalanced, its depth could grow linearly with the number of elements. In fact, in the extreme case, our splendid binary search tree becomes nothing more than a sorted linked list—all the nodes have a single child in the same direction as shown in Figure 5-13.

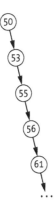

Figure 5-13: An example of an unbalanced binary search tree

Highly unbalanced trees can easily occur in many real-world applications. Imagine we are storing our coffee log in a binary search tree indexed by timestamp. Every time we drink a cup of coffee, we insert the relevant information into our tree. Things go bad quickly. Due to the monotonically increasing timestamps, we insert every entry in sorted order, and we create a linked list using only the right-hand child pointers.

Operations on an unbalanced tree can be extremely inefficient. Consider a tree with N nodes. If our tree is balanced, our operations take time logarithmic in N. In the opposite case, where our tree is a list, our operations can take time linearly proportional to N.

There are a variety of augmentations, such as red-black trees, 2-3 trees, and B-trees, that we can use to keep trees balanced while undergoing dynamic insertions and deletions. The tradeoff for any of these approaches is increased complexity in the tree operations. We consider B-trees in more detail in Chapter 12 and show how their structure keeps them balanced.

The next section introduces a straightforward approach to building a balanced binary search tree from an initial set of values. *Bulk construction* allows the algorithm to choose which nodes split the data so as to balance the number of nodes on each side. This is a good approach when we have many of the values up front but need to be careful with future insertions, as they could result in an unbalanced tree.

Bulk Construction of Binary Search Trees

We can easily construct a binary search tree by iteratively adding nodes: we create a single new node and label that our root, then for each remaining value, create a new node and add that node to the tree. This approach has the advantages of being simple and reusing the algorithms that we defined previously. Unfortunately, it can lead to unbalanced trees. As we saw above, if we add values in sorted order, we end up with a sorted linked list. We can do better when creating a tree from an initial set of numbers.

We create balanced binary search trees from a sorted array, such as the one shown in Figure 5-14, by recursively dividing the elements into smaller subsets. At each level, we choose the middle value to be the node at that level. If there is an even number of elements, we can use either of the two middle elements.

1	2	3	4	5	6	7	8	9	10	11	12

Figure 5-14: A sorted array used for bulk construction of a binary search tree

We create a new node with the value equal to the middle element in our array and split the remaining elements among the two child nodes, as shown in Figure 5-15. We recursively create subtrees for each of those child nodes using the same process. Values less than the middle element go on the left, while larger values go on the right.

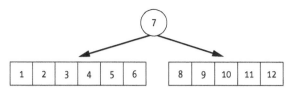

Figure 5-15: After the first split, we have a single node and two separate arrays.

We don't need to create new copies of the input array at each split. Instead, we can take a page from the binary search algorithm and just track the current range of the array under consideration, as shown in Figure 5-16. Each of our splits partitions the array into coherent halves, so we only need to worry about two bounds: the indices of the highest and lowest values that fall into the current branch.

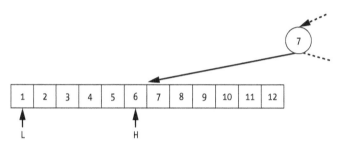

Figure 5-16: A high and low index can be used to track the subset of the array currently under consideration.

Once we've created the new node, we use the same approach to build each of the left and right subtrees independently. Specifically, we select the middle value, create a new node from that value, partition the remaining ranges, and use those ranges to create the subtrees. The process ends when there is only a single value left in our range. In that case, we create a new leaf node with that value and no children.

Why This Matters

Binary search trees demonstrate how we can adapt dynamic data structures to specific problems. The trees use a branching structure to capture and maintain ordering information in the data values. This allows them to facilitate efficient searches. Further, the pointer-based structure of binary search trees allows them to continuously adapt as new data is added. This interplay of data, problem, and computation provides the foundation that allows us to solve increasingly complex computational challenges.

Throughout later chapters, we will continue to build on the concepts of dynamic data structures, adapting the structure of the data to the problem itself and using branching data structures to allow efficient pruning. These techniques pop up in a range of different data structures. Understanding the fundamentals, such as how these techniques allow efficient searches in dynamic binary search trees, is critical to understanding how to work with more advanced data structures and algorithms. The next chapter introduces the trie, showing how the tree-based concepts of the binary search tree can be extended to multiway branches in order to improve the efficiency of certain types of searches.

6

TRIES AND ADAPTING DATA STRUCTURES

Binary search trees, while incredibly powerful, are only one way of using a tree structure to better organize data. Instead of splitting our data sets based on less-than or greater-than comparisons, we can optimize how the tree splits the data for the specific search problem at hand. In this chapter, for example, we tackle the problem of storing and searching strings in trees. Extending the binary search tree's general branching approach to capture additional structure within the data enables us to search efficiently for target strings in a set of strings.

We begin by discussing how binary search trees can be directly applied to string data but have greater cost than other datatypes. Taking the sequential nature of strings into account, we'll then adapt our search trees to store strings more efficiently. The result is a branching structure that may one day motivate the world's most gloriously excessive filing cabinet: the trie (pronounced "try").

Tries are data structures that branch on a *single* character of the string at each level. This splitting strategy greatly reduces the cost of comparisons at each node. Through this lens, we explore how foundational concepts of various algorithms and data structures can be adapted to a new type of problem.

Binary Search Trees of Strings

When considering whether we can improve an algorithm, we should first understand the limitations of our current approach—otherwise, there's no reason to build a more complex data structure. Therefore, before we dive into string-specific data structures, we'll examine where binary search trees fall short when used to store strings. First, let's see how binary search trees can be used for this search.

Strings in Trees

Binary search trees can store not just numbers but anything sortable, from shoes (sorted by size or smell) to zombie movies (sorted by box office revenue or scariness) to food items (sorted by price, spiciness, or likelihood to cause vomiting within the next 24 hours). Binary search trees are quite versatile that way. All we need is the ability to order the items.

To store strings in a binary search tree, we can sort elements in alphabetical order. For example, each node of the binary search tree in Figure 6-1 is a single string partitioning its subtree into strings that come before and after it in the dictionary. We reuse the greater than and less than notation from binary search trees, where X < Y indicates that string X comes before string Y in the alphabet.

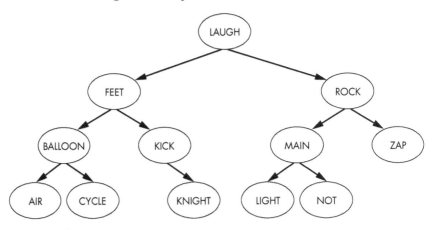

Figure 6-1: A binary search tree constructed with words

We search binary search trees of strings just as we did for numbers. For example, to find the string LIGHT in Figure 6-1, we begin at the root node. We then compare the target value to the node's value, using alphabetical ordering, and progress down either the left or right branch:

1. LIGHT > LAUGH: We proceed down the right branch.
2. LIGHT < ROCK: We proceed down the left branch.

3. LIGHT < MAIN: We proceed down the left branch.

4. LIGHT == LIGHT: We have found the target value and can terminate the search.

In Figure 6-2, the shaded ovals indicate the 4 out of 12 nodes explored during the search.

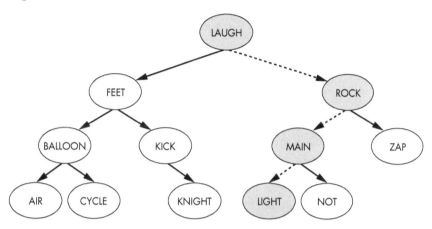

Figure 6-2: The path of traversal when searching a binary search tree of strings for the string LIGHT

At first glance, binary search trees seem to provide a simple, efficient mechanism for searching string data—no modification required. If our tree is balanced, the worst-case cost of the search will scale proportional to the logarithm of the number of entries. In Figure 6-2, we were able to limit our search to checking the target against only 4 out of 12 nodes.

However, we are forgetting one critical factor—the cost of each comparison. As we saw in Chapter 1, comparing two strings is more expensive than comparing a pair of numbers. In fact, in the worst case, the cost of the string comparison operation scales with the length of the strings themselves. Now the cost of our tree search depends on both the number of strings and their lengths, meaning we've added a new dimension of complexity.

To fix this problem and achieve even greater computational savings than provided by a binary search tree, we must take into account two important aspects of string data's structure: the sequential ordering of strings and the limited number of letters or characters involved.

The Cost of String Comparison

So far, we have been ignoring two important pieces of information in our quest to search strings. The first is the sequential nature of string comparisons. To determine the alphabetical order of strings, we start at the first character in a string and sequentially compare characters until we find a difference. That one difference then determines the string's relative order in the search tree—it doesn't matter what the rest of the characters are.

In the example in Figure 6-3, ZOMBIE comes before ZOOM because of the characters in the third position: M comes before O. We don't care about the relationship of remaining characters, BIE and M, and can ignore them.

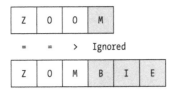

Figure 6-3: The comparison of two strings progresses character by character until the first nonmatching pair is found.

As we saw in Chapter 1, the sequential comparison required for strings in binary search trees is inherently more expensive than the comparison of two numbers. Even comparing the two relatively short strings in Figure 6-3 requires three separate comparisons: Z versus Z, O versus O, and O versus M. By the time we get to longer strings, such as our favorite movie quotes, the cost can become significant. The situation becomes even more dire when the strings have a high degree of overlap. Imagine a binary search tree that indexes our coffee collection by name. If we insert a few hundred coffees under the brand name "Jeremy's Gourmet High Caffeine Experience," we would need to compare quite a few characters to decide whether "Jeremy's Gourmet High Caffeine Experience: Medium Roast" comes before or after "Jeremy's Gourmet High Caffeine Experience: City Roast." Our binary search tree algorithm pays that cost at each node.

The second key piece of information we haven't considered as we strive to improve search efficiency is that, in many languages, each position can only contain a small number of letters. English words use just 26 letters (ignoring capitalization). Even if we include numbers and other characters, the set of valid characters is limited in practice. This means that, at each position, we have a limited number of ways the string can proceed—a limited number of next steps. As we'll see shortly, this insight allows us to define a partitioning function that creates multi-way splits over the next character in the string.

We can combine these insights to build a data structure that operates similarly to comparing strings in the real world. The resulting data structure, a trie, is optimized to account for the additional structure in strings.

Tries

Tries are tree-based data structures that partition strings along different branches based on their prefixes. Computer scientist René de la Briandais proposed the general approach behind tries as a method to improve file searching on computers with slow memory access, and Edward Fredkin, a computer scientist and physicist, proposed their name. Instead of partitioning the data into two sets at each node, we branch the tree based on the prefix so far (sequential comparisons). Further, we allow the tree to split into more than a measly two branches (limited number of characters). In fact, for English words, we can let the tree branch 26 ways at each node— one branch for each of the possible next letters. Each node in the trie thus represents a prefix so far.

Like binary search trees, the trie starts at a root node, in this case representing the empty prefix. Each branch then defines the next character in the string. Naturally, this means each node can have more than two children, as shown in Figure 6-4.

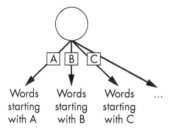

Figure 6-4: A trie node branches out on each possible character in the current position.

We can implement the branches of each trie node as using an array of pointers, with one array bin for each character. In some cases, we may be able to use representations more memory-efficient than arrays within our data structure. After all, even for English words, most non-trivial prefixes will have significantly fewer than 26 valid options for the next letter. For now, however, we will stick with an array implementation for simplicity's sake. The discussions and example implementations in this chapter also focus primarily on English words (26 letters and a 26-element array of children), though the algorithms apply to other character sets as well.

Think of a trie's branching structure as the registration table of a major event. Upon showing up at the world's premier conference on Coffee Analogies for Computer Science, we visit the registration table to get our own personalized packet of information and free conference goodie (hopefully a coffee mug). With a huge number of participants, the organizers split up the packets into manageable groups so as to prevent a single line from snaking around the convention center. Instead of creating a series of pairwise splits (such as "Does your last name come before or after Smith?"), the organizers divide attendees into 26 different lines according to the first letter of their last name. In a single step, the crush of attendees shrinks to 26 more manageable lines. A trie performs that spectacular many-way branching at every node.

As with a binary search tree, we do not need to create nodes for empty branches of the tree. Figure 6-5 shows an example of this structure, where the shaded letters represent empty branches of the trie. We do not create child nodes for those branches. Using the same terminology as for binary search trees, we call nodes with at least one child *internal nodes* and nodes without any children *leaf nodes*. As a result, although we have the potential to branch 26 times at each node (when using only English letters), our trie will be relatively sparse. Later nodes may only branch a small number of times.

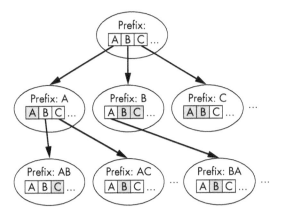

Figure 6-5: Tries only create nodes for non-empty branches of the tree, allowing the data structure to avoid wasting space on unused branches.

Unlike in binary search trees, not every node in a trie represents a valid entry. While every leaf node is a valid entry, some internal nodes might be prefixes along the route to a full string. For example, a trie containing the string COFFEE would include an intermediate node representing the prefix COFFE. Although this is the spelling the author often uses when he's consumed too much coffee, it is not actually a valid word or entry. We don't want our data structure to imply that COFFE is acceptable just because there is a node corresponding to that prefix. At other points, however, an internal node might be a completely valid entry. If a trie contains the strings CAT and CATALOG, the node for CAT will be internal, because it has at least one child that lies along the path to the node for CATALOG.

To resolve this ambiguity, we store within the trie node an indicator of whether the current prefix represents a valid entry. This could be as simple as a Boolean is_entry that is True for any node corresponding to a valid entry and False otherwise:

```
TrieNode {
    Boolean: is_entry
    Array of TrieNodes: children
}
```

In this example, the node for COFFE would have is_entry = False, while the node for COFFEE would have is_entry = True.

Alternately, we could store something more useful in the trie node, such as the count of how many times a given entry has been inserted. Or, if we are tracking auxiliary data for each entry, such as a word's definition or a list of hysterical puns, we could use the existence of this data as an indicator itself. Prefixes that do not represent valid entries can point to `null` or empty data structures. It may seem harsh, but only real words qualify for our best puns.

As with the binary search tree, we can clean up the trie's interface by wrapping the root node in a trie object:

```
Trie {
    TrieNode: root
}
```

Unlike the binary search tree, our trie always has a (non-null) root. We create this root at the same time we create the trie data structure itself. Even for completely empty tries, we allocate a root node (with is_entry = False) that indicates the start of the string. Not only will the `Trie` data structure wrap the root node into a convenient container, but it will allow us to hide some additional bookkeeping needed for various operations.

One useful physical analogy for tries is an ultimate real-world filing system. Imagine a building that acts as storage system for detailed files on every topic in the world—a monument to efficient filing schemes. We partition the topics based on their first letter, like books of an encyclopedia, so our building has 26 stories. We reserve each floor of the building for each first letter, so the floors provide our first-level split. We then pack each floor with 26 rooms, one for each second letter of the topic. Each room would contain 26 filing cabinets that split for the third letter; each cabinet has 26 drawers (fourth letter), and 26 sections per drawer (fifth letter), and so on. At each level we are grouping together entries by their common prefixes. As long as we have high-speed elevators, we can find any topic relatively easily.

Searching Tries

Searching tries is similar to searching binary search trees, in that we start at the top of the tree at the root node and progress downward, choosing branches that lead to the search target. In the case of a trie, however, we choose the branch that corresponds to the next letter in the string. We don't need to compare full strings, or even the beginning of the prefix. That was done at previous nodes. We only need to consider the next character—a single comparison at each level.

Returning to the filing building analogy, imagine searching for information on your favorite author. After arriving at the floor K, you face 26 rooms labeled A through Z that represent the prefixes KA through KZ. Your next step depends only on the second letter of the author's name. You do not need to waste time even considering the first letter again—that was already done on the elevator. Every room on this floor starts with K. You confidently head toward the room labeled U.

One complication with implementing this approach in code is that the comparisons we perform change at each level of the search. At the first level, we check the first character for a match—but at the second level, we need to check the second character. Our search no longer compares the entire target against the value at the node. We need additional information, the placement of the character that we are checking for at this level. We can track this additional state by passing the index to check into our recursive search function and incrementing it with each level of recursion.

The trie wrapper allows us to hide both the reference to the root node and the initial counter required by the recursive function, simplifying the code seen by the trie's users:

```
TrieSearch(Trie: trie, String: target):
    return TrieNodeSearch(tr.root, target, 0)
```

This wrapper guarantees that subsequent search function is called with a non-null node and the correct initial index.

The code for recursively searching a trie is a bit more complex than the code for searching a binary search tree, because we must deal with target values of different lengths:

```
TrieNodeSearch(TrieNode: current, String: target, Integer: index):
❶ IF index == length(target):
        IF current.is_entry:
            return current
        ELSE:
            return null

❷ Character: next_letter = target[index]
❸ Integer: next_index = LetterToIndex(next_letter)
   TrieNode: next_child = current.children[next_index]
❹ IF next_child == null:
        return null
    ELSE:
        return TrieNodeSearch(next_child, target, index+1)
```

This code starts by checking the length of the target string against the current depth in order to determine whether the target should be located at this level ❶. If the index is equal to the length of the string (and thus one *past* the last character in the string), the code then checks whether the current node is itself a valid entry. This check is particularly necessary when the search terminates at an internal node, since we need to confirm that this node represents a valid entry in its own right, not just the prefix of another entry.

If the code has not reached the end of the target string, it continues the search by examining the next character in our target ❷. We can define a helper function to map the character to the correct index in the array ❸. The code then checks whether the corresponding child exists ❹. If there isn't a corresponding child, the code returns null, confident that target is not in the trie. If there is a corresponding child, the code follows that branch.

For an example of this search procedure, consider a trie of exclamations like YIKES and ZOUNDS from a recent episode of our favorite

Saturday morning cartoon, as in Figure 6-6. We can record auxiliary data such as the frequency of the word and who said it, allowing us to correct people's references at parties. After all, what's the use of data structures if they don't help us win pedantic arguments?

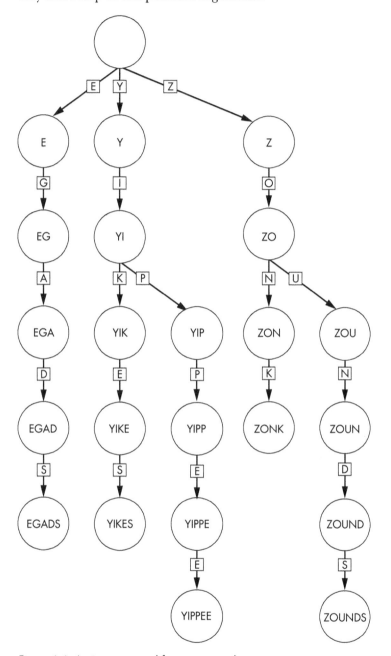

Figure 6-6: A trie constructed from cartoon phrases

To check whether this week's episode contained our all-time favorite cartoon word, ZONK, we can simply search the trie. We start at the top of the trie and take the corresponding branches for each character, as shown in Figure 6-7.

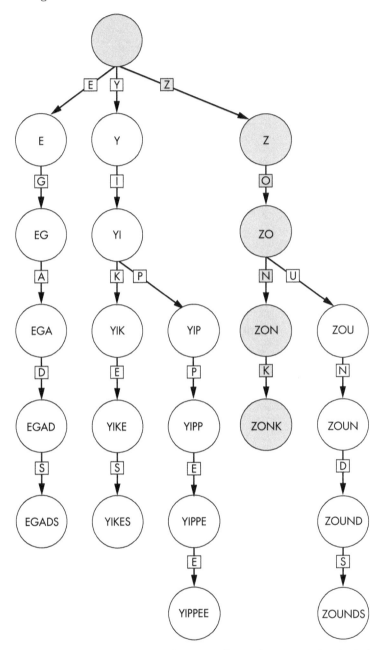

Figure 6-7: A search of the trie of cartoon phrases for ZONK. The shaded nodes indicate the path taken during the search.

Since tries include only nodes that have data, we can determine whether a string is not in the trie by watching for dead ends. For example, we know ZIPPY did not occur in the episode because we hit a dead end after the prefix Z. There is no branch for the prefix ZI. If some know-it-all proclaims that their favorite line contained the exclamation ZIPPY, we can prove them wrong with a simple search.

At first glance, it may appear that adding a large number of internal nodes increases the cost of searching. However, this new structure actually improves our search enormously. At each character in our target string, we perform a single lookup in the current node, checking for an existing child for that character, then proceed to the appropriate child node; thus, the number of lookups and comparisons scales with the length of our target string. Unlike a binary search tree, the number of comparisons for a successful trie search is independent of the number of strings stored in the trie. We could fill the trie with an entire dictionary and still only need to visit six nodes to check for the string EGADS.

Of course, as with everything in computer science, this efficiency does not come for free. We pay a significant cost in memory usage. Instead of storing one node for each string and pointers to two children, we now store one node for each character in the string and a large number of pointers to potential children. Overlapping prefixes help reduce the memory cost per string. If multiple entries share the same prefix, such as ZO for ZOUNDS and ZONK in Figure 6-6, those entries share nodes for those initial overlapping characters.

Adding and Removing Nodes

Like binary search trees, tries are dynamic data structures that adapt as we add or remove nodes, allowing them to accurately represent the data as it changes. Adding a string to a trie works much like adding data to a binary search tree. We progress down the tree as though searching for the string. Once we hit a dead end, we can create a subtree below that node to capture the remaining characters in that string. Unlike insertions in binary search trees, we may add multiple new internal nodes while inserting a single entry.

The top-level Trie function sets up the insertion by calling the recursive search function with the (non-null) root node and the correct initial depth:

```
TrieInsert(Trie: tr, String: new_value):
    TrieNodeInsert(tr.root, new_value, 0)
```

We don't need to treat the creation of the root node as a special case, as we allocate an initial root node during the creation of the trie itself.

The code for insertion is similar to that of the search function:

```
TrieNodeInsert(TrieNode: current, String: new_value, Integer: index):
❶ IF index == length(new_value):
     current.is_entry = True
  ELSE:
     Character: next_letter = new_value[index]
     Integer: next_index = LetterToIndex(next_letter)
     TrieNode: next_child = current.children[next_index]
  ❷ IF next_child == null:
        current.children[next_index] = TrieNode()
      ❸ TrieNodeInsert(current.children[next_index],
                    new_value, index + 1)
     ELSE:
      ❹ TrieNodeInsert(next_child, new_value, index + 1)
```

This code starts by checking the current position against the length of the inserted string ❶. When it has hit the end of the string, it marks the current node as a valid entry. Depending on the use case, the code might also need to update the node's auxiliary data. Where the code has not yet hit the end of the string, it looks up the next character and checks whether the corresponding child exists ❷. If not, the code creates a new child node. Then it recursively proceeds to call TrieNodeInsert on the correct child node (❸ or ❹).

For example, if we wanted to add the string EEK to our list of cartoon exclamations, we would add two nodes: an internal node for the prefix EE and a leaf node for the full string EEK. Figure 6-8 illustrates this addition, with shaded nodes indicating the trie nodes created during the insertion.

Removing nodes follows a similar process, but in reverse: starting at the node for the final character, we progress up the tree, deleting nodes that we no longer need. We stop deleting nodes once we hit an internal node that either has at least one non-empty child branch, thus representing a valid prefix for other strings in the trie, or is itself a string stored in the tree and thus represents a valid leaf node in its own right.

As with search and insertion, we start with the wrapper code that starts the deletion at the root node and with the correct index:

```
TrieDelete(Trie: tr, String: target):
   TrieNodeDelete(tr.root, target, 0)
```

The function does not return a value.

The code for removing nodes builds on the code for search and insertion, initially walking down the tree until it reaches the entry to delete. As it returns back up the trie, additional logic prunes empty branches. The code returns a Boolean value indicating whether or not the current node can safely be deleted, allowing the parent node to prune the branch.

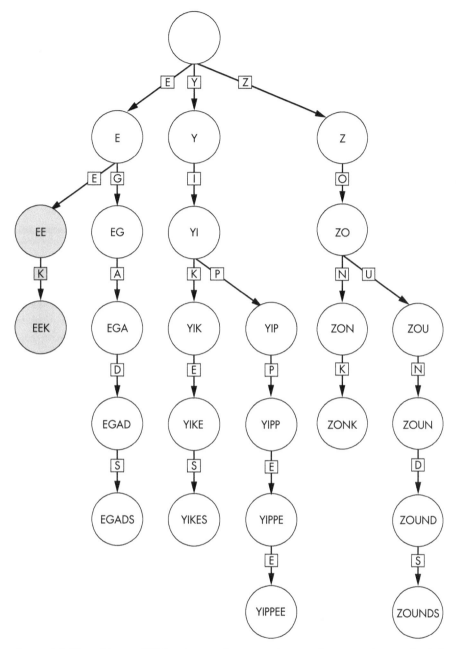

Figure 6-8: The addition of EEK to the trie of cartoon phrases. The new nodes are shaded.

```
TrieNodeDelete(TrieNode: current, String: target, Integer: index):
❶ IF index == length(target):
       IF current.is_entry:
           current.is_entry = False
    ELSE:
       ❷ Character: next_letter = target[index]
         Integer: next_index = LetterToIndex(next_letter)
         TrieNode: next_child = current.children[next_index]
         IF next_child != null:
             ❸ IF TrieNodeDelete(next_child, target, index+1):
                 current.children[next_index] = null

     # Do not delete this node if it has either an entry or a child.
❹ IF current.is_entry:
       return False
❺ FOR EACH ptr IN current.children:
       IF ptr != null:
           return False
    return True
```

This code starts by comparing the length of the deleted string to the current level and changing the value of is_entry if the current node is being removed ❶. Otherwise, the algorithm recursively progresses down the tree, using the same logic as both our search and insertion functions ❷. It looks up the next character, finds the corresponding node, checks whether the node exists, and, if so, recursively descends to that node. If the node doesn't exist, the target string is not in the trie, and the code will not continue downward. The code then deletes empty branches from the parent node. Each TrieNodeDelete call returns a Boolean to indicate whether it is safe to delete the corresponding node. If TrieNodeDelete returns True, then the parent immediately deletes the child node ❸.

The function ends with logic to determine whether it is safe for the parent to delete the current node. It returns False if is_entry == True ❹, indicating a valid entry, or if the current node has at least one non-null child ❺. It performs this last check using a FOR loop to iterate through each child and check whether it is null. If any child is not null, the code immediately returns False because it is a necessary internal node. Note that the code returns False in cases where the target string is not in the trie, because the code never sets is _entry to False for any node and thus there are no new pruning opportunities.

Consider removing the string YIPPEE from our example trie. If the trie also contains the word YIP as an entry, we'd delete all nodes following the one for YIP as shown in Figure 6-9. The node for YIPPEE itself is marked safe to delete because it is a leaf and is_entry was marked False as part of the deletion. When the function returns to the node for YIPPE, it immediately deletes its only child (branch E). The node for YIPPE is now a leaf with is_entry == False and can be deleted by its parent. The process continues up the tree until we hit the node for YIP, which has is_entry == True, because the string YIP is in the trie.

Since deletion requires making a round trip from the root to a single leaf, the cost is again proportional to the length of the target string. As with search and insertion, cost is independent of the overall numbers of strings stored in the trie.

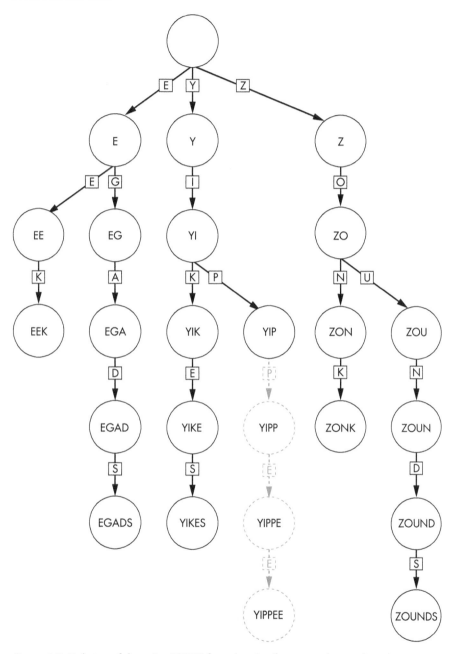

Figure 6-9: Deletion of the string YIPPEE from the trie of cartoon phrases that also contains the string YIP. The deleted nodes have dashed lines and are grayed out.

Why This Matters

We can now see how tries solve the problem with binary search trees that we posed earlier on: the cost of their search depends on both the number and length of words. In the brief examples in this chapter, tries do not provide much of an advantage. In fact, the overhead from additional branches may make them less efficient than binary search trees or sorted lists. However, tries become more and more cost-effective as we add more and more strings and the number of strings with similar prefixes increases. There are two reasons for this: first, the cost of a lookup in a trie scales independent of the number of entries, and second, string comparisons themselves can be expensive. In a binary search tree, these two factors compound, as we pay the cost of comparing two strings at each of the nodes.

In the real world, for example, we might use a trie inside a word processor to track the words in a dictionary. Auxiliary data at each node might include the definition or common misspellings. As the user types and edits, the program can efficiently check whether each word is in the dictionary and highlight it if otherwise. This program greatly benefits from the shared prefixes and limited number of characters in a natural language.

If we are composing an in-depth essay on the history of encyclopedias, for example, we do not want to pay excessive cost comparing *encyclopedia* to the neighboring words *encyclopedias*, *encyclopedic*, *encyclopedist*, and so forth. Remember that, as shown in Figure 6-10, the algorithm to compare the alphabetical ordering of two strings consists of iterating over those strings, comparing each character. Although the program stops once it finds a differing character, the cost of comparing similar prefixes adds up. Within an active word processor document, we might need to modify the set of words constantly. Each insertion or edit will require a lookup in our data structure.

E	N	C	Y	C	L	O	P	E	D	I	C
=	=	=	=	=	=	=	=	=	=	=	>
E	N	C	Y	C	L	O	P	E	D	I	A	S

Figure 6-10: An example of an expensive string comparison

An even better use for a trie might be a data structure that tracks structured labels—such as serial numbers, model numbers, or SKU codes—that are often formatted as short alphanumeric strings. For example, we could create a simple trie to store product registration information indexed by serial number. Even allowing for billions of products sold, the cost of all operations scales linearly with the length of the serial number. If our serial numbers contain structure, such as a prefix representing the device's model, we can realize further savings by limiting the branching factor at initial nodes (since many strings will use the same prefix). Auxiliary data could include information about where or when the device was purchased.

More importantly than any particular application, tries demonstrate how we can use further structure within the data to optimize the cost of operations. We adapted the branching structure of binary search trees to use the sequential nature of strings. This improvement once again illustrates a core theme of this book: we can often use the structure inherent in data to improve algorithmic efficiency.

7

PRIORITY QUEUES AND HEAPS

Priority queues are a class of data structures that retrieve items ordered by given scores for each item. Whereas both stacks and queues from Chapter 4 depended solely on the order in which data was inserted, priority queues use an additional piece of information to determine the retrieval order—the item's priority. As we will see, this new information allows us to further adapt to the data and, among other useful applications, allows us to process urgent requests first.

For example, imagine a new coffee shop, Dynamic Selection Coffee, has opened in your neighborhood. Bursting with excitement, you venture into the store and see 10 types of coffee beans you've never sampled. Before diving in and trying them, you spend the next hour carefully charting the relative merits of each new brand based on their woefully inadequate menu descriptions, leaving you with a ranked list of coffees to try. You select the most promising brand from the top of the list, purchase it, and go home to savor the experience.

The next day, you return to Dynamic Selection Coffee to try the second item on your list, only to find they've added another two coffees to the menu. When you ask the barista why they've made this change, they point to the shop's sign, which explains that Dynamic Selection Coffee serves a constantly expanding selection of coffees. Their goal is to eventually serve over a thousand varieties. You are at once thrilled and terrified. Every day you will need to prioritize the new coffees and insert them into your list so that you know which coffee to try next.

The task of retrieving items from a prioritized list is one that pops up regularly in computer programs: given a list of items and associated priorities, how can we efficiently retrieve the next item in priority order? Often, we need to do this retrieval in a dynamic context where new items arrive all the time. We might need to choose which network packet to process based on priority, offer the best suggestion in spellcheck based on common spelling errors, or choose the next option in a best-first search. In the real world, we might use our own mental priority queues to decide which urgent task to perform next, which movie to watch, or which patient to see first in a crowded emergency room. Once you start looking, prioritized retrievals are everywhere.

In this chapter, we introduce the priority queue, a class of data structures for retrieving prioritized items from a set, and then discuss the most common data structure for implementing this useful tool: the heap. Heaps make the central operations for a priority queue extremely efficient.

Priority Queues

Priority queues store a set of items and enable the user to easily retrieve the item with the highest priority. They are dynamic, allowing insertions and retrievals to be intermixed. We need to be able to add and remove items from our prioritized task list. If we were stuck using a fixed data structure, the author might spend the day consulting his static list and repeatedly performing the highest-priority task of "Get morning coffee." Without the ability to remove that task after it was accomplished, it would stay at the top of the author's list. While this might make for an enjoyable day, it is unlikely to be a productive one.

In their most basic form, priority queues support a few primary operations:

- Add an item and its associated priority score.
- Look up the item with the highest priority (or null if the queue is empty).
- Remove the item with the highest priority (or null if the queue is empty).

We can also add other useful functions that allow us to check whether a priority queue is empty or to return the number of items currently stored.

We set the items' priorities according to the problem at hand. In some cases, the priority values might be obvious or determined by the algorithm. When processing network requests, for example, each packet might come with an explicit priority, or we might choose to process the oldest request first. Deciding what to prioritize isn't always a simple endeavor, however. When prioritizing which brand of coffee to try next, we might want to create a priority based on price, availability, or caffeine content—it depends on how we plan to use our priority queue.

It's possible, but not ideal, to implement priority queues with primitive data structures like sorted linked lists or sorted arrays, adding new items into the list according to their priority. Figure 7-1 shows an example of adding the value 21 into a sorted linked list.

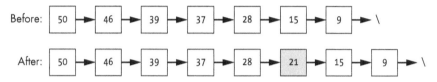

Figure 7-1: Adding an element (21) into a sorted linked list representing a priority queue

A sorted linked list keeps the highest-priority item at the front of the list for easy lookup. In fact, in this case, a lookup takes constant time regardless of the length of the priority queue—we just look at the first element. Unfortunately, adding new elements can be expensive. We might need to traverse the entire list each time we add a new item, costing us time proportional to the length of the priority queue.

The author uses a real-world version of this sorted-list approach to organize his refrigerator, storing items front-to-back in order of increasing expiration date. The closest item is always the highest priority, the one that will expire the soonest. Retrieving the correct item is easy—just grab whatever is in front. This scheme is particularly beneficial when storing milk or cream for morning coffee: no one wants to spend the first few bleary moments of the morning reading expiration dates. However, inserting new items behind old ones can take time and require an annoying amount of shifting.

Similarly, we could maintain the priority queue in an *unsorted* linked list or array. New additions are trivial—just tag the element onto the back of the list, as illustrated in Figure 7-2.

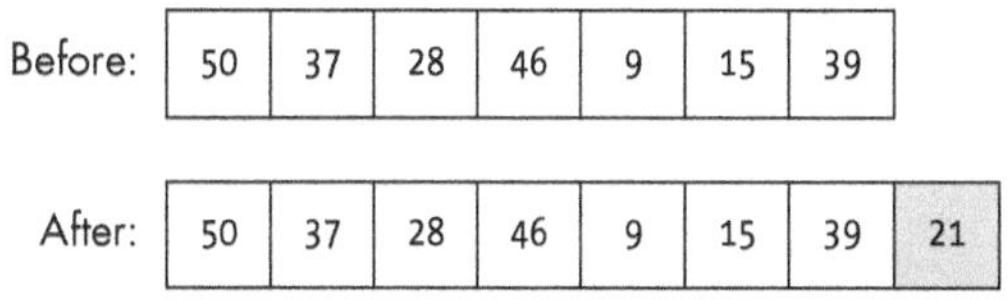

Before: | 50 | 37 | 28 | 46 | 9 | 15 | 39 |

After: | 50 | 37 | 28 | 46 | 9 | 15 | 39 | 21 |

Figure 7-2: Adding an element (21) into an unsorted array representing a priority queue

Unfortunately, we now pay a high cost in looking up the next element. We must scan the entire list in order to determine which element has the highest priority. If we are removing it, we also shift everything over to fill in the gap. This approach corresponds to scanning the full set of items in the author's fridge to find whichever is closest to expiring. This might work for a fridge with just a few milk cartons, but imagine the overhead of picking through every single item of food or drink in a large grocery store.

Implementing priority queues as sorted lists may work better than using unsorted lists or vice versa, depending on how we plan to use the priority queue. If additions are more common than lookups, we prefer the unsorted list. If lookups are more common, we should pay the cost of keeping the elements sorted. In the case of refrigerators, lookups are much more common—we pick up a single carton of milk to use it more often than we buy a new carton, so it pays to keep the milk in sorted order. The challenge arises when both additions and lookups are common; prioritizing one operation over the other will lead to overall inefficiency, so we need a method that balances their costs. A clever data structure, the heap, helps us solve this problem.

Max Heaps

A *max heap* is a variant of the binary tree that maintains a special ordered relationship between a node and its children. Specifically, a max heap stores the elements according to the *max heap property*, which states that the value at any node in the tree is larger than or equal to the values of its child nodes. For simplicity's sake, we will often use the more general terms *heaps* and *heap property* to refer to max heaps and the max heap property throughout the remainder of the chapter.

Figure 7-3 shows a representation of a binary tree organized according to the max heap property.

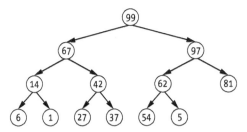

Figure 7-3: A heap represented as a binary tree

There's no special preference or ordering between the left and right children, aside from their being lower priority than their parent. For comparison, imagine an elite coffee lover's mentorship program, the Society for the Improvement of Coffee-Related Knowledge. Each member (node) agrees to mentor up to two other coffee lovers (child nodes). The only condition is that each of the mentees must not know more about coffee than their mentor does—otherwise, the mentorship would be a waste.

Computer scientist J. W. J. Williams originally invented heaps as a component of a new sorting algorithm, heapsort, which we'll discuss later in the chapter. However, he recognized that heaps are useful data structures for other tasks. The max heap's simple structure allows it to efficiently support the operations required for priority queues: (1) allowing a user to efficiently look up the largest element, (2) removing the largest element, and (3) adding an arbitrary element.

Heaps are often visualized as trees but are often implemented with arrays for efficiency. In this chapter, we present these two representations in parallel to allow the reader to make mental connections between them. However, it is not required that we use arrays for implementation.

In the array-based implementation, each element in the array corresponds to a node in the tree with the root node at index 1 (we skip index 0 to stay consistent with common convention for heaps). Child node indexes are defined relative to the indexes of their parents, so a node at index i has children at indexes $2i$ and $2i + 1$. For example, the node at index 2 has a child at index $2 \times 2 = 4$ and index $2 \times 2 + 1 = 5$, as shown in Figure 7-4.

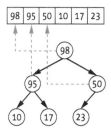

Figure 7-4: The heap's position corresponds to index locations.

Similarly, we compute the index of a node's parent as Floor(i/2). The indexing scheme allows the algorithm to trivially compute the index of a child based on that of the parent, and the index of a parent based on its child.

The root node always corresponds to the maximum value in a max heap. Since we store the root node in a fixed spot in the array (index = 1), we can always find this maximum value in constant time. It's just an array lookup. The layout of the data itself thus addresses one of the necessary priority queue operations.

Since we'll be adding and removing arbitrary elements in our priority queue, in order to avoid constantly resizing the array, we want to preallocate an array that is large enough to accommodate the number of items we expect to add. Remember from Chapter 3 that dynamically resizing an array can be expensive, forcing us to create a new array and copy over the values, and in this case wasting the precious efficiency of the heap. Instead, we can initially allocate a large array, track the index of the last filled element of the array, and call that index the virtual end of the array. This allows us to append new elements by simply updating the index for the last element.

```
Heap {
    Array: array
    Integer: array_size
    Integer: last_index
}
```

Of course, the cost of this overallocation is a chunk of potentially unused memory if our heap doesn't grow as large as expected.

Using an array to represent a tree-based data structure is an interesting step in its own right. We can use packed arrays and a mathematical mapping to represent a heap instead of relying on pointers, allowing us to store the heap with less memory. By maintaining a mapping from a node's index to its children's, we can re-create a tree-based data structure without the pointers. As we will see below, this array-based representation is feasible for heaps because the data structure always maintains a nearly complete and balanced tree. This results in a packed array with no gaps. While we could use the same array representation for other trees, such as binary search trees, those data structures often have gaps throughout and would require very large (and possibly mostly empty) arrays to store trees with deep branches.

Adding Elements to a Heap

When adding a new element to a heap, we must ensure that the structure retains the heap property. Just as you would not assign a decorated general to report to a fresh lieutenant, you wouldn't put a heap node with high priority under a low priority node. We must add the element to the heap's tree structure such that all elements below the addition have a priority less than or equal to that of the new node. Similarly, all nodes above the new addition should have priorities that are greater than or equal to that of the new node.

Part of the brilliance of the array implementation of a heap is that it retains this property while storing the nodes as a packed array. In previous chapters, adding nodes to the middle of an array was expensive, requiring us to shift later entries down. Fortunately, we don't need to pay this linear cost each time we add a new element to a heap. Instead, we add elements by first breaking the heap property and then swapping elements along a single branch of the tree to restore it.

In other words, to add a new element to the heap, we add it to the first empty space in the bottom level of the tree. If this new value is larger than the value of its parent node, we bubble it up the tree until it is smaller than or equal to its parent, restoring the heap property. The structure of the heap itself allows us to do this efficiently. In the array implementation of a heap, this corresponds to appending the new element to the back of the array and swapping it forward.

Consider the example in Figure 7-5, which shows the structure of the heap as both an array and a tree at each step. Figure 7-5(a) shows the heap before the new element is added. In Figure 7-5(b), we append the new element, 85, to the back of the array, effectively inserting it in the bottom of the tree. After the first comparison in Figure 7-5(c), we swap the new element with its parent node, since 85 is greater than 50. The swap is shown in Figure 7-5(d). The second comparison, in Figure 7-5(e), reveals that the new node is now in the correct place in the hierarchy: 98 is greater than 85, so there is no need for the new node to switch with its parent a second time. Figure 7-5(f) shows the heap after the addition is complete.

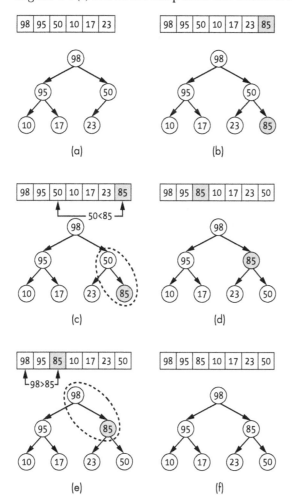

Figure 7-5: Adding an element (85) to a heap

The code for implementing this addition uses a single WHILE loop to progress up the levels of the heap until it has reached the root or found a parent larger than or equal to the new node's value:

```
HeapInsert(Heap: heap, Type: value):
❶ IF heap.last_index == heap.array_size - 1:
      Increase Heap size.
```

```
❷ heap.last_index = heap.last_index + 1
  heap.array[heap.last_index] = value

  # Swap the new node up the heap.
❸ Integer: current = heap.last_index
  Integer: parent = Floor(current / 2)
❹ WHILE parent >= 1 AND (heap.array[parent] <
                          heap.array[current]):
    ❺ Type: temp = heap.array[parent]
      heap.array[parent] = heap.array[current]
      heap.array[current] = temp
      current = parent
      parent = Floor(current / 2)
```

Since we are using an array to store the heap, the code starts by checking that it still has room in the array to add a new element ❶. If not, it increases the size of the heap, perhaps by applying the array-doubling technique described in Chapter 3. Next, the code appends the new element to the end of the array and updates the position of the last element ❷. The WHILE loop starts at the freshly added element ❸, progresses up each layer of the heap by comparing the current value to that of its parent ❹, and switching if necessary ❺. The loop terminates when we either reach the top of the heap (parent == 0) or find a parent greater than or equal to the child.

We might compare this process to an oddly designed, yet efficient, package distribution center as shown in Figure 7-6. The employees organize packages in neat rows on the floor using the heap property: in the front row is a single package with the highest priority, the next to be shipped. Behind that package sit two lower-priority packages. Behind each of these are two more packages (for a total of four in that row) such that each pair has priorities less than or equal to the corresponding package in front of them. With each new row, the number of packages doubles so that the arrangement spreads out wider and wider as you move toward the back of the warehouse. Each package has at most two lower- or equal-priority packages sitting behind it and at most one higher- or equal-priority package in front. Painted rectangles on the warehouse floor helpfully indicate the possible locations for packages in each of the rows.

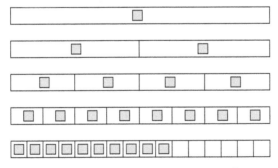

Figure 7-6: A warehouse floor organized as a heap

New packages are brought in from the back of the warehouse. Each delivery person mumbles something about the weird sorting scheme, relieved that at least they don't have to carry their package to the very front, drops the package in the frontmost available spot, and leaves as quickly as possible. The warehouse employees then spring into action, comparing the priority of the new package with the one immediately in front of it (ignoring the rest of the packages in that row). If they find an inversion, they switch the packages. Otherwise, they leave the package where it is. This continues until the new package occupies the appropriate place in the hierarchy, with the package in front of it having a higher or an equal priority. Since the packages are heavy and spread out, the employees minimize their work with at most one comparison and switch per row. They never shuffle packages within a row. After all, nobody wants to move boxes unnecessarily.

Intuitively, we can see that heap additions are not terribly expensive. In the worst case, we would have to swap the new node all the way to the root of the tree, but this only means swapping a small fraction of the array's values. By design, heaps are *balanced* binary trees: we fill out a complete level of the tree before inserting a node into the next level. Since the number of nodes in a full binary tree doubles with each level, the addition operation requires, in the worst case, $\log_2(N)$ swaps. This is significantly better than the worst case of N swaps required to maintain a sorted list.

Removing the Highest-Priority Elements from Heaps

Looking up and removing the highest-priority element from a priority queue is a core operation that allows us to process items in order of their priority. Perhaps we are storing a list of pending network requests and want to process the highest-priority one. Or we could be running an emergency room and looking to see the most urgent patient. In both cases, we want to remove this element from our priority queue so that we can go on to extract the next highest priority element.

To remove the highest-priority node, we must first break, then restore, the heap property. Consider the example in Figure 7-7. We start by swapping the highest-priority node with the last node in the lowest level of the tree (Figure 7-7(b)), effectively making the last element the new root node. However, this epic promotion for the new root node is almost guaranteed not to stand up to scrutiny. In the array implementation, this corresponds to swapping the first and last elements in the array. This swap plugs the gap at the front of the array that would be created by removing the first element and thus maintains a packed array.

Next, the original max value of 98, which is currently the last element in the tree, is deleted as in Figure 7-7(c). We have now deleted the correct node, but likely broken the heap property in the process. We may have moved a low-urgency package all the way to the front of the warehouse.

NOTE *It is also possible that swapping the first and last elements in the heap will not break the heap property, especially in the case of duplicate priorities or small heaps.*

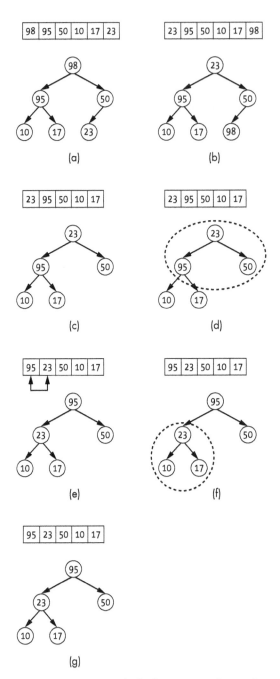

Figure 7-7: Removing the highest-priority element from a heap

To fix the heap property, we start at the new (incorrect) root node of 23 and walk down the tree, restoring the heap property at every level. The incorrectly placed package is shifted one row at a time toward the back of the warehouse, the opposite of an added package's shifting forward row by row. Admittedly, this traversal isn't as exciting as moving an urgent package to the front of the line, but it's for the good of the heap structure. At each level, we compare our moving package's priority to that of both its children, the two packages in the next row (Figure 7-7(d)). If it's smaller than either of its children, we move the new root node backward to restore the heap property by swapping places with the larger of its two children (Figure 7-7(e)). This represents the package's higher-priority successor moving forward to take its place.

The downward swaps terminate when there are no larger children. Figure 7-7(f) shows a comparison made when the current node is in the correct position. The heap property has been restored, and all the nodes are satisfied with their relative position. Figure 7-7(g) shows the final heap, once the removal is complete.

While fixing the location for the root node, we follow a single path down the tree, checking and restoring the heap property for only the descendant branch where we made the swap. There is no need to check the other branch. It is already guaranteed to maintain the heap property since we haven't done anything to break it. Again, this means that, in the worst case, we need to make $\log_2(N)$ swaps.

Here's the code for removing the max element:

```
HeapRemoveMax(Heap: heap):
❶ IF heap.last_index == 0:
      return null

   # Swap out the root for the last element and shrink heap.
❷ Type: result = heap.array[1]
   heap.array[1] = heap.array[heap.last_index]
   heap.array[heap.last_index] = null
   heap.last_index = heap.last_index - 1

   # Bubble the new root down.
   Integer: i = 1
❸ WHILE i <= heap.last_index:
      Integer: swap = i
    ❹ IF 2*i <= heap.last_index AND (heap.array[swap] <
                                     heap.array[2*i]):
         swap = 2*i
    ❺ IF 2*i+1 <= heap.last_index AND (heap.array[swap] <
                                       heap.array[2*i+1]):
         swap = 2*i+1

    ❻ IF i != swap:
         Type: temp = heap.array[i]
         heap.array[i] = heap.array[swap]
         heap.array[swap] = temp
         i = swap
      ELSE:
         break
   return result
```

This code starts by checking that the heap is not empty ❶. If it is, there is nothing to return. The code then swaps the first element (index == 1) with the last element (index == heap.last_index), breaking the heap property to prepare the max element for removal ❷. The code then uses a WHILE loop to traverse down the heap in a series of comparisons, repairing the heap property ❸. During each iteration, it compares the current value to both children and swaps with the larger one if necessary ❻. We must add additional checks ❹ ❺ to ensure that the code is only comparing the current value to an existing child. We don't want it to try to compare against an entry that is past the array's last valid index. The loop terminates when it has hit the bottom of the heap or has gone an iteration without a swap (via the break statement).

Storing Auxiliary Information

Much of the time, we need our heap to store additional information for each entry. In our task list, for example, we need to store information about the tasks to be done, not just their priority. It doesn't help us to know that we need to do the priority = 99 task next, if we don't know what that task is. We might as well just scan through the original list manually.

Augmenting the heap to store composite data structures or objects, such as a TaskRecord, is simple:

```
TaskRecord {
    Float: Priority
    String: TaskName
    String: Instructions
    String: PersonWhoWillYellIfThisIsNotDone
    Boolean: Completed
}
```

We modify the previous code to handle comparisons based on the priority field of this composite record. We could do this by directly modifying the code (such in the HeapInsert function):

```
    WHILE parent >= 1 AND (heap.array[parent].priority <
                            heap.array[current].priority):
```

However, this requires us to potentially specialize the heap implementation to the particular composite data structure. A cleaner approach is to add a composite data structure specific helper function, such as:

```
IsLessThan(Type: a, Type: b):
  return a.priority < b.priority
```

We'd use this function instead of the mathematical less-than sign in the code for HeapInsert:

```
    WHILE parent >= 1 AND IsLessThan(heap.array[parent],
                            heap.array[current]):
```

Similarly, we would modify the comparisons in the HeapRemoveMax function to use the helper function.

```
IF 2*i <= heap.last_index AND IsLessThan(heap.array[swap],
                                          heap.array[2*i]):
    swap = 2*i
IF 2*i+1 <= heap.last_index AND IsLessThan(heap.array[swap],
                                           heap.array[2*i+1]):
    swap = 2*i+1
```

These small changes allow us to build heaps from composite data structures. As long as we can define an IsLessThan function to order the elements, we can build an efficient priority queue for them.

Updating Priorities

Some use cases might demand another mode of dynamic behavior: allowing the algorithm to update the priorities of elements within the priority queue. Consider a bookstore database that prioritizes which books to restock by the number of patrons who have requested each title. The system builds the heap over an initial list of books and uses that to determine which title to order next. But, after a popular blog article points out the vital importance of data structures in computational thinking, the store suddenly sees a dramatic—though entirely understandable—increase in patrons requesting books about data structures. Its priority queue must be equipped to handle this sudden influx.

To meet this need, we use the same approaches we applied to addition and removal. When we change an item's value, we check whether we are increasing or decreasing the priority. If we are increasing the item's value, we need to bubble the item up the max heap in order to restore the heap property. Similarly, if we are decreasing the item's value, we let it sink down the max heap into its rightful position.

```
UpdateValue(Heap: heap, Integer: index, Float: value):
    Type: old_value = heap.array[index]
    heap.array[index] = value

    IF old_value < value:
        Bubble the element up the heap using the
        procedure from inserting new elements
        (swapping with parent).
    ELSE:
        Drop the element down the heap using the
        procedure from removing the max element
        (swapping with the larger child).
```

We can even break out the code for letting elements bubble up or sink down so that the exact same code can be used for updating as for addition and removing the max.

How do we find the element we want to update in the first place? As mentioned, heaps aren't optimized for finding specific elements. If we have no information on our element of interest other than its value, we might need to search through a substantial portion of the array to find it. Often, we can solve this problem by using a secondary data structure, such as a hash table (discussed in Chapter 10), to map from the item's key to its element in the heap. In the example in this section, we assume that the program already has the item's current index.

Min Heaps

So far, we have focused on the max heap, which uses the property that the value at any node in the tree is larger than (or equal to) the values of its children. The *min heap* is a version of the heap that facilitates finding the item with the lowest value. With a min heap, the root of the tree is the smallest value, allowing us to easily find the item with the lowest score. For example, instead of ordering network packets by priority, we might want to sort them by arrival time, processing packets with an earlier time of arrival before packets received more recently. More importantly, if we run out of space on our coffee shelf, we'll need to remove our least favorite brand. After a gut-wrenching internal debate on whether it would be better to increase the size of our coffee storage by discarding a shelf's worth of plates or bowls rather than part with any of our precious coffee grounds, we instead decide to discard the lowest-ranked coffee. We consult our list of enjoyability scores for each coffee and select the one with the lowest value.

We could, in theory, continue to use a max heap by just negating the values. However, a cleaner strategy is to make a minor tweak to our heap property and solve the problem outright. The *min heap property* is that the value at any node in the tree is smaller than (or equal to) the values of its children. An example min heap is shown in Figure 7-8. When we insert new elements, the ones with the lowest score bubble up the hierarchy. Similarly, we always extract and return the element with the lowest score.

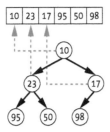

Figure 7-8: The min heap's position corresponds to index locations.

Of course, the algorithms for adding and removing elements in the min heap need to modified accordingly. For insertion, we change the comparison function in the WHILE loop to check whether the parent value is greater than the current value:

```
MinHeapInsert(MinHeap: heap, Type: value):
    IF heap.last_index == heap.array_size - 1:
```

```
    Increase Heap size.

  heap.last_index = heap.last_index + 1
  heap.array[heap.last_index] = value

  # Swap the new node up the heap.
  Integer: current = heap.last_index
  Integer: parent = Floor(current / 2)
❶ WHILE parent >= 1 AND (heap.array[parent] >
                        heap.array[current]):
      Type: temp = heap.array[parent]
      heap.array[parent] = heap.array[current]
      heap.array[current] = temp
      current = parent
      parent = Floor(current / 2)
```

The majority of the code is identical to that for insertion into a max heap. The only change is to replace < with > when comparing a node to its parent ❶.

We make a similar change for the two comparisons during the removal operation:

```
MinHeapRemoveMin(Heap: heap):
    IF heap.last_index == 0:
        return null

    # Swap out the root for the last element and shrink heap.
    Type: result = heap.array[1]
    heap.array[1] = heap.array[heap.last_index]
    heap.array[heap.last_index] = null
    heap.last_index = heap.last_index - 1

    # Bubble the new root down.
    Integer: i = 1
    WHILE i <= heap.last_index:
        Integer: swap = i
      ❶ IF 2*i <= heap.last_index AND (heap.array[swap] >
                                       heap.array[2*i]):
            swap = 2*i
      ❷ IF 2*i+1 <= heap.last_index AND (heap.array[swap] >
                                         heap.array[2*i+1]):
            swap = 2*i+1

        IF i != swap:
            Type: temp = heap.array[i]
            heap.array[i] = heap.array[swap]
            heap.array[swap] = temp
            i = swap
        ELSE:
            break
    return result
```

Here, the only changes are replacing < with > when determining whether to swap nodes ❶ ❷.

Heapsort

Heaps are powerful data structures across a range of computer science tasks, not limited to implementing priority queues and efficiently returning the next item in a prioritized list. Another exciting lens through which to view heaps, and data structures in general, is in terms of the novel algorithms that they enable. J. W. J. Williams initially proposed heaps themselves in the context of a new algorithm to sort arrays: *heapsort*.

As its name implies, heapsort is an algorithm for sorting a list of items using the heap data structure. The input is an unsorted array. The output is an array containing those same elements, but in *decreasing* sorted order (for a max heap). At its core, heapsort consists of two phases:

1. Building a max heap from all the items
2. Extracting all the items from the heap in decreasing sorted order and storing them in an array

It's that simple.

Here's the heapsort code:

```
Heapsort(Array: unsorted):
    Integer: N = length(unsorted)
    Heap: tmp_heap = Heap of size N
    Array: result = array of size N

    Integer: j = 0
❶ WHILE j < N:
        HeapInsert(tmp_heap, unsorted[j])
        j = j + 1

    j = 0
❷ WHILE j < N:
        result[j] = HeapRemoveMax(tmp_heap)
        j = j + 1
    return result
```

This code consists of two WHILE loops. The first one inserts each item into a temporary heap ❶. The second loop removes the largest element using the HeapRemoveMax function and adds it to the next position in the array ❷. Alternatively, we can implement heapsort to produce an answer in *increasing* sorted order by using a min heap and HeapRemoveMin.

Suppose we want to sort the following array: [46, 35, 9, 28, 61, 8, 38, 40] in decreasing order. We start by inserting each of these values into our heap. Figure 7-9 shows the final arrangement of the array (and its equivalent tree representation) after the insertion. Remember that we always begin by inserting new items at the back of the array, then swap them forward until the heap property is restored. In Figure 7-9, arrows represent the new element's path through the array to its final position. The tree representation is also shown, with shading indicating the nodes that have been modified.

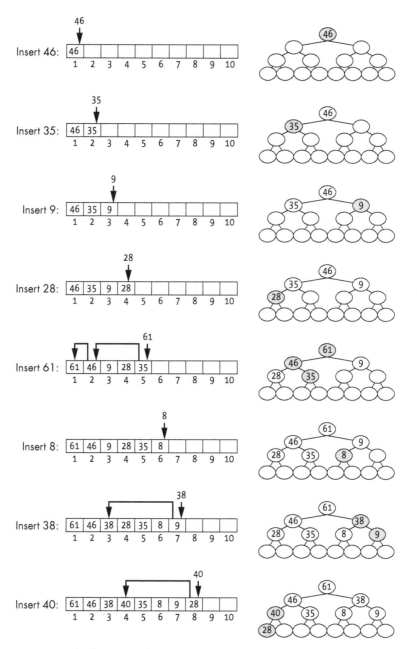

Figure 7-9: The first stage of heapsort where elements in the unsorted array are added to the heap one at a time

We bound the runtime of creating the heap using the worst-case runtime of a single insertion. As we saw earlier in the chapter, in the worst case, inserting a new item into a heap containing N items can scale proportional to $\log_2(N)$. Thus, to construct a heap out of N items, we bound the worst-case runtime as proportional to $N\log_2(N)$.

Now that we've built our heap, we proceed to the second stage and extract each item, as shown in Figure 7-10.

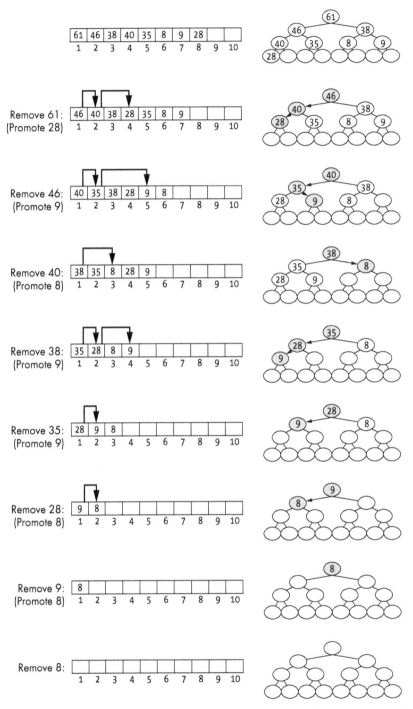

Figure 7-10: The second stage of heapsort, where the maximal element is repeatedly removed from the heap with each iteration

We remove the items from the heap one by one in order of decreasing priority. This is what produces the decreasing sorted order. At each step, the root is extracted, the last item in the heap is swapped to the root's position, and then the new root sinks back down into a position that restores the heap property. The figure shows the state of the array (and the equivalent tree representation) at the end of each iteration. The arrows in the diagrams and the shaded nodes illustrate the overpromoted node's journey down though the heap. As we extract the items, we add them directly to the array storing our result. Once we have emptied the heap, we throw it away. It has served its purpose.

As with the insertions, we can bound the worst-case runtime as proportional to $N\log_2(N)$. Each extraction requires at most $\log_2(N)$ to restore the heap property, and we need to extract all N items for our sorted list. Thus, the total worst-case runtime of the heapsort algorithm is proportional to $N\log_2(N)$.

Why This Matters

Heaps are a simple variation of binary trees that allow a different set of computationally efficient operations. By changing the binary search tree property into the heap property, we can change the behavior of the data structure and support a different set of operations.

Both addition of new elements and deletion of the maximum element require us to walk at most one path between the top and bottom of the tree. Since we can approximately double the number of nodes in a heap while adding only a single level of new nodes to the bottom, even large heaps allow speedy operations. Doubling the number of nodes in this way adds only one additional iteration to insertion and deletion! Furthermore, both operations guarantee that the tree remains balanced so that future operations will be efficient.

However, there's always a tradeoff: by moving from the binary search tree property to the heap property, we can no longer efficiently search for a specific value. Optimizing for one set of operations often prevents us from optimizing from others. We need to think carefully about how we will use the data and design its structure accordingly.

8

GRIDS

In this chapter, we look at what happens as
we consider multidimensional values and
targets. The data structures we've examined
so far have all shared a common constraint—
they organize data based on a single value. Many
real-world problems involve multiple important dimensions, and we need
to extend our data structures to handle searches over such data.

This chapter starts by introducing nearest-neighbor search, which will
serve as our motivating use case for multidimensional data. As we will see, the
generality of nearest-neighbor search makes it very flexible and applicable to a
wide range of spatial and non-spatial problems. It can help us find the cup of
coffee closest to our current location or the brand best suited to our tastes.

We then introduce the grid data structure and show how it facilitates
nearest-neighbor search over two dimensions, using spatial relationships
within the data to prune out infeasible regions of the search space. We
briefly discuss how these approaches can be extended to more than two
dimensions. We will also see how these data structures fall short, providing
the motivation for further spatial data structures.

Introducing Nearest-Neighbor Search

As its name implies, *nearest-neighbor search* consists of finding a particular data point closest to a given search target—for example, the coffee shop nearest our current location. Formally, we define nearest-neighbor search as follows:

> Given a set of N data points $X = \{x_1, x_2, \ldots, x_N\}$, a target value x', and a distance function $dist(x,y)$, find the point $x_i \in X$ that minimizes $dist(x',x_i)$.

Nearest-neighbor search is closely related to the target value search we used to motivate binary search in Chapter 2. Both algorithms search for a specific data point within a set of data. The key difference lies in the success criteria. Whereas binary search tests for an exact match within a data set, which may or may not be present, nearest-neighbor search is only concerned with finding the closest match.

This framing makes nearest-neighbor search useful for many types of multiple-dimensional data. We could be searching a map for nearby coffee shops, a list of historical temperatures for days similar to the current date, or a list of "close" misspellings of a given word. As long as we can define a distance between the search target and other values, we can find nearest neighbors.

In past chapters, we primarily considered targets that are individual numeric values, like the data stored in binary search trees and heaps. While we sometimes included auxiliary data, the targets themselves remained simple. In contrast, nearest-neighbor search is most interesting when dealing with multidimensional data, which may be stored in a variety of other data structures such as arrays, tuples, or composite data structures. Later in this chapter, we look at example two-dimensional search problems and their targets. For now, though, let's introduce a basic algorithm for this search.

Nearest-Neighbor Search with Linear Scan

As a baseline algorithm for nearest-neighbor search, we start with a modified version of the linear scan algorithm from Chapter 2. The linear scan algorithm isn't particularly exciting; you can implement it with a simple loop in most programming languages. Yet, because of its simplicity, linear scan provides a good starting point from which to examine more complex and efficient algorithms.

Consider the problem of nearest-neighbor search with numbers using the absolute distance: $dist(x,y) = |x - y|$. Given a list of numbers and a search target, we want to find the closest number on the list. Perhaps we wake up in a new city and need to find our first cup of coffee in the morning. The hotel's concierge provides a list of coffee shops on the same street, along with a helpful map. Not recognizing any of the businesses, we resolve to prioritize expedience and visit the coffee shop closest to the hotel.

We can visualize this search with a number line shown in Figure 8-1. The points represent different coffee shops and their location with respect to the start of the map, while the X represents our hotel with a location of 2.2 miles along the street.

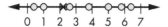

Figure 8-1: A one-dimensional nearest-neighbor
search represented as a number line

In a program, the points in Figure 8-1 might represent unsorted values
within an array. However, visualizing these values along a real-valued number line has two advantages in the context of nearest-neighbor search. First,
it clarifies the importance of distance: we can see the gaps between our target value and each data point. Second, it helps us generalize the techniques
beyond a single dimension, as we'll see in the next section.

For now, the linear scan proceeds through each data point, as shown in
Figure 8-2, computing the distance for the current data point and comparing
it to the minimum distance found so far. Here we consider the points in sorted
order since they are already along the number line, but linear scan does not
require a particular ordering. It uses the data's ordering within the list.

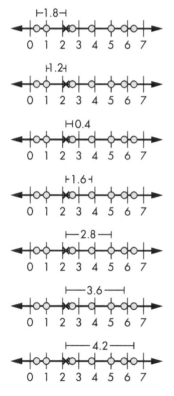

Figure 8-2: A linear scan through the data points
in a one-dimensional nearest-neighbor search

In the first comparison in Figure 8-2, we find a point at distance 1.8.
This becomes our best option so far, our *candidate nearest neighbor*. It might
not be a *good* neighbor—1.8 miles is a bit far to walk for our morning cup
of joe—but it's the best we've seen. The next two steps discover better

candidates at distances 1.2 and 0.4, respectively. Alas, the remaining four comparisons don't produce a better candidate; the point at distance 0.4 remains the closest we've found. In the end, the algorithm returns that third point on our number line as the nearest neighbor. We head to the coffee shop, confident we're heading to the closest one on the street.

Listing 8-1 shows the code for a linear scan using an arbitrary distance function. We use floating-point values for the one-dimensional case but can extend the function to multiple dimensions by using composite data structures or other representations.

```
LinearScanClosestNeighbor(Array: A, Float: target, Function: dist):
    Integer: N = length(A)
 ❶ IF N == 0:
        return null

 ❷ Float: candidate = A[0]
    Float: closest_distance = dist(target, candidate)

    Integer: i = 1
 ❸ WHILE i < N:
        Float: current_distance = dist(target, A[i])
      ❹ IF current_distance < closest_distance:
            closest_distance = current_distance
            candidate = A[i]
        i = i + 1
 ❺ return candidate
```

Listing 8-1: The code for a linear scan nearest-neighbor algorithm

The code starts by checking whether the array is empty and, if so, returning null ❶, since there is no closest point. The code then picks the first item in the array as the initial candidate nearest neighbor and computes the distance from that point to the target ❷. This information provides a starting point for our search: we compare all future points against the best candidate and distance so far. The remainder of the code uses a WHILE loop to iterate over the remaining elements in the array ❸, computing the distance to the target and comparing that to the best distance found so far. The code updates the best candidate and best distance found whenever it finds a closer candidate ❹, then returns the closest neighbor ❺.

Beyond providing a simple implementation of nearest-neighbor search, the linear scan algorithm also trivially supports different distance functions or even higher-dimensional points. First, let's look at some example problems in this two-dimensional space.

Searching Spatial Data

Imagine that you are multiple hours into a cross-country road trip and desperately need a coffee refill. Panic floods your mind as you realize that you haven't mapped out the optimal coffee shops along your route. You take a few deep breaths, pull out the map shown in Figure 8-3, and locate numerous towns with known coffee establishments. Prioritizing expedience over quality, you vow to find the closest café.

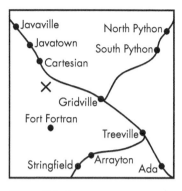

Figure 8-3: A map as an example of two-dimensional data

The data consists of two-dimensional points—towns with x, y coordinates. These data points can be stored as an ordered tuple (x, y); a small, fixed-size array $[x, y]$; or even a composite data structure for two-dimensional spatial points:

```
Point {
    Float: x
    Float: y
}
```

When determining which town is closest, we'll focus on just the straight-line distance to the coffee shop. In any real-world navigation task, we'd also need to consider obstacles standing between us and our coffee. For now, though, let's just consider the Euclidean distance to the coffee shops. If our current point is (x_1, y_1) and the coffee shop is at (x_2, y_2), then the distance is:

$$dist = \sqrt{((x_1 - x_2)^2 + (y_1 - y_2)^2)}$$

We could use the linear-scan algorithm in Listing 8-1. The algorithm computes the distance from our target to each candidate point, as shown in Figure 8-4.

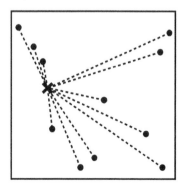

Figure 8-4: A linear scan nearest-neighbor search computes the distance from the target to each candidate point.

The point with the smallest distance to the target, shown in Figure 8-5, is the target's nearest neighbor. The dashed line represents the distance to the closest point, and the dotted circle shows the area of our map that is closer than (or equal to) the closest point. No other points lie closer than the nearest neighbor.

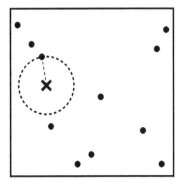

Figure 8-5: The point with the smallest distance to the target is that target's nearest neighbor.

As we've seen multiple times, though, this type of linear scan search quickly becomes inefficient as the number of points increases. If the current edition of the *Coffee Lover's Guide to Roadside Coffee* lists 100,000 coffee shops, it would be needlessly time-consuming to check each one.

We shouldn't need to look at every single data point in two-dimensional space. Some points are too far away to matter. We would never consider Alaskan coffee shops when driving through Florida. This is not to disparage Alaskan cafés—I'm sure there are plenty that equal their Floridian peers in terms of taste and quality. It's simply a matter of expedience. We can't survive an hour without our coffee, let alone a multi-day drive. If we are driving through northern Florida, we need to focus on northern Floridian coffee establishments.

As we saw in binary search, we can often use structure within the data to help eliminate large numbers of candidates. We can even adapt binary search to find nearest neighbors in one-dimensional space. Unfortunately, a simple sort will not help in the two-dimensional case. If we sort and search either x or y dimensions, as shown in Figure 8-6, we get the wrong answer—the closest neighbor in the one-dimensional space is not the same as the closest two-dimensional neighbor.

We need to use information from all relevant dimensions to make accurate pruning decisions. A point close to our target along a single dimension might be staggeringly far away in other dimensions. If we sort our list of coffee shops by latitude, our search for locations near our current latitude in northern Florida might return quite a few "close" results from Houston. Similarly, if we sort by longitude, we might be swamped with entries from Cleveland. We need to explore new approaches, adapted from our experience with one-dimensional data but also making use of the structure inherent in higher dimensions.

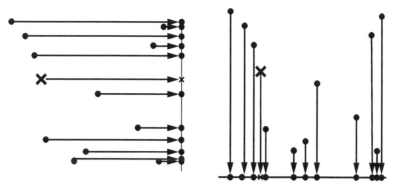

Figure 8-6: Projecting the data to one dimension along either the y-axis (left) or x-axis (right) removes important spatial information about the other dimension.

Grids

Grids are data structures for storing two-dimensional data. Like arrays, grids consist of a fixed set of *bins*, or *cells*. Since we are initially covering two-dimensional data, we use a two-dimensional arrangement of bins and index each bin with two numbers, *xbin* and *ybin*, representing the bin numbers along the x-axis and y-axis respectively. Figure 8-7 shows an example grid.

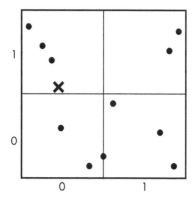

Figure 8-7: A 2×2 grid of spatial data points

Unlike arrays, we can't restrict each bin to hold a single value. Grid cells are defined by spatial bounds—a high and low edge along each dimension. No matter how finely we draw the grid, multiple points might fall within the same cell, so we need our bins to store multiple elements apiece. Each bin stores a list of *all* data points that fall within that bin's range.

We can visualize the difference between grids and arrays as different forms of refrigerator storage. The egg carton is an array with one individual space for each egg. In contrast, the vegetable drawer is like a grid bin. It contains multiple items of the same type, all vegetables. We might stuff a single drawer with twenty-five onions. The egg carton, on the other hand, contains only a fixed number of eggs, each in its designated place. While vegetable drawers may generate intense debates about where to correctly store tomatoes or cucumbers, the bounds of a grid cell are defined with mathematical precision.

Grids use the points' coordinates to determine their storage, allowing us to use the data's spatial structure to limit our searches. To see how this is possible, we first need to consider the details of the grid's structure.

Grid Structure

The top-level data structure for our grid contains some extra bookkeeping information. As shown in Figure 8-8, we need to include multiple pieces of information along each dimension. In addition to the number of bins along the x- and y-dimensions, we must track the spatial bounds along each dimension. We use x_start and x_end to indicate the minimum and maximum values of x included in our grid. Similarly, y_start and y_end capture the spatial bounds for y.

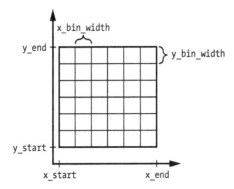

Figure 8-8: A grid with specified starting and ending values along each dimension

We can derive some top-level information from the number of bins and the spatial bounds, but we often want to store that additional information about the grid for convenience. Precomputing the width of the bins along each dimension simplifies later code:

```
x_bin_width = (x_end - x_start) / num_x_bins
y_bin_width = (y_end - y_start) / num_y_bins
```

Other useful information might include the total number of points stored in the grid or the number of empty bins. We can track all this information in a composite data structure. For two-dimensional data, our typical data structure would look like this:

```
Grid {
    Integer: num_x_bins
    Integer: num_y_bins
    Float: x_start
    Float: x_end
```

```
    Float: x_bin_width
    Float: y_start
    Float: y_end
    Float: y_bin_width
    Matrix of GridPoints: bins
}
```

For a fixed-size grid, we can map from a point's spatial coordinates to the grid's bin using a simple mathematical computation:

```
xbin = Floor((x - x_start) / x_bin_width)
ybin = Floor((y - y_start) / y_bin_width)
```

The switch from "one bin, one value" to "spatial partitioning" has important consequences beyond index mapping. It means that we can no longer store the data as a set of fixed bins in the computer's memory. Each square could contain an arbitrary number of data points. Each grid square needs its own internal data structure to store its points. One common and effective data structure for storing points within the bin is a linked list like the one in Figure 8-9.

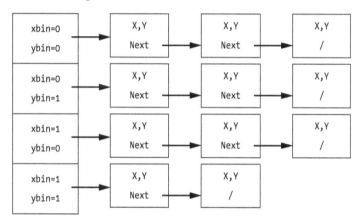

Figure 8-9: A representation of the data structure used to store points in a grid

Each bin stores the pointer to the head of a linked list, which contains all the points in that bin. We accomplish this with another, internal data structure to store individual points:

```
GridPoint {
    Float: x
    Float: y
    GridPoint: next
}
```

Alternatively, we could use the LinkedListNode data structure from Chapter 3 and store a pair to represent the x, y coordinates.

Building Grids and Inserting Points

We construct a grid for our data set by allocating an empty grid data structure and iteratively inserting points using a single FOR loop over the data points. The high-level structure of the grid itself (the spatial bounds and number of bins along each dimension) is fixed at time of creation and does not change with the data added.

As shown in Listing 8-2, inserting a point consists of finding the correct bin and prepending the new point to the beginning of the linked list for that bin.

```
GridInsert(Grid: g, Float: x, Float: y):
❶ Integer: xbin = Floor((x - g.x_start) / g.x_bin_width)
  Integer: ybin = Floor((y - g.y_start) / g.y_bin_width)

  # Check that the point is within the grid.
❷ IF xbin < 0 OR xbin >= g.num_x_bins:
      return False
  IF ybin < 0 OR ybin >= g.num_y_bins:
      return False

  # Add the point to the front of the list.
❸ GridPoint: next_point = g.bins[xbin][ybin]
  g.bins[xbin][ybin] = GridPoint(x, y)
  g.bins[xbin][ybin].next = next_point

❹ return True
```

Listing 8-2: A function to insert a new point into a grid

The code first computes the x and y bins for the new point ❶ and confirms that the new point falls within a valid bin ❷. While it's always important to confirm that you are accessing an in-bounds array index whenever using an array, spatial data structures present additional concerns. We might not be able to predefine a fixed, finite grid that works for every possible future point. Therefore, it is important to consider what happens when previously unseen points fall outside the range covered by your spatial data structure. In this example, we return a Boolean to indicate whether or not the point could be inserted ❹. However, you might prefer other mechanisms, such as throwing an exception, depending on the programming language.

Once we have determined that point does fit within our grid, the code finds the appropriate bin. The code prepends the new point to the front of the list, creating a new list if the bin was previously empty ❸. The function concludes by returning True ❹.

Deleting Points

We can use a similar approach to insertion for deleting points from a grid. One additional difficulty is determining which point in the bin to delete. In many use cases, the user might insert arbitrarily close or even duplicate points into the grid. For example, if we are storing a list of ground coffees available to purchase, we might insert multiple points for a single coffee shop. Ideally, we use other identifying information, such as the name or ID number of the coffee, to determine which of the points to delete. In this section, we present the simple and general approach of deleting the first matching point in our linked list.

Due to the limited precision of floating-point variables, we also might not be able to use a direct equality test. In Listing 8-3, we use a helper function to find a point that is close enough. The approx_equal function returns True if both points are within a threshold distance in both dimensions.

```
approx_equal(Float: x1, Float: y1, Float: x2, Float: y2):
    IF abs(x1 - x2) > threshold:
        return False
    IF abs(y1 - y2) > threshold:
        return False
    return True
```

Listing 8-3: Code to check whether two data points, represented as a pair of floating-point numbers, are equal

The code checks each dimension independently and compares the distance to a threshold. The threshold will depend on the use case and the numerical precision of your programming language. Generally, we want these thresholds to be just large enough to account for the float's numerical precision.

Deletion consists of finding the correct bin, traversing the linked list until we find a match, and removing the match by splicing it out of the list. Our delete function returns True if a point was found and deleted and False otherwise.

```
GridDelete(Grid: g, Float: x, Float: y):
❶ Integer: xbin = Floor((x - g.x_start) / g.x_bin_width)
   Integer: ybin = Floor((y - g.y_start) / g.y_bin_width)

   # Check that the point is within the grid.
❷ IF xbin < 0 OR xbin >= g.num_x_bins:
       return False
   IF ybin < 0 OR ybin >= g.num_y_bins:
       return False

   # Check if the bin is empty.
❸ IF g.bins[xbin][ybin] == null:
       return False

   # Find the first matching point and remove it.
❹ GridPoint: current = g.bins[xbin][ybin]
   GridPoint: previous = null
   WHILE current != null:
     ❺ IF approx_equal(x, y, current.x, current.y):
         ❻ IF previous == null:
               g.bins[xbin][ybin] = current.next
           ELSE:
               previous.next = current.next
```

```
        return True
❼ previous = current
    current = current.next
return False
```

The code first computes the x and y bins for the new point ❶ and confirms that the new point falls within a valid bin ❷. Next it checks whether the target bin is empty ❸, returning False if it is.

NOTE   *While the code above checks a single bin for simplicity, we could theoretically see (extremely rare) edge cases where the deleted point lies right on the bin's boundary. We could further account for the limited precision of floats in that case with additional checks.*

If there are points to check, the code iterates through the list ❹. Unlike the code for insertion, we track both the current node and the previous one so that we can splice the target node out of the list. The code uses the approx_equal helper function from Listing 8-3 to test each point ❺. When it finds a matching point, it splices it out of the list, taking care to correctly handle the special case of the first node in the list ❻, and returns True. Thus, only the *first* matching point in the list is removed. If the current point does not match, the search continues to the next node in the list ❼. If the search finishes the entire list, the function returns False to indicate that no matching node was deleted.

Searches Over Grids

Now that we've learned how to construct grid data structures, let's use them to improve our nearest-neighbor searches. First, we examine the problem of pruning grid cells that are too far away, which will allow us to avoid unnecessary computations within grid cells. We then consider two basic searches: a linear scan over all the bins and an expanding search.

Pruning Bins

The grid's spatial structure allows us to limit how many points we need to check, excluding those outside the range we're interested in (northern Florida). Once we have a candidate neighbor and its associated distance, we can use that distance to *prune bins*. Before checking the points in a bin, we ask whether *any* point within the bin's spatial bounds could be closer than the current best distance. If not, we can ignore the bin.

Determining whether *any* point within a bin lies within a given distance from our target point may sound like a daunting task. However, if we are using Euclidean distance $dist = \sqrt{(x_1 - x_2)^2 + (y_1 - y_2)^2}$, which we can encapsulate in this simple helper function:

```
euclidean_dist(Float: x1, Float: y1, Float: x2, Float: y2):
    return sqrt((x1-x2)*(x1-x2) + (y1-y2)*(y1-y2))
```

then the test boils down to simple mathematics. We start by finding the closest possible point in the grid cell and use that for our pruning test. Specifically, if the closest possible point in the grid cell is further than our current best candidate, there is no reason to check any of the actual points stored in the bin. They all must be further away. If a target point falls within the cell—that is, if its x and y values are within the cell's x and y ranges, respectively—the distance to the cell (and thus the closest possible point) is zero.

If the point falls outside the cell, then the closest possible point in the cell must lie on the edge of the cell. Figure 8-10 shows a variety of points outside the grid cell and the corresponding closest points within the cell. For points outside the grid cell, we need to compute the distance to the closest edge point.

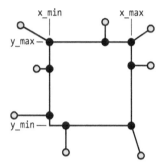

Figure 8-10: Points outside a grid cell (gray circles) and the corresponding closest points within the cell (solid circles)

We can compute the Euclidean distance between a point and the nearest edge of a grid's bin by considering each dimension independently. We find the minimum distance needed to shift the x value within the bin's range and the minimum distance to shift the y value within the bin's range. For the grid bin (*xbin*, *ybin*), the minimum and maximum x and y dimensions are:

```
x_min = x_start + xbin * x_bin_width
x_max = x_start + (xbin + 1) * x_bin_width
y_min = y_start + ybin * y_bin_width
y_max = y_start + (ybin + 1) * y_bin_width
```

We can compute the distance as follows (in the case of Euclidean distance):

$$MinDist = \sqrt{x_{dist^2} + y_{dist^2}}$$

where

IF $x < x\_min$ THEN $x_{dist} = x\_min - x$

IF $x\_min \leq x \leq x\_max$ THEN $x_{dist} = 0$

IF $x > x\_max$ THEN $x_{dist} = x - x\_max$

and

$$\text{IF } y < y\_min \text{ THEN } y_{\text{dist}} = y\_min - y$$

$$\text{IF } y\_min \leq y \leq y\_max \text{ THEN } y_{\text{dist}} = 0$$

$$\text{IF } y > y\_max \text{ THEN } y_{\text{dist}} = y - y\_max$$

If the minimum distance to any possible point in the bin is greater than that of our current closest point, then nothing in the bin could replace the current closest point. We can ignore the entire bin!

The code for computing the minimum distance from a point to a bin can be encapsulated into the following helper function. This function implements the mathematical logic above.

```
MinDistToBin(Grid: g, Integer: xbin, Integer: ybin, Float: x, Float: y):
    # Check that the bin is valid.
❶ IF xbin < 0 OR xbin >= g.num_x_bins:
        return Inf
    IF ybin < 0 OR ybin >= g.num_y_bins:
        return Inf

❷ Float: x_min = g.x_start + xbin * g.x_bin_width
    Float: x_max = g.x_start + (xbin + 1) * g.x_bin_width
    Float: x_dist = 0
    IF x < x_min:
      x_dist = x_min - x
    IF x > x_max:
      x_dist = x - x_max

❸ Float: y_min = g.y_start + ybin * g.y_bin_width
    Float: y_max = g.y_start + (ybin + 1) * g.y_bin_width
    Float: y_dist = 0
    IF y < y_min:
      y_dist = y_min - y
    IF y > y_max:
      y_dist = y - y_max
    return sqrt(x_dist*x_dist + y_dist*y_dist)
```

Listing 8-4: A helper function that computes the closest distance from a target point to a given bin

The code starts by checking that the bin indices are valid ❶. In this example, we use an infinite distance to indicate that the function's caller has referenced an invalid bin. This logic allows us to use this lookup function in pruning computations that might ask about invalid bins. However, this may lead to confusion: Why is the function returning any distance for an invalid bin? Depending on the usage, it might be preferable to throw an error indicating that the bin indices are invalid. Either way, the function's behavior should be clearly documented for users.

The remainder of the code proceeds through the distance logic above for the x and y dimensions (❷ and ❸, respectively). The code computes the minimum and maximum values for the bin, compares them with the point's value along that dimension, and computes the distance.

To visualize this distance test, imagine that a raucous game of catch sends a ball over our fence into the yard of our friendly, but exceedingly lazy, neighbor. They will return the ball, of course, but without exerting any more effort than absolutely necessary. What is the shortest distance they need to throw the ball in order for it to (just barely) return to our yard? If their longitude already falls within the bounds of our yard, they will throw in a pure north or south direction so as not to add any unnecessary east/west distance. In the end, their throw always lands exactly on the fence such that it falls back into our property. Our neighbor may be lazy, but they have some impressive throwing skills.

Linear Scan Over Bins

The simplest approach to searching a grid would iterate through all the grid's bins using a linear scan and only check those that could contain a potential nearest neighbor. This is not a particularly good algorithm, but it provides an easy introduction to working with and pruning bins.

The linear search algorithm simply applies the aforementioned minimum distance test to each bin before checking its contents:

```
GridLinearScanNN(Grid: g, Float: x, Float: y):
❶ Float: best_dist = Inf
   GridPoint: best_candidate = null

   Integer: xbin = 0
❷ WHILE xbin < g.num_x_bins:
       Integer: ybin = 0
       WHILE ybin < g.num_y_bins:

           # Check if we need to process the bin.
         ❸ IF MinDistToBin(g, xbin, ybin, x, y) < best_dist:

               # Check every point in the bin's linked list.
               GridPoint: current = g.bins[xbin][ybin]
             ❹ WHILE current != null:
                   Float: dist = euclidean_dist(x, y, current.x, current.y)
                 ❺ IF dist < best_dist:
                       best_dist = dist
                       best_candidate = current
                   current = current.next
           ybin = ybin + 1
       xbin = xbin + 1
❻ return best_candidate
```

Listing 8-5: A nearest-neighbor search that uses a linear scan over a grids bin with pruning tests on each bin.

The code starts by setting the best distance to infinity to indicate that no best point has been found so far ❶. Then the algorithm scans through each bin using a pair of nested WHILE loops that iterate over the x and y bins ❷. Before checking the individual points in the bin, the code performs a minimum distance test to check whether *any* point in the bin could be a better neighbor ❸. If the bin may contain better neighbors, the code uses a third WHILE loop to iterate through the linked list of points in the bin ❹. It tests the distance to each point and compares it with the best distance found so far ❺. The function completes by returning the best candidate found, which may be null if the grid is empty ❻.

The algorithm in Listing 8-5 allows us to prune out entire bins, along with all the points they contain, whenever we determine that minimum distance to any point in the bin is greater than the distance to the best point seen so far. If we have a large number of points per bin, this can lead to significant savings. However, if the grid is sparsely populated, we might end up paying more to check each of the bins than we would have if we'd checked each point individually.

Unlike the GridInsert function in Listing 8-2, our linear scan works with target points inside or outside the grid's spatial bounds. GridLinearScanNN does not need to map the target point to a bin and therefore does not care if the target is on the grid itself. It will still return the nearest neighbor from the grid (or null if the grid is empty). This provides an additional level of flexibility to our nearest-neighbor search that can be useful when encountering new, non-typical targets.

Ideal Expanding Search over Bins

While the linear scan algorithm allows us to prune out entire bins based on their minimum distance to our target point, we're still not using all the spatial information at our disposal. We waste a significant amount of computation by testing bins that are far from our target point. We can do better if we prioritize bins by their proximity to their target, first searching the bins closest to our target point and halting the search when the remaining bins are further than the nearest neighbor we have found so far. We call this an *expanding search*, because we effectively expand out from the bin containing the target point until we have found the nearest neighbor.

To visualize this improved scanning method, imagine a panicked search for our car keys in the morning. We start with the area (comparable to a grid cell) where the car keys would be if we had stored them correctly. We inspect every inch of the kitchen counter before admitting that we must have misplaced the keys. Spiraling out to other parts of the house (that is, other bins), we check nearby locations, such as the coffee table and the floor, before venturing further and further away. This search continues, exploring less and less likely locations, until we find the keys mysteriously sitting in the sock drawer.

For an example of an expanding scan in action, consider our map overlaid with a four-by-four grid, as shown in Figure 8-11. We find the closest bin to our target point by asking, "Into which bin does our target point fall?"

and using the grid index-mapping equations. Since it is possible that our target point falls outside the grid, we might also need to shift the computed bin indices into the valid range. In Figure 8-11, the target point is in the third bin up in the leftmost column ($xbin = 0$ and $ybin = 2$ in our notation).

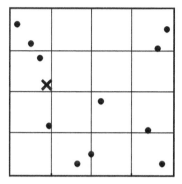

Figure 8-11: A 4×4 grid of two-dimensional points

We can start our search in the target point's bin and test every point in that bin. As long as the bin isn't empty, we are guaranteed to find our first *candidate* nearest neighbor, as shown in Figure 8-12. Unfortunately, since we're not organizing or sorting the points within each bin, we can't do better in this case than a linear scan through that bin's points. Of course, if the initial bin is empty, we must progress our search outward to neighboring bins, incrementally trying further and further bins until we find one containing a data point to be our candidate nearest neighbor.

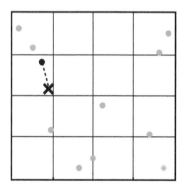

Figure 8-12: An initial candidate nearest neighbor
found in the same bin as the target point

Once we obtain this initial candidate for nearest neighbor, we are still not done. The candidate is just that—a candidate. It's possible there could be a closer point in one of the adjacent bins. This is more likely if our target point is near the edge of a bin. In Figure 8-13, the dashed circle represents the space of all points that are closer to or at the same distance from the current candidate. Any other point that falls within the circle could be the true nearest neighbor. The shaded grid cells are those that overlap this region.

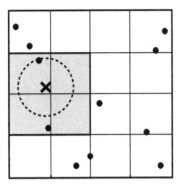

Figure 8-13: A candidate nearest neighbor and the grid cells that could contain points closer to the target

To visualize why we need to continue to check other bins, imagine you want to determine the closest person to you at an outdoor party. You're telling a particularly embarrassing story, involving the use of spoiled milk in your coffee, and want to make sure that only the intended audience hears you. Your best friend standing by the house might appear to be closest to you, but, if you're near your fence, you also need to consider people on the other side. If your neighbor is planting flowers along their side of the fence, they might actually be closer and hear all of the humiliating details. You can't discount them because there is a fence in the way. This is why we always check neighboring bins—and why you should always be careful about telling embarrassing stories in public.

We continue to expand out the search to include *all* nearby bins until we can guarantee that no possible point in the remaining bins could be closer than our candidate nearest neighbor. Once we have checked all the bins within the radius of our nearest-neighbor candidate, we can ignore any bins beyond that. We don't even need to check their distance.

The tradeoff for this improved grid search is algorithmic complexity. Instead of scanning across every one of the bins—an algorithm we could implement with a nested pair of FOR loops—the optimized search spirals out from a single bin, exploring further and further away until we can prove that none of the unexplored bins could contain a better neighbor. This requires additional logic in the search order (outward spiral), bounds checking (avoiding testing bins off the edge of the grid), and termination criteria (knowing when to stop). The next section presents a simple example of an expanding search for illustrative purposes.

Simplified Expanding Search

Let's consider a simplified (and non-optimized) version of an expanding search that moves outward in a diamond-shaped pattern. Instead of executing a perfect spiral out from the initial bin, the search uses an increasing distance from an initial bin. For simplicity of implementation, we will use a Manhattan distance on the grid indices that counts the steps between grid cells:

$$d = |xbin_1 - xbin_2| + |ybin_1 - ybin_2|$$

While this search pattern is unlikely to be efficient for grids with drastically different bin widths along each dimension, it provides an easy-to-follow illustration.

Figure 8-14 shows the first four iterations of the search. During the first iteration in Figure 8-14(a), we search the bin containing the target point (zero steps away). During the next iteration in Figure 8-14(b), we search all bins a single step away. On each subsequent iteration, we search all the bins that are one step further out.

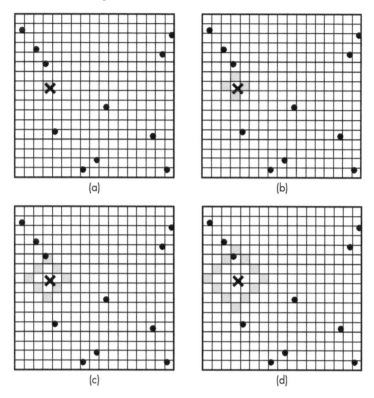

(a) (b)

(c) (d)

Figure 8-14: The first four iterations of a simplified expanding search on a grid

We start with a helper function that checks whether any points within a specified bin are closer to our target point (x, y) than a given threshold. This function encodes our linear scan through the bin's points. If there is at least one point closer than threshold, the function returns the closest such point. The use of a threshold value will allow us to use the helper function to compare the bin's points to the best candidates from other bins.

```
GridCheckBin(Grid: g, Integer: xbin, Integer: ybin,
             Float: x, Float: y, Float: threshold):
    # Check that it is a valid bin and within the pruning threshold.
 ❶ IF xbin < 0 OR xbin >= g.num_x_bins:
        return null
    IF ybin < 0 OR ybin >= g.num_y_bins:
        return null
```

```
    # Check each of the points in the bin one by one.
    GridPoint: best_candidate = null
❷  Float: best_dist = threshold
    GridPoint: current = g.bins[xbin][ybin]
❸  WHILE current != null:
❹      Float: dist = euclidean_dist(x, y, current.x, current.y)
        IF dist < best_dist:
            best_dist = dist
            best_candidate = current
        current = current.next
❺  return best_candidate
```

Listing 8-6: A helper function that returns the closest point in a bin to the target point as long as it is below the given threshold

The code starts with a safety check that we are accessing a valid bin ❶. If not, it returns null to indicate that there are no valid points. The code then uses a WHILE loop to iterate through each point in the bin ❸, computing its distance from the target point, comparing it to the best distance seen so far, and saving it as the new best candidate if it is closer ❹. The code finishes by returning the closest point ❺. Since the code initially set best_dist to the threshold value before checking any points ❷, it will only mark points with a distance less than threshold as new candidates. The function returns null if none of the bin's points are closer than threshold.

The code for performing the expanding search works by iterating through a different number of steps and checking all bins that can be reached in that number of steps. As in previous searches, we track the best candidate seen so far. The search concludes after iteration *d* if there are no valid grid cells *d* steps away that could contain a closer neighbor.

```
GridSearchExpanding(Grid: g, Float: x, Float: y):
    Float: best_d = Inf
    GridPoint: best_pt = null

❶  # Find the starting x and y bins for our search.
    Integer: xb = Floor((x - g.x_start) / g.x_bin_width)
    IF xb < 0:
        xb = 0
    IF xb >= g.num_x_bins:
        xb = g.num_x_bins - 1

    Integer: yb = Floor((y - g.y_start) / g.y_bin_width)
    IF yb < 0:
        yb = 0
    IF yb >= g.num_y_bins:
        yb = g.num_y_bins - 1
```

```
    Integer: steps = 0
    Boolean: explore = True
❷ WHILE explore:
        explore = False

    ❸ Integer: xoff = -steps
      WHILE xoff <= steps:
        ❹ Integer: yoff = steps - abs(xoff)
        ❺ IF MinDistToBin(g, xb + xoff, yb - yoff, x, y) < best_d:
            ❻ GridPoint: pt = GridCheckBin(g, xb + xoff, yb - yoff,
                                            x, y, best_d)
              IF pt != null:
                  best_d = euclidean_dist(x, y, pt.x, pt.y)
                  best_pt = pt
            ❼ explore = True

        ❽ IF (MinDistToBin(g, xb + xoff, yb + yoff, x, y) < best_d
              AND yoff != 0):
              GridPoint: pt = GridCheckBin(g, xb + xoff, yb + yoff,
                                            x, y, best_d)
              IF pt != null:
                  best_d = euclidean_dist(x, y, pt.x, pt.y)
                  best_pt = pt
            ❾ explore = True

          xoff = xoff + 1
      steps = steps + 1
    return best_pt
```

This code starts by finding the closest bin within the grid to our target point, taking care to map targets outside the grid to their closest bin in the grid ❶. The resulting bin (xb, yb) will be the starting point for the search. By mapping bins outside the grid to a valid bin, the function can return the nearest neighbor for target points that lie outside the grid itself.

The code then uses a WHILE loop to explore outward from this initial bin by increasing amounts ❷. The variable steps tracks the distance used for the current iteration. The WHILE loop is conditioned on the variable explore, which indicates that the next iteration may include a valid bin and we should thus continue exploring at the next value of steps. As we will see shortly, the WHILE loop terminates as soon as it completes a full iteration where *none* of the bins visited could have held a closer neighbor.

Within the main WHILE loop, the code iterates across the different x-index offsets from -steps to steps as though scanning horizontally across the grid ❸. The total number of steps in the x-direction and y-direction are fixed by steps, so the code can programmatically compute the remaining number of steps to use in the (positive or negative) y-direction ❹. Starting with the negative y-direction, the code uses MinDistToBin from Listing 8-4 to check whether the bin indices are valid and, if so, determine the distance to that bin ❺. It can skip any bins that are invalid or too far away. If the bin could contain a closer point than our current candidate, the code uses GridCheckBin from Listing 8-6 to check for such a point ❻. Whenever a closer point has been found, the code saves it as the new closest candidate and updates its estimate of the closest distance. The second IF block performs the same checks in the positive y-direction as long as the y-offset is not zero (in which case we have already checked the bin in the negative y-direction) ❽.

During an iteration of the outer WHILE loop ❷, the code resets explore to False. It later updates explore to True if any of the calls to MinDistToBin indicate that a bin could contain a closer neighbor (❼ and ❾). Thus, the outer loop continues until it reaches a number of steps where every bin is either further than best_d or lies off the grid (and is therefore invalid). While other termination criteria may provide more exact tests and terminate earlier, we use this rule in the code due to its simplicity.

The Importance of Grid Size

The size of our grid's bins has a massive impact on the efficiency of our search. The larger our bins, the more points we may need to check per bin. Remember that our grid searches still do a linear scan through the points within each visited bin. However, partitioning the grid into finer bins has tradeoffs both in terms of memory and the number of empty bins we may encounter. As we shrink the size of the grid's bins, we often need to search more individual bins before we even find the first candidate nearest neighbor and the cost of checking bins increases.

Figure 8-15 shows an extreme case where the grid is too fine.

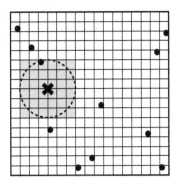

Figure 8-15: A fine grid in which most of the bins are empty

In Figure 8-15, we must search 36 bins in order to find the nearest neighbor. This is clearly more expensive than the example in Figure 8-13, where we only needed to check four bins and two individual points. Sadly, it might even be more expensive than the linear scan search, which checked every one of the 11 data points.

Consider this in the context of our search for coffee shops. If we partition the space too finely, such as in 1 m by 1 m squares, we'll be facing a grid that contains mostly empty bins. If we partition the space more coarsely, such as 5 km by 5 km squares, we might bucket entire cities and their multitudes of coffee shops in a single bin while still leaving (to our utmost horror) a large number of bins nearly or completely empty.

The optimal grid size often depends on multiple factors, including the number of points and their distribution. More complex techniques, such as non-uniform grids, can be used to dynamically adapt to the data. In the next chapter, we will consider several tree-based data structures that dynamically enable this type of adaptation.

Beyond Two Dimensions

The grid-based techniques developed for two dimensions can be scaled to higher dimensional data as well. We might need to search a multi-floor office building for the closest available conference room. We can search for nearest neighbors in three-dimensional data by incorporating the z coordinate into our distance computation:

$$dist = \sqrt{((x_1 - x_2)^2 + (y_1 - y_2)^2 + (z_1 - z_2)^2)}$$

Or, more generally, we can define Euclidean distance over d-dimensional data as:

$$dist(x_1, x_2) = \sqrt{(\Sigma_d \, (x_1[d] - x_2[d])^2)}$$

where $x_i[d]$ is the dth dimension of the ith data point.

Higher-dimensional data comes with another challenge for the grid-based approach we've considered in this chapter: it requires us to partition the space along more dimensions. The space required to store such data structures explodes quickly as we consider higher dimensions. For data with D dimensions and K bins per dimension, we need K^D individual bins! This can require a huge amount of memory. Figure 8-16 shows a three-dimensional example, a 5×5×5 grid, which already includes a large number of individual bins.

Worse, as we increase the number of grid bins, we're likely increasing the percentage of empty bins. Checking those empty bins is wasted work. For this reason, grids aren't ideal for higher-dimensional problems. In the next chapter, we will introduce a better approach for scaling to higher-dimensional data—the k-d tree.

While it is difficult to think of an everyday spatial problem using more than three dimensions, we can use our nearest-neighbor formulation on data beyond spatial points. In the next section, we will see how nearest-neighbor search can be used to help us find similar coffee or days with similar weather conditions.

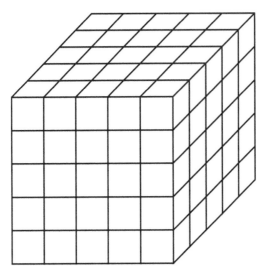

Figure 8-16: A grid of three-dimensional points

Beyond Spatial Data

Spatial data, such as locations on a map, provides a simple visual example for both nearest-neighbor search and grids themselves. We're accustomed to thinking about locations in terms of proximity, since we regularly ask ourselves questions like "What is the closest gas station?" or "Where is the closest hotel to the conference center?" Yet the nearest-neighbor problem extends beyond spatial data.

Let's consider the critical problem of selecting the next-best brand of coffee to purchase when our favorite brand is out of stock. To find something similar to our favorite brew, we might consider what attributes we liked about that coffee, such as strength or acidity level, and then look for other coffees with similar attributes. We can extend nearest-neighbor search to find these "close" coffees. To do so, we first record every coffee we have ever sampled in a coffee log, noting such properties as strength and acidity, as shown in Figure 8-17.

Over the years, we build a comprehensive mapping of the coffee landscape. Performing a nearest-neighbor search on this data allows us to find varieties of coffee similar to a target value. Looking for a strong, low-acidity brew to fuel the hurried work before a tight deadline? We can picture exactly the coffee we want, that sublime brew we had once in Hawai'i. Unfortunately, the upcoming deadline does not provide enough slack to justify a quick trip to Hawai'i. But have no fear! We use our thorough analysis of the coffee's attributes, as captured in our coffee log, to define a search target and then search for a local brand that might be similar enough.

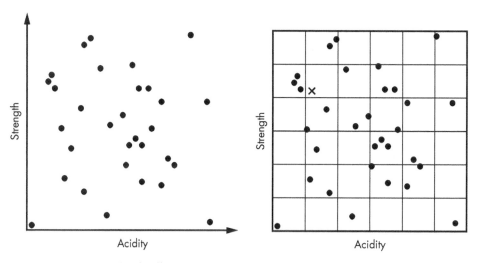

Figure 8-17: An example of coffee attributes as two-dimensional data (left) and those points in a grid (right)

To perform this search, we just need a way to compute distances for attributes like coffee strength or acidity. The nearest-neighbor algorithm relies on our ability to distinguish "near" versus "far" neighbors. While it is possible to define distance measures over other types, such as strings, we restrict our discussion in this chapter to real-valued attributes for consistency.

With spatial data points, we have simple standard measures of the distances between two points (x_1, y_1) and (x_2, y_2), such as the Euclidean distance used earlier. But the optimal distance measure for any problem will depend on the problem itself. When evaluating brands of coffee, we might want to weight the attributes differently in different situations. Before our impending deadline, caffeine content takes precedence over factors such as the acidity level.

One common distance measure for non-spatial data is weighted Euclidean distance:

$$dist(x_1, x_2) = \sqrt{(\Sigma_d\, w_d(x_1[d] - x_2[d])^2)}$$

where $x_i[d]$ is the dth dimension of the ith data point and w_d is the weighting for the dth dimension. This formulation allows us to weight the impact of the different dimensions. In this case, we might set the weight of caffeine content to twice that of acidity, skewing the search toward coffees that are similarly caffeinated. We can even vary the weights per search.

Of course, our search makes no guarantees as to the suitability of other aspects of the coffee. We're only measuring proximity along the specified dimensions. If we are searching for an everyday coffee by matching only strength and acidity, then we do not consider roast level, batch size, growing conditions, caffeine content, or even the concentration of nutrients in the soil. If the nearest neighbor turns out to be decaf, our search wouldn't account for this travesty. We'd be left with substandard coffee and tears of disappointment. It is important to make sure your distance computation takes into consideration all the dimensions of interest.

Why This Matters

Nearest-neighbor search allows us to find points that are "close" to some target value, whether spatial or non-spatial. From an algorithmic point of view, nearest-neighbor search moves us from searching for an exact target to searching based on distance metrics. The details of search get more complex as we step away from one-dimensional data sets into the realm of multidimensional data. As we saw with the shift from arrays to grids, this extension opens a range of new questions in terms of how we organize and search the data. It's no longer possible to consider a simple ordering, as we did with a binary search for one-dimensional data. We need to adapt our data structures to a new type of multidimensional structure. Grids provide a new way to structure data based on aggregating points within the same spatial regions into the same bin.

At the same time, grids illustrate a different structure than the one-bucket, one-value structure we have seen with arrays. Grids use linked-list or other internal data structures to store multiple values per bin, a technique we will reuse in future chapters. By using this structure, grids also introduce a new tradeoff to consider—the size of the bins. By increasing the size of the bins, we can shift cost from evaluating many small bins to scanning through a large number of points per bin. Choosing the right number of bins is an example of the common task of *tuning* our data structure for the specific problem at hand.

In the next chapter, we'll take spatial partitioning further by combining the adaptive properties of trees with the spatial properties of grids. In doing so, we'll address some of the major drawbacks of grids—and make the search for a good cup of coffee significantly more efficient.

9

SPATIAL TREES

The previous chapter showed how nearest-neighbor search allows us to find nearby or close data points, broadening our ability to answer coffee-related questions, such as finding the closest physical location or finding items with similar attributes. In this chapter, we build on the concepts of tree-based data structures and spatial partitioning to further improve our nearest-neighbor searches.

Chapter 8 discussed how we can adapt the algorithmic concepts for finding a specific value to the more general problem of finding nearest neighbors. We also saw how operations become more difficult as we transition from a single dimension to multiple dimensions. Maybe we want to find nearby coffee shops in two-dimensional space or similar friends (based on empathy, willingness to listen, and the ever-important coolness factor). Grids replace the simple arrays, and it's no longer sufficient to sort along a single dimension.

This chapter introduces two new tree-based data structures: uniform quadtrees and k-d trees. The term *quadtree* is often used to describe an entire class of two-dimensional data structures, based on the original quadtree proposed by computer scientists Raphael Finkel and Jon Bentley, that partition each two-dimensional node into four subquadrants at each level. We focus on a uniform quadtree such as the structure proposed by researcher and inventor David P. Anderson. This structure has equal-sized subregions that mirror the grid structure, thus building upon our discussions in the previous chapter. In contrast, *k-d trees*, invented by Jon Bentley, use a more flexible binary partitioning scheme that can further adapt to the data and allow us to scale to higher dimensions. Through examining quadtrees and k-d trees, we learn to generalize and modify tree-based data structures—and examine these data structures by comparison with the projects of city planners.

Quadtrees

While grids provide a convenient data structure for storing two-dimensional data, they come with their own host of complexities. As we saw in the previous chapter, both the overhead and usefulness of grids depend heavily on how finely we partition the space. Using a large number of grid bins (by creating a finely grained grid) takes significant memory and may require us to search many bins. On the other hand, coarsely grained partitioning can result in a large number of points per bin, as in Figure 9-1, resembling a simple linear scan over a large number of individual points.

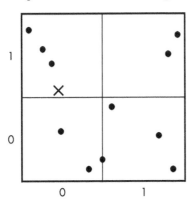

Figure 9-1: A grid with a small number of bins

We can think of the grids in terms of different approaches to home organization. If we throw all our kitchen equipment into a single massive drawer, it takes forever to find a given item. This is equivalent to having a single large grid bin. To improve matters, suppose we separate utensils into different drawers and cookware into various cupboards depending on their usage. We even put cereals on one shelf and spices on another. This is equivalent to using finer-grained bins. Suddenly things are looking up—we no longer need to search under the frying pans to find the cinnamon. A little additional structure makes our cooking routine significantly easier.

However, we can take the idea too far. Perhaps we have too many utensils and it takes too long to search the packed drawer. We might improve efficiency by splitting the utensils into a drawer for scooping utensils and one for non-scooping utensils. But imagine the overhead of storing each utensil in its own drawer—or worse, allocating a drawer for each potential utensil we might buy. Soon we're staring at a whole wall of drawers, wondering how many we'll need to check to find something to beat our eggs. This is what happens when we use grids with overly fine bins.

The solution to this conundrum is to partition space dynamically relative to the data. We only bring in additional structure, and its corresponding overhead, when we need it. We start with a coarse-grained partition of the space. Maybe we wait to allocate a separate drawer for spatulas until we have at least five. Until then we can store them with the ladles and whisks. When we need more granularity, we subpartition our space further. To provide this dynamism, we can turn to *uniform quadtrees.*

A uniform quadtree brings the branching structure of trees to grids. Each node in the tree represents a region of space. The root node represents the entire space covered by the tree and all points contained within this space. Each node is partitioned into four equal-sized quadrants, with a child node for each non-empty quadrant. The term *uniform* refers to the fact that nodes are partitioned into equal-sized spatial regions and thus partition the space within the node uniformly. Figure 9-2 illustrates a quadtree split.

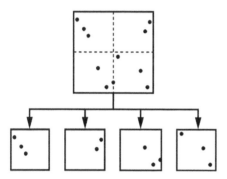

Figure 9-2: A quadtree node can have up to four children representing four equal-sized quadrants of that space.

When discussing the four subtrees, it's common to label them NorthWest, NorthEast, SouthWest, and SouthEast to reflect their spatial positions in the original region.

Internal quadtree nodes store pointers to up to four children, along with associated metadata such as the number of points in the branch or the region's spatial bounds (the minimum and maximum values for the node along the x- and y-dimension). Leaf nodes store a list of points that fall within that region, along with any desired metadata. We can use a single data structure for both internal and leaf nodes by keeping both a 2×2 grid of pointers to child nodes (for internal nodes) and an array for points (for leaf nodes). We either set the child entries to null in a leaf node or use an empty array for internal nodes.

The following is an example of a composite data structure for the QuadTreeNode:

```
QuadTreeNode {
    Boolean: is_leaf
    Integer: num_points
    Float: x_min
    Float: x_max
    Float: y_min
    Float: y_max
    Matrix of QuadTreeNodes: children
    Array of Points: points
}
```

We use a simple composite data structure for the points:

```
Point {
    Float: x
    Float: y
}
```

As in the previous chapter, we could alternatively store the points in arrays or ordered tuples.

Technically, we don't need to store the spatial bounds of the node explicitly. We can instead derive the bounds for each node from bounds of the root node and the sequence of splits, since each node partitions its points along the middle of each dimension, slicing the space into four predictably sized subregions. Given the root node's original bounds and the series of branches, we can compute the bounds for any child node precisely. However, precomputing and storing the bounds has one distinct advantage: at any given node we can simply look up the bounds instead of deriving them, making implementing our search algorithms significantly easier. I've often found that the value of storing this type of additional spatial information outweighs the additional memory costs.

The power of quadtrees is that branching at each level (where there are enough points) effectively creates an adaptive, hierarchical grid. Figure 9-3 shows an example of one quadtree's spatial partitioning.

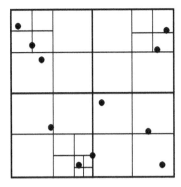

Figure 9-3: The spatial partition created by a quadtree

Imagine the successive partitions of a quadtree and how we search them as the interactive geographical search software in a sci-fi thriller. The protagonists crowd the command room and stare at a large screen representing the entire city. Tense music plays. As new information pours in, the operator selects a quadrant from the screen. Someone says, "Zoom in there and enhance," and the operator does so. Regardless of the dialogue, this operation is the equivalent to descending a level in the quadtree. In an instant, the command room's screen displays a subset of the city. The entire range under display is a single quadrant of the previous level. Everyone stares at the new geo-subset intently, before they select a further subquadrant and zoom in again. The search concludes when our heroes have found the transmitter closest to the target points.

As with other trees, we can add a wrapper data structure around the uniform quadtree to simplify bookkeeping:

```
QuadTree {
    QuadTreeNode: root
}
```

The root node is created as an empty node with the correct dimensions at the time the tree itself is created, so we do not need to worry about its being null.

Building Uniform Quadtrees

We build these magical quadtrees by recursively dividing our allocated space into smaller and smaller subregions. Since data can contain arbitrarily close or even duplicate points, we need additional logic to determine when to stop subdividing and designate a node with multiple points as a leaf. At each level, we check whether we need to make the current node an internal node (with child nodes) or a leaf node (with a list of points). There are different mechanisms we can use for this test, but here are the most common:

Are there enough points to justify a split?   If we have too few points, the cost of checking the distance to the child nodes is higher than exhaustively checking each of the points. It's not worth the overhead.

Are the spatial bounds large enough to justify a split?   What if we have 10 points in exactly the same location? We could split and split and split without ever partitioning the points. It's a waste of time and memory.

Have we hit a maximum depth?   This provides an alternate check to prevent us from wasting time and memory on excessive subdivision by capping how deep our tree can be.

We can visualize this process as an unconventional city planner's attempt to divide up the land such that each parcel has a building. Unacquainted with modern geographical partitioning techniques, the planner always divides regions into four equal-sized quadrants. Each time they look at a plot of land, they ask, "Are there too many buildings on this land?" and "Is this plot big enough to divide up further? I can't sell a 2-foot by 2-foot lot. People would laugh." The third criterion (maximum depth) represents how much subdividing the planner is willing to do before they give up. After four levels, the planner might call it "good enough" and move on. If the criteria for stopping aren't met, the planner sighs, mumbles "Really? Again?" and subdivides the plot.

When partitioning a level, we divide the current space into four equal quadrants, partition the points according to quadrant, and recursively examine each one. If we set the minimum of points to 1 and the maximum depth to 4 (including the root), we'd construct the tree in Figure 9-4. As shown by the illustration, we can save memory by only storing the non-empty children for each node. If a quadrant doesn't have a child, we can set its pointer to null.

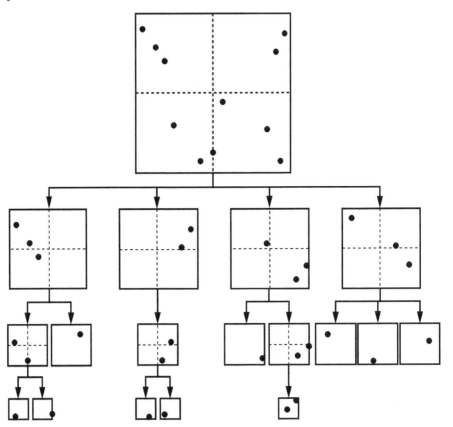

Figure 9-4: An example quadtree with four levels

The code for bulk construction of quadtrees is very similar to the code presented in the next section for adding points. In fact, iteratively adding points to an empty quadtree is a good approach for constructing it.

Adding Points

Since quadtrees are dynamic data structures, we can efficiently add points while maintaining the tree structure. We start with the wrapper function for the QuadTree data structure:

```
QuadTreeInsert(QuadTree: tree, Float: x, Float: y):
    IF x < tree.root.x_min OR x > tree.root.x_max:
        return False
    IF y < tree.root.y_min OR y > tree.root.y_max:
        return False
    QuadTreeNodeInsert(tree.root, x, y)
    return True
```

This wrapper guarantees we are always calling QuadTreeNodeInsert with a non-null node. The code also checks that the inserted point falls within the quadtree's bounds. This is critical, as uniform quadtrees use equal-sized bins and cannot be dynamically resized. All points must fall within the root node's spatial bounds. The code returns False if the point is out of range, but, depending on the implementation, you might want to use another mechanism such as returning an error or throwing an exception.

As shown in the following code, adding points to a node consists of traversing the tree to find the new point's location. This search can end in one of two ways: at a leaf node or at an internal dead end. If we terminate the search at a leaf node, we can add the new point there. Depending on our splitting criteria (spatial bounds, max depth, and number of points), we might need to split the node into subnodes. If we end at an internal dead end, then we have found a path that previously didn't contain any points. We can create the appropriate node.

```
QuadTreeNodeInsert(QuadTreeNode: node, Float: x, Float: y):
 ❶ node.num_points = node.num_points + 1

    # Determine into which child bin the point should go.
 ❷ Float: x_bin_size = (node.x_max - node.x_min) / 2.0
    Float: y_bin_size = (node.y_max - node.y_min) / 2.0
    Integer: xbin = Floor((x - node.x_min) / x_bin_size)
    Integer: ybin = Floor((y - node.y_min) / y_bin_size)

    # Add the point to the correct child.
 ❸ IF NOT node.is_leaf:
     ❹ IF node.children[xbin][ybin] == null:
            node.children[xbin][ybin] = QuadTreeNode(
                node.x_min + xbin * x_bin_size,
                node.x_min + (xbin + 1) * x_bin_size,
                node.y_min + ybin * y_bin_size,
                node.y_min + (ybin + 1) * y_bin_size)
        QuadTreeNodeInsert(node.children[xbin][ybin], x, y)
        return
```

```
# Add the point to a leaf node and split if needed.
❺ node.points.append(Point(x, y))
❻ IF we satisfy the conditions to split:
       node.is_leaf = False
    ❼ FOR EACH pt IN node.points:
           QuadTreeNodeInsert(node, pt.x, pt.y)
    ❽ node.num_points = (node.num_points -
                             length(node.points))
       node.points = []
```

The code starts by incrementing num_points to represent the new point ❶. The function then determines which of the four bins the new point falls into by computing the size of the bins and using that to map the x and y indices to either 0 or 1 ❷. If the node is not a leaf, the code needs to recursively add the point to the correct child ❸. It starts by checking whether the child exists. If not (if the child's pointer is null), it creates the child ❹. We use the fact that both xbin and ybin are either 0 or 1 to simplify the logic. Instead of enumerating all four cases, we can compute the child's bounds with arithmetic. Finally, at leaf nodes, the code inserts the points directly into the node ❺.

We aren't done yet, though. The code needs to check whether the splitting conditions are met ❻; if so, it splits the current leaf node. Luckily, we can reuse the same insertion function for splitting as we did to add a point. The code marks the node as a non-leaf (node.is_leaf = False) and reinserts the points one at a time using a FOR loop ❼. Because the current node is no longer a leaf node, the reinserted points now fall through to the correct children, with new children created as needed. However, since we used the function twice for each point, we have to correct num_points to avoid double-counting the reinserted points ❽ (due to the counter increment at ❶). The code also clears the list of points at the newly internal node.

Figure 9-5 shows what happens if we add two points to the tree. The inserted open-circle point causes one node to split before triggering the max-depth condition. The resulting leaf node holds two points. The inserted open-square point adds a single new child node corresponding to its parent NorthWest quadrant. The code does not split again because of the minimum number of points condition.

As noted in the previous section, we can use this approach to construct a uniform quadtree from a set of points. First, we create an empty root node with the necessary spatial bounds. Then we incrementally add each point from our set. Since splits are always based at the halfway point along each dimension, the tree structure does not change due to the order in which we insert the points.

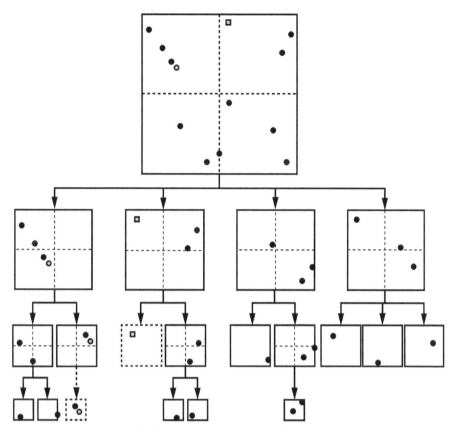

Figure 9-5: An example of adding two points, indicated by a shaded circle and shaded square, to a quadtree

Removing Points

Removing points from a node follows a similar, but more complex, process as inserting points. We delete the point from the list in the leaf node. We can then proceed back up the tree, removing splits that are no longer warranted by our criteria. This can involve recursively extracting the points from each of the node's children (which may themselves have children) and merging them into a single list at the next leaf node.

One additional difficulty is determining which point to delete. As with grids, the user might insert arbitrarily close or even duplicate points. In the code below, we delete the first matching point in the leaf node's list. Due to floating-point errors (rounding due to a floating-point variable's limited precision), we also cannot use a direct equality test. Therefore, we use a helper function to find a point that is close enough. We can reuse the approx_equal function from Listing 8-3 for this test.

We also use a helper function to collapse nodes that no longer meet our splitting criteria. The code collapses a node with children and returns an array with all the subtree's points:

```
QuadTreeNodeCollapse(QuadTreeNode: node):
❶ IF node.is_leaf:
       return node.points

❷ FOR i IN [0, 1]:
       FOR j IN [0, 1]:
           IF node.children[i][j] != null:
               Array: sub_pts = QuadTreeNodeCollapse(node.children[i][j])
               FOR EACH pt IN sub_pts:
                   node.points.append(pt)
               node.children[i][j] = null
❸ node.is_leaf = True
❹ return node.points
```

The code starts by checking whether the current node is already a leaf and, if so, directly returning the array of points ❶. Otherwise, the node is internal, and the code needs to aggregate the individual data points from each child. The code loops through each of the four children, checking whether they are null and, if not, recursively calling QuadTreeNodeCollapse to aggregate the points ❷. The function finishes by setting the current node to be a leaf ❸ and returning the points ❹.

With that helper function, we can move on to the deletion function. We start with the wrapper.

```
QuadTreeDelete(QuadTree: tree, Float: x, Float: y):
    IF x < tree.root.x_min OR x > tree.root.x_max:
        return False
    IF y < tree.root.y_min OR y > tree.root.y_max:
        return False
    return QuadTreeNodeDelete(tree.root, x, y)
```

The wrapper function starts by checking that the point lies within the bounds of the tree and thus could be in the tree. If so, it calls the recursive deletion function.

The recursive deletion code proceeds down the tree as though searching for the point. When it reaches a leaf, it deletes the point if it exists. It then returns up the tree, collapsing nodes as needed. The function returns True if a point was deleted.

```
QuadTreeNodeDelete(QuadTreeNode: node, Float: x, Float: y):
❶ IF node.is_leaf:
       Integer: i = 0
    ❷ WHILE i < length(node.points):
        ❸ IF approx_equal(node.points[i].x, node.points[i].y, x, y):
               remove point i from node.points
               node.num_points = node.num_points - 1
               return True
```

```
        i = i + 1
    return False

    # Determine into which child bin the point to be removed would go.
❹ Float: x_bin_size = (node.x_max - node.x_min) / 2.0
    Float: y_bin_size = (node.y_max - node.y_min) / 2.0
    Integer: xbin = Floor((x - node.x_min) / x_bin_size)
    Integer: ybin = Floor((y - node.y_min) / y_bin_size)

❺ IF node.children[xbin][ybin] == null:
    return False

❻ IF QuadTreeNodeDelete(node.children[xbin][ybin], x, y):
    node.num_points = node.num_points - 1

    ❼ IF node.children[xbin][ybin].num_points == 0:
        node.children[xbin][ybin] = null

    ❽ IF node no longer meets the split conditions
        node.points = QuadTreeNodeCollapse(node)
    return True
❾ return False
```

The code starts by checking whether the recursion has reached a leaf node ❶. If so, it iterates through the array of points ❷, checking whether each one matches the target point ❸. If the code finds a matching point, it removes it from the array, decrements the count of points in this node, and returns True to indicate a successful deletion. Note that only a single matching point is ever deleted. If the code does not find a matching point at the leaf, it returns False.

The search then progresses down into the bin into which the target point would be assigned ❹. The code checks whether the correct child exists and, if not, returns False to indicate the point is not in the tree ❺. Otherwise, the code recursively calls QuadTreeNodeDelete on the child ❻.

NOTE *As in Chapter 8, due to the numerical precision for floating-point values, we might need to extend the check of the child bin to handle cases where the point falls right on the split threshold. For simplicity of illustration, we will just check a single bin for now. But additional checks may be needed for production code.*

If the recursive call to QuadTreeNodeDelete returns True, then the code has deleted a point from one of its children. It updates the count of points and checks whether the child is empty ❼. If so, it deletes the child node. Then the code checks whether the current node continues to meet the criteria for being an internal node ❽. If not, it collapses the node. The code returns True to indicate the deletion was successful. If the recursive call did not return True, then no point was deleted. The function finishes by returning False ❾.

Searching Uniform QuadTrees

We begin our search of the quadtree at the root node. At each node, we first ask whether the node could contain anything closer than our current candidate. If so, for an internal node we explore the children recursively, and for a leaf node we test the points directly. However, if we determine that the current node could *not* contain our nearest neighbor, we can prune the search by ignoring not only that node but its entire subtree.

We check the compatibility of points within a node using the same test we applied to grid cells in Chapter 8. We have similar information at our disposal: the location of the point and the bounding box of the region. As described in the previous chapter, the distance computation is:

$$MinDist = \sqrt{x_{dist}2 + y_{dist}2}$$

where

$$\text{IF } x < x_{min} \text{ THEN } x_{dist} = x_{min} - x$$

$$\text{IF } x_{min} \leq x \leq x_{max} \text{ THEN } x_{dist} = 0$$

$$\text{IF } x > x_{max} \text{ THEN } x_{dist} = x - x_{max}$$

and

$$\text{IF } y < y_{min} \text{ THEN } y_{dist} = y_{min} - y$$

$$\text{IF } y_{min} \leq y \leq y_{max} \text{ THEN } y_{dist} = 0$$

$$\text{IF } y > y_{max} \text{ THEN } y_{dist} = y - y_{max}$$

In short, we're checking the distance from our search target to the closest possible point contained in the node's spatial region. To revisit the example from the last chapter, we're once again asking how far our lazy neighbor would need to throw a ball in order to just barely return it to our yard. This check only tests whether a point at this distance could exist within the node. We need to explore the node to see what points exist.

Consider searching for the nearest neighbor of the point marked with an X in Figure 9-6. This figure shows the same distribution of points as our original map of coffee shop locations in Figure 8-3, where the X is our current location and the other points are nearby cafés.

We start at the root node with a dummy candidate point with infinite distance. We haven't seen any candidate neighbors yet, so we need something with which to start our search. Using a dummy point with infinite distance allows the algorithm to accept the first point it finds as the new candidate without requiring any special logic. Any point we find is going to be closer than infinitely far away, and every region will contain closer points. In the case of searching for coffee shops, this corresponds to starting with an imaginary café that is infinitely far away. Any real café on our list is guaranteed to be closer than this imaginary point.

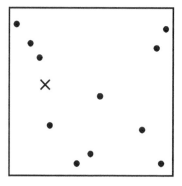

Figure 9-6: An example data set for nearest-neighbor search

NOTE *It's possible to begin our quadtree search with something other than an infinite-distance dummy candidate, like the first point in the data set (as we did with linear scan in Listing 8-1) or a random point from out data set. All that really matters is that we have some point and distance for use in our comparisons at each node.*

Since our (dummy) candidate point has infinite distance, our compatibility test for the root node passes. At least one of the points in the root node *could* be less than infinitely far away. Although this test is mathematically identical to the one we used for grid cells, it has one big practical difference: the size of the cells we are testing varies at each level of the tree. At higher levels, each node covers a large amount of space. As we descend lower, the spatial bounds tighten.

We prioritize which child node to search first based on the childrens' proximity to the query point. After all, we ultimately want to find the closest point and prune as much as possible. So we consider the x and y splits and ask "Into which of the four quadrants would our target point fall?" In this case, our query point falls in the NorthWest quadrant, as shown in Figure 9-7, so we start there.

We proceed down the pointer to the NorthWest child and find ourselves focusing on a subset of both the space and the points as shown in Figure 9-8. The grayed-out nodes represent nodes that have not been explored, and the grayed-out points have not been checked.

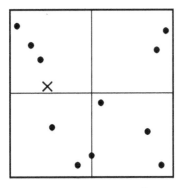

Figure 9-7: The query point falls within the
NorthWest quadrant of the quadtree's root node.

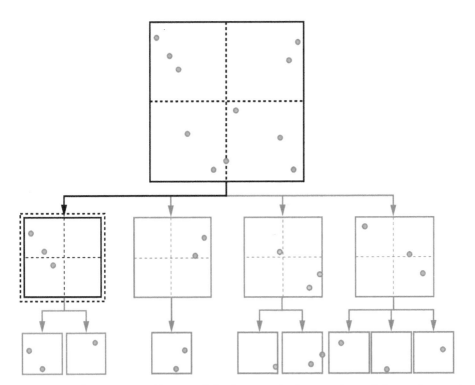

Figure 9-8: The nearest-neighbor search for the example shown in Figure 9-6 starts by searching
the subtree corresponding to the NorthWest quadrant of the root node.

Again, our test of spatial compatibility reveals that this node *could* contain our nearest neighbor. The minimum distance to the any point in the node is less than that of our current (dummy) candidate. We're at another internal node, which means that the space is further partitioned into four subregions.

Our search continues to the SouthWest child of the internal node in question, as illustrated in Figure 9-9. We choose this node because it is the closest to our query point. For the third time, the compatibility test passes.

Since we're at a leaf node, we explicitly check the distance to each point in that node. In this case, there is only a single point, and it is closer than our dummy candidate.

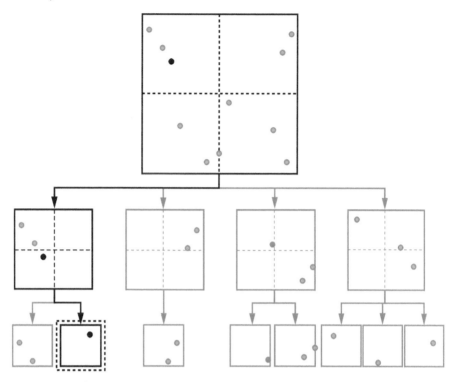

Figure 9-9: At the second level of the quadtree, our search starts with the closest quadrant to the target point, SouthWest.

We've found our first real candidate nearest neighbor! Its distance becomes our minimum distance so far. We can be pickier about all future points. In our running example of finding a nearby coffee shop, this first neighbor represents the closest coffee shop found so far. The distance to this point is the maximum distance that we'll need to travel to get a cup of coffee. We might find closer coffee shops later in our search, but at least we don't have to travel infinite miles. The relief is palpable.

Once we've tested all the points in a leaf node, we return to the (internal) parent node and check the remainder of the children. Now that we have a real candidate and distance, our pruning tests have power. We check the compatibility of all remaining child quadrants: NorthWest, NorthEast, and SouthEast. Our distance test shows that we can skip the NorthWest quadrant: as shown in Figure 9-10, the closest possible point in its spatial bounds is further than the candidate we already have. It can't possibly contain a better neighbor.

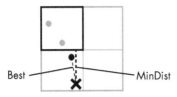

Figure 9-10: An illustration of the relative distance between the best candidate seen so far and the current node's NorthWest quadrant

We can also skip the empty NorthEast and SouthEast quadrants. Since they don't have any points, they can't have a better neighbor either. Our search can discard both quadrants without a distance test because their pointers will be null to indicate that no such child exists. We've managed to prune three of the four quadrants in this node as illustrated by the grayed-out quadrants in Figure 9-11. The two data points in the NorthWest quadrant also remain gray, because we never tested them.

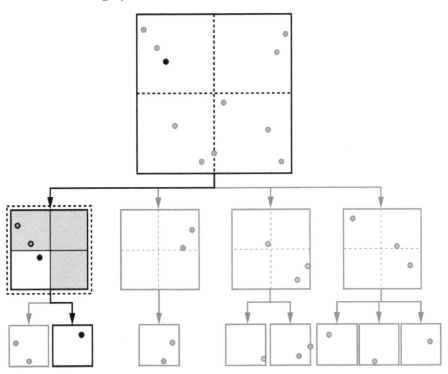

Figure 9-11: The nearest-neighbor search is able to skip three of the node's four quadrants.

Once we've finished checking the quadrants within an internal node, we return to its parent and repeat the process. The next closest quadrant is SouthWest, which our pruning test confirms is close enough to possibly contain a better neighbor, as shown in Figure 9-12.

Any time we find a child that, according to our simple distance test, *could* contain a closer point, we proceed down that pathway to check if there are indeed closer neighbors. In this case, our search descends into the SouthWest quadrant.

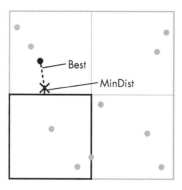

Figure 9-12: A pruning test where the candidate quadrant could include a closer neighbor than the current best point

At the next level, four potential quadrants again vie for our attention. Armed with a real candidate point and its corresponding distance, we can aggressively prune our search, as shown in Figure 9-13. We check the NorthWest quadrant (and its single point) because it falls within our distance threshold. We can skip the other three quadrants; the NorthEast and SouthWest quadrants are both empty and thus have null child pointers, and we use a distance test to confirm that the SouthEast quadrant is too far away to contain a better neighbor.

This time when we return to the root node, we can prune out the two remaining children, as shown in Figure 9-14.

The remote expanses of both the NorthEast and SouthEast quadrants lie well outside our distance threshold.

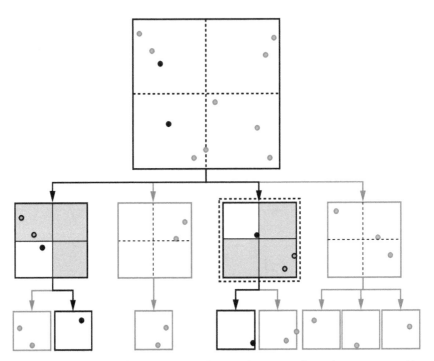

Figure 9-13: While checking the root node's SouthWest quadrant, the nearest-neighbor search can again skip three of the four subquadrants.

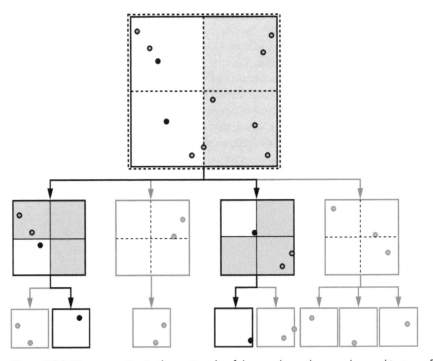

Figure 9-14: Upon returning to the root node of the quadtree, the search can skip two of that node's quadrants.

Nearest-Neighbor Search Code

To simplify our implementation of the nearest-neighbor search code, we start with a helper function to compute the distance from the target point (x, y) to a node. The code for checking the minimum distance to a node is similar to the minimum distance code presented for grids in the last chapter:

```
MinDist(QuadTreeNode: node, Float: x, Float: y):
    Float: x_dist = 0.0
    IF x < node.x_min:
        x_dist = node.x_min - x
    IF x > node.x_max:
        x_dist = x - node.x_max

    Float: y_dist = 0.0
    IF y < node.y_min:
        y_dist = node.y_min - y
    IF y > node.y_max:
        y_dist = y - node.y_max

    return sqrt(x_dist*x_dist + y_dist*y_dist)
```

However, in this case, the code does not need to compute the minimum and maximum bounds for the node, since each node stores them explicitly.

The main search algorithm uses the same recursive formulation described for other tree-based methods. Our implementation of this search algorithm includes a parameter best_dist that represents the distance so far. By passing best_dist to our search function, we can simplify the pruning logic. If the minimum distance to the current node is greater than the best distance so far, we can terminate that branch of the search. The function then returns a *closer* point if it finds one and null otherwise. It's important to note that in this implementation, a return value of null means that there are no points in the current node closer than best_dist.

We use a thin wrapper that passes along the root node and an initial infinite distance:

```
QuadTreeNearestNeighbor(QuadTree: tree, Float: x, Float: y):
    return QuadTreeNodeNearestNeighbor(tree.root, x, y, Inf)
```

Our wrapper function for nearest-neighbor search does not check that the target point falls within the quadtree bounds. This allows us to use the code to find neighbors within the tree for target points that fall outside the tree's bounds, increasing the usefulness of the code.

Here's the code for recursively searching the nodes:

```
QuadTreeNodeNearestNeighbor(QuadTreeNode: node, Float: x,
                            Float: y, Float: best_dist):
    # Prune if the node is too far away.
❶ IF MinDist(node, x, y) >= best_dist:
        return null
    Point: best_candidate = null
```

```
        # If we are in a leaf, search the points.
❷ IF node.is_leaf:
      FOR EACH current IN node.points:
          Float: dist = euclidean_dist(x, y, current.x, current.y)

          IF dist < best_dist:
              best_dist = dist
              best_candidate = current
      return best_candidate

    # Recursively check all 4 children starting with the closest.
❸ Float: x_bin_size = (node.x_max - node.x_min) / 2.0
  Float: y_bin_size = (node.y_max - node.y_min) / 2.0
  Integer: xbin = Floor((x - node.x_min) / x_bin_size)
  IF xbin < 0:
      xbin = 0
  IF xbin > 1:
      xbin = 1

  Integer: ybin = Floor((y - node.y_min) / y_bin_size)
  IF ybin < 0:
      ybin = 0
  IF ybin > 1:
      ybin = 1

❹ FOR EACH i IN [xbin, (xbin + 1) % 2]:
      FOR EACH j IN [ybin, (ybin + 1) % 2]:
          IF node.children[i][j] != null:
              Point: quad_best = QuadTreeNodeNearestNeighbor(
                                    node.children[i][j],
                                    x, y, best_dist)
            ❺ IF quad_best != null:
                  best_candidate = quad_best
                  best_dist = euclidean_dist(x, y, quad_best.x,
                                    quad_best.y)
  return best_candidate
```

The function starts with the pruning test, skipping the node and returning null if no point could be closer than best_dist ❶. The code then checks if it is at a leaf node ❷. If it has reached a leaf, it uses a FOR loop to check whether each point is closer than best_dist, updating best_dist and best_candidate if so. At the end of this loop, we return best_candidate, which has the value null if we haven't found a new closer point.

The next block of code handles the logic for an internal node. We have only made it this far if the node isn't a leaf and thus doesn't have any candidate points. Some basic numerical tests and integer manipulation control the order that the code searches the children, allowing the code to search the closest child first and then expand to the rest of the children. The code starts by computing into which x and y bin the candidate point should fall ❸, adjusting the value so that xbin and ybin both fall within [0, 1], and thus indicates the closest child node. This adjustment is necessary because, for many internal nodes, our target point will lie completely outside the 2×2 grid represented by the current node.

We then recursively explore the non-null children using a pair of nested FOR loops to iterate over the pairs ❹. Each time we check whether we find a closer point (represented by quad_best != null) and, if so, update both best_candidate and best_dist ❺. At the end of the function, we return best_candidate. As in the case of the leaf node, best_candidate may be null if we haven't found a point closer than the original best_dist.

k-d Trees

We've solved the problem of dynamic splits for two dimensions, so now it's time to turn our attention to searching for points or nearest neighbors in three or more dimensions using k-d trees. We've already seen the disappointment that can result when we don't account for all the relevant attributes in our coffee. Higher-dimensional problems are common whenever we're looking for similar points in data sets, such as searching for similar conditions (temperature, pressure, humidity) in a weather data set.

In theory, we could scale quadtrees by simply splitting along more dimensions. *Octtrees*, for example, are three-dimensional versions that split into eight subnodes at each level. Eight-way splits may not seem too bad, but this approach clearly doesn't scale gracefully with the number of dimensions. If we want to build a tree over D-dimensional data, we need to split along all D dimensions at once, giving us 2^D children for each internal node. If we were building a data structure over weather data containing temperature, pressure, humidity, precipitation, and wind speed, we would be using five-dimensional points and splitting 32 subtrees at each level! This immense overhead is the same problem we found when scaling grids to higher dimensions.

To effectively scale to higher dimensions, we need to rein in the branching factor. There are a variety of powerful data structures designed to enable efficient proximity search in higher dimensions. One example is the k-d tree, which builds off similar concepts as the quadtree.

k-d Tree Structure

A *k-d tree* is a spatial data structure that combines the spatial partitioning of quadtrees with the binary branching factor of a binary search tree, giving us the best of both worlds. Instead of splitting along every dimension at every level, the k-d tree chooses a single dimension and splits the data along that dimension. Each internal node thus partitions the data into exactly two children: a left child whose points fall below (or equal to) the split value, and a right child whose points fall above the split value.

When working with k-d trees, we lose the regular grid-like structure of the uniform quadtree, but, in exchange, we return to the two-way branching factor we know and love from binary search trees. This ability to partition along a single dimension in turn allows the k-d tree to scale to higher-dimensional data sets. We no longer need to split into 2^D children at each level. Figure 9-15 shows an example k-d tree.

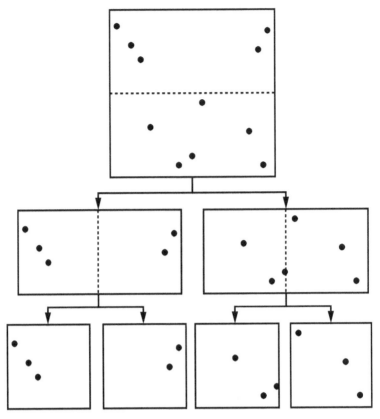

Figure 9-15: A k-d tree split along a single dimension at each level

A k-d tree can adjust more flexibly to the structure of the data than quadtrees. We're not constrained to split in the midpoint of every dimension at once. Instead of partitioning space into 2^D equally sized grid cells, we can choose a split dimension and value that are best suited to the data at each node. Each internal node thus stores both the dimension along which we're partitioning (split_dim) and the value (split_val), with points assigned to the left child if their value in that one dimension is less than or equal to the node's split value:

```
pt[split_dim] <= split_val
```

Rather than split along alternating axes, producing partitioning similar to that of the quadtree in Figure 9-15, we can tailor our tree structure by choosing splits based on the composition of the data points within the current node, thus allowing us to make splits that will better aid our future searches. We might choose the split value based on the overall bounds of the node, such as splitting in the middle of the widest dimension. Or we could choose the split value based on the distribution of data points, such as splitting at the middle of the range or the median of the points' values along the split dimension. The difference between these two options is illustrated in Figure 9-16.

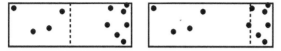

Figure 9-16: A node split at the middle (left) and median (right)

The flexible structure of the k-d tree means we need to take additional care when dealing with nodes' spatial bounds. Unlike the uniform quadtree's square grid cells, the nodes of a k-d tree cover multidimensional rectangles of the overall search space. The width in each dimension can be completely different. Some nodes might be square-ish, while others might be long and thin. We represent a node's area by explicitly tracking the multidimensional rectangle defining its spatial bounds—the minimum and maximum values in each dimension. Since we can have an arbitrary number of dimensions, we store the bounds in two arrays, x_min and x_max, where x_min[d] represents the lowest value along dimension d contained within the current node and x_max[d] represents the highest. All points within the node satisfy:

```
x_min[d] <= pt[d] <= x_max[d] FOR ALL d
```

As a result of its complexity, each k-d tree node stores a significant amount of information. While this might initially seem like expensive overhead, as we'll see in this section, the cost is offset by the power and flexibility of tree itself. As with every other data structure in this book, we are making an explicit tradeoff in terms of memory, data structure complexity, and later algorithmic efficiency.

Here is an example composite data structure for the KDTreeNode:

```
KDTreeNode {
    Boolean: is_leaf
    Integer: num_dimensions
    Integer: num_points
    Array of Floats: x_min
    Array of Floats: x_max
    Integer: split_dim
    Float: split_val
    KDTreeNode: left
    KDTreeNode: right
    Array of Arrays: points
}
```

In this case, we use an array to represent each point, allowing it to have arbitrary dimensions.

As with other trees in this book, we can wrap the nodes in an outer data structure such as a KDTree.

```
KDTree {
    Integer: num_dimensions
    KDTreeNode: root
}
```

It is helpful to store the number of dimensions in this wrapper data structure to check for consistency during operations such as insertion, deletion,
or search. The value of num_dimensions is set at time of the k-d tree's creation
and remains fixed for this tree.

This flexibility of choosing a strategy for splitting nodes illustrates
the true power of the k-d tree: we're augmenting the spatial partitioning of quadtrees to further adapt to the data. If our points are clustered,
we choose splits that provide the most information by focusing on those
regions. Figure 9-17 demonstrates this dynamic partitioning.

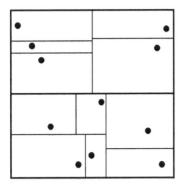

Figure 9-17: The spatial partition created by a k-d tree

Consider our ongoing task of locating nearby coffee shops. If we are
taking a road trip along Interstate 95 from Florida to Maine, we could
preprocess the data to store only those coffee shops within 50 miles of the
highway. Figure 9-18 shows an example distribution of this shape.

This prefiltering helps limit the search space to only coffee shops
near the highway, yet we can make our searches even more efficient by
storing these locations in a spatial data structure. We want to narrow
our search to the appropriate region along the highway as well. After all,
there is no need to check coffee shops in Massachusetts while we are still
in South Carolina. We quickly see that a uniform partitioning scheme is
far from ideal: our trip covers over 1,500 miles of mostly northward driving. Since we have already filtered to only shops along the highway, we
do not gain as much pruning from partitioning uniformly east and west
as well. We can increase the amount of pruning, and thus decrease the
search cost, by biasing our partitions along the north-south direction.

To give another analogy, if quadtrees are the daily routine of a city
planner following rigid regulations to divide up a map, k-d trees represent
a city planner with a wider range of tools at their disposal. They're no longer constrained to divide each plot into perfect squares. Instead, they have

the flexibility to partition the space according to the distribution of actual points. Our city planner chooses the widest dimension to split in order to minimize long, narrow zones. They also use the median point along this dimension to provide a balanced tree. The result might not always look as orderly as the quadtrees squares, but it can be much more effective.

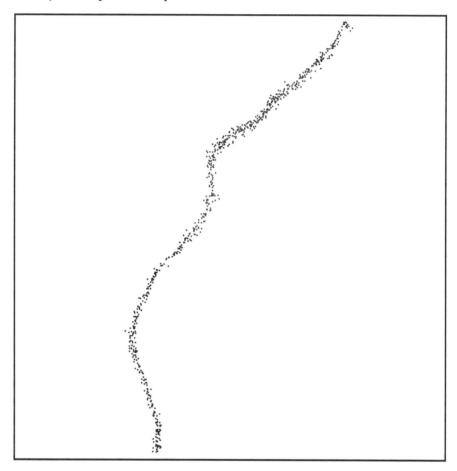

Figure 9-18: An example of how coffee shops might be distributed along a major highway

Tighter Spatial Bounds

We can often further improve a spatial tree's pruning power by tracking the bounding box of all the points falling within a given node instead of the node's total spatial bounds. This changes our pruning question from "Could a nearest-neighbor candidate exist in the space covered by the node?" to "Could a nearest-neighbor candidate exist in the bounding boxes of actual points within the node?" While this might seem like a small change, depending on what logic we use to split the nodes, we can see significant savings, as shown in Figure 9-19.

Figure 9-19: The bounding box of
points within a k-d tree node

If we use these tighter bounding boxes during node construction, we
can better adapt to the data. We are no longer splitting based on the entire
possible spatial region, but rather on the region occupied by actual points.
The resulting k-d tree structure looks like the one in Figure 9-20. The black
boxes indicate the tight bounding boxes at each node. The gray points and
lines are shown to place the nodes' bounds in the context of the rest of the
data set.

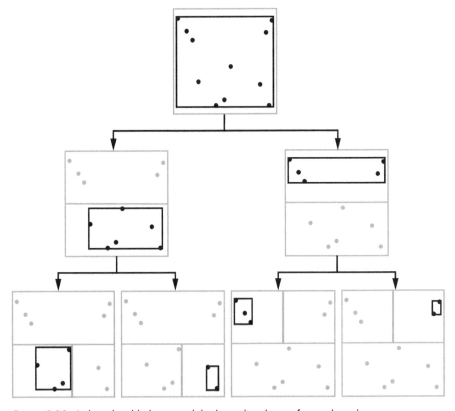

Figure 9-20: A three-level k-d tree and the bounding boxes for each node

During a search, we use the black boxes (tight bounding boxes) for
pruning. As you can see from the figure, the resulting regions can be significantly smaller, allowing us to prune much more aggressively. Since the
tight bounding box is smaller, it will often have a greater minimum distance
to our query point.

We can use a simple helper function to compute the tight bounding boxes from a set of points represented as arrays (Listing 9-1):

```
ComputeBoundingBox(Array of Arrays: pts):
❶ Integer: num_points = length(pts)
  IF num_points == 0:
      return Error
  Integer: num_dims = length(pts[0])

❷ Array: L = Array of length num_dims
  Array: H = Array of length num_dims
  Integer: d = 0
❸ WHILE d < num_dims:
      L[d] = pts[0][d]
      H[d] = pts[0][d]
      d = d + 1

  Integer: i = 1
❹ WHILE i < num_points:
      d = 0
      WHILE d < num_dims:
          IF L[d] > pts[i][d]:
              L[d] = pts[i][d]
          IF H[d] < pts[i][d]:
              H[d] = pts[i][d]
          d = d + 1
      i = i + 1
❺ return (L, H)
```

Listing 9-1: A helper function to compute the tight bounding box of the points in a node

The code extracts the number of points and number of dimensions from the input data ❶. It then creates new arrays L and H to hold the low and high bounds, respectively, ❷ and seeds them with the coordinates of the first point in our array ❸. The code then iterates through the remaining points in the array and checks whether any of them fall outside the bounds ❹. If so, it extends the bounds. The code ends by returning the two arrays ❺.

This helper function also illustrates the benefit of prechecking that all our points contain the correct number of dimensions in the KDTree's wrapper function. This check ensures that we do not try to access our invalid array entries for our data points.

Of course, tracking these additional bounds adds significant complexity when we start dealing with dynamic changes. Adding points to a k-d tree can increase the bounds for a given node. Similarly, removing nodes may shrink the bounds.

Building k-d Trees

Construction of a k-d tree uses a recursive process similar to the one for binary search trees, but with a few major differences. We start with all the data points and divide them into two subsets by picking a splitting dimension and value. This process repeats at each level until we hit our termination criteria: a minimum number of points left at the node, a minimum width, or a max depth. Generally, we use two of these tests, minimum number of points and minimum width, but using at least one of the last two tests is essential to avoid infinite recursion when you have duplicate data points.

We start with a wrapper function to check that our data is valid:

```
BuildKDTree(KDTree: tree, Array of Arrays: pts):
  FOR EACH pt IN pts:
      IF length(pt) != tree.num_dimensions:
          Return an error.
  IF length(pts) > 0:
      tree.root = KDTreeNode()
      RecursiveBuildKDTree(tree.root, tree.num_dimensions, pts)
  ELSE:
      tree.root = null
```

The code starts by checking that all points have the correct dimensionality. It then checks that there are points from which to build the tree. If so, it allocates a new root node (overwriting the previous tree) and recursively builds the k-d tree using the function below. Otherwise, it sets the root to null to indicate an empty tree.

The primary difference between k-d tree and quadtree construction is that k-d trees require us to choose a single split dimension at each level. If we are using tight bounding boxes, we also need to compute the bounding boxes over *D* dimensions. While these changes make the code a little longer (with extra loops over *D*), they don't add any real complexity. The code for building a k-d tree recursively partitions our set of points among the child nodes until we reach the termination criteria.

```
RecursiveBuildKDTree(KDTreeNode: node, Integer: num_dims,
                     Array of Arrays: pts):
❶ node.num_points = length(pts)
  node.num_dimensions = num_dims
  node.left = null
  node.right = null
  node.points = empty array
  node.split_dim = -1
  node.split_val = 0.0
  node.is_leaf = True

  # Compute the bounding box of the points.
❷ (node.x_min, node.x_max) = ComputeBoundingBox(pts)

  # Compute the width of the widest dimension.
❸ Float: max_width = 0.0
  Integer: d = 0
  WHILE d < node.num_dimensions:
      IF node.x_max[d] - node.x_min[d] > max_width:
          max_width = node.x_max[d] - node.x_min[d]
      d = d + 1
```

```
    # If we meet the conditions for a leaf, append the
    # remaining points to the node's point list.
❹ IF we do not satisfy the conditions to split:
    FOR EACH pt IN pts:
        node.points.append(pt)
    return

    # Choose split dimension and value.
❺ node.split_dim = chosen split dimension
    node.split_val = chosen split value along node.split_dim
    node.is_leaf = False

    # Partition the points into two sets based on
    # the split dimension and value.
    Array of Arrays: left_pts = []
    Array of Arrays: right_pts = []
❻ FOR EACH pt IN pts:
    IF pt[node.split_dim] <= node.split_val:
        left_pts.append(pt)
    ELSE:
        right_pts.append(pt)

    # Recursively build the child nodes.
❼ node.left = KDTreeNode()
    RecursiveBuildKDTree(node.left, num_dims, left_pts)

    node.right = KDTreeNode()
    RecursiveBuildKDTree(node.right, num_dims, right_pts)
```

This code starts with bookkeeping to fill in the information needed at each node. We record the essential details, such as the number of points and number of dimensions of the current points ❶. Then the function loops over all the points, computing the tight bounding box for the node ❷ using the helper function in Listing 9-1.

Once we have the bounds, the code loops over each of the dimensions to find the widest dimension ❸. We use this loop for one of the stopping conditions for the recursion (not splitting a node that is too small). If the node does not meet the conditions to keep splitting, the code stores all the points in a list at the leaf ❹. Otherwise, the code picks a split dimension and a split value for the node ❺. The code iterates over the current set of points, partitioning them into two arrays, left_pts and right_pts, according to the split dimension and value ❻. Those arrays are used to recursively build the two children nodes ❼.

One approach for choosing split_dim and split_val is to split along the middle of the widest dimension. The code for this is relatively simple and most of it can be incorporated into the initial block that finds the widest dimension ❸:

```
Float: max_width = 0.0
Integer: split_dim = 0
Integer: d = 0
```

```
WHILE d < node.num_dimensions:
    IF node.x_max[d] - node.x_min[d] > max_width:
        max_width = node.x_max[d] - node.x_min[d]
        split_dim = d
    d = d + 1
```

and then later setting the split dimension and the value at ❺:

```
node.split_dim = split_dim
node.split_val = (node.x_min[node.split_dim] +
                  node.x_max[node.split_dim]) / 2.0
```

Bulk construction of k-d trees has a significant advantage over dynamically inserting and removing points. By considering all the data points during construction, we can better adapt the structure of the tree to the data. We choose splits based on all the data points instead of the subset inserted so far.

k-d Tree Operations

The basic operations of inserting points, deleting points, and searching the k-d tree follow the same approach as with quadtrees. We start all operations at the top of the tree (root node) and use the split values to navigate down the appropriate branches. The major difference is that, instead of picking which of four quadrants to explore, we use split_dim and test against split_val to choose one of two children. As the high-level concepts are similar to those presented for the quadtree, we will not go into the code in detail for each one. Instead, let's look at some of the differences.

Insertion   When inserting points into a k-d tree node, we use split_dim and split_val to determine which branch to take. We split leaf nodes if they meet our split condition using the same approach as we would use during bulk construction. Finally, if we are tracking the tight bounding box for each node, we need to update the bounds to account for the new point. Since we are adding points, this update will always increase the size of the bounding box.

```
Integer: d = 0
WHILE d < node.num_dimensions:
    IF x[d] < node.x_min[d]:
        node.x_min[d] = x[d]
    IF x[d] > node.x_max[d]:
        node.x_max[d] = x[d]
    d = d + 1
```

This code iterates over each dimension of the new point, checks whether it falls outside the bounding box, and, if so, updates the bounds.

Deletion   When deleting points in a k-d tree, we use split_dim and split_val to determine which branch to take during our search for the point. After deleting a node, we return to the root of the tree. At each node along the way, we check whether the bounds can be tightened (using the points in a leaf or the two children's bounding boxes for an internal node). We also check whether internal nodes can be collapsed.

Search The key difference in the search operations between a quadtree and a k-d tree is in testing whether we can prune nodes. For example, we can compute the Euclidean distance between a point x and the closest possible point in a node's (non-uniform, D-dimensional) bounding box using an extension of the formula $MinDist = \sqrt{(\Sigma_d dist_d{}^2)}$ that we used for quadtrees and grids. We start by competing the minimum distance from the point to the node's spatial bounds along each individual dimension:

IF $x[d] < x_{min}[d]$ THEN $dist_d = x_{min}[d] - x[d]$

IF $x_{min}[d] \leq x \leq x_{max}[d]$ THEN $dist_d = 0$

IF $x[d] > x_{max}[d]$ THEN $dist_d = x[d] - x_{max}[d]$

where $x[d]$ represents the query point's dth dimension, and $x_{min}[d]$ and $x_{max}[d]$ represent the node's low and high bounds in the dth dimension. Then we compute the sum of squared distances along each dimension and take the square root. We can implement this entire computation as a WHILE loop over the dimensions:

```
KDTreeNodeMinDist(KDTreeNode: node, Point: pt):
    Float: dist_sum = 0.0
    Integer: d = 0
    WHILE d < node.num_dimensions:
        Float: diff = 0.0
        IF pt[d] < node.x_min[d]:
            diff = node.x_min[d] - pt[d]
        IF pt[d] > node.x_max[d]:
            diff = pt[d] - node.x_max[d]
        dist_sum = dist_sum + diff * diff
        d = d + 1
    return sqrt(dist_sum)
```

Note that k-d trees can be more sensitive to additions and deletions than quadtrees. While both trees can become unbalanced due to the splitting rules and the distribution of points, k-d trees' splits are chosen based on the data at the time. If we significantly change the distribution of points, the original split values may no longer be good ones. During bulk construction, we can adapt the splits to the data at hand, considering such factors as the depth of the tree, whether it is balanced, and the tightness of the nodes' spatial bounds. This illustrates another tradeoff we see with data structures— the performance of a structure may degrade as the data changes.

Why This Matters

The quadtree and k-d trees are examples of how we can combine the power of dynamic data structures with the spatial structure in our search problem. By branching along multiple dimensions at once, quadtrees allow us to adapt the resolution of a grid to the density of data points in a local area. High-density areas result in deeper branches and thus a finer-grained grid. At the same time, retaining a regular grid structure introduces new costs for higher dimensions. Examining how quadtrees, octtrees, and their variants scale across different data sets provides an important lens for how we think about utilizing spatial structure.

A k-d tree represents a combination of the concepts we have built up over the past few chapters to solve the problem of nearest-neighbor search. It solves the problem of having a high branching factor by returning to the core concepts of binary search trees and choosing a single dimension along which to split at each node. In addition, it allows more flexibility to adapt to the structure of the data, increasing pruning power.

Quadtrees and k-d trees aren't the only data structures for facilitating nearest-neighbor searches. There are a wealth of other tree-based and non-tree-based approaches. The topic of spatial data structures could fill multiple books. As with almost everything in computer science, each approach comes with its own tradeoffs in terms of program complexity, computational cost, and memory usage. For the purpose of this book, quadtrees and k-d trees serve as excellent examples of how we can combine the spatial pruning of nearest-neighbor search with tree-based structures to allow the spatial trees to adapt to the data at hand.

10

HASH TABLES

This chapter introduces *hash tables*, dynamic data structures hyper-optimized for insertions and lookups. Hash tables use mathematical functions to point us toward the data's location. They are particularly useful in pure storage cases where the goal is to find and retrieve information quickly.

This is the type of tradeoff we might want to make for our coffee pantry. Forget trying to sort coffees by expiration date or tastiness—we are true coffee aficionados who effortlessly remember the smallest details of every bean in our pantry. For any given attribute (or combination of attributes), we can instantly remember the coffee's name. By the time we walk to the coffee pantry, we've already decided which coffee we want. Storing our coffee selection in sorted order along these other dimensions will just slow us down. What we need is efficient retrieval: given just the name of the coffee we want to drink, we want to find those beans with minimal effort. Hash tables enable exactly this type of rapid retrieval by name.

Arrays provide a compact structure for storing individual pieces of data and a mechanism for efficient retrieval—but only when we know the item's index. With an index, we can look up any element in constant time. As we saw in Chapter 2, without an index, the process for looking up items in an array becomes more complicated. If we only have the item's value, then we need to search through the array to find its correct location. We can find items efficiently with binary search only at the cost of keeping the array in sorted order, which makes for inefficient insertions and deletions.

After the past chapters of exploring data structures and algorithms to efficiently search for target values, imagine we could build a magical function that mapped our target value directly to its index (with a few caveats, of course). This is the core idea behind hash tables. Hash tables use mathematical functions to compute a value's index in our data structure, allowing us to map directly from value to an array bin. The downside is that no mapping is perfect. We will see how different values can map to the same location, causing collisions. We will then examine two approaches to resolving collisions.

As with all data structures, hash tables are not a perfect solution for every problem—we'll examine both the benefits and the tradeoffs, including the use of memory and worst-case performance. In doing so, we'll examine a new way to organize data by using mathematical mappings.

Storage and Search with Keys

Before we delve into the mechanics of hash tables, let's consider an idealized indexing scheme for efficient retrieval of integer values—maintaining an individual array bin for each *possible* value and indexing that bin with the value itself. This structure is shown in Figure 10-1. To insert the value 9, we simply place it in the bin at index 9. Under this arrangement, we can insert or retrieve items in constant time.

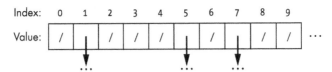

Figure 10-1: A large array with a bin for every potential entry

The obvious downside of our idealized data structure is the absurd cost of maintaining an array of every possible key. Consider the case of storing all possible 16-digit credit card numbers. We'd need several quadrillion bins, 10^{16} to be exact. That is a lot of memory. Worse, it's unlikely that we would even use this many bins. If we are writing a program to track the corporate credit cards for a 1,000-person company, we need only a tiny fraction of the available bins—one bin out of every 10^{13} we've allocated. The rest are wasted. They sit empty, hoping that someday they'll have data to store. Similarly, we wouldn't want to reserve a spot in the library for every possible book, a room in a hotel for every possible patron, or a spot in our coffee pantry for every known coffee. That'd be absurd (except maybe for the coffee).

But, as a thought experiment, let's consider how this idealized data structure could work for other types of data. We immediately run into the question of what value to use for more complex data types, such as strings or even composite data types. Suppose we're looking to create a simple database of coffee records. Chapter 3 showed how to use an array of pointers to store such dynamically sized data, as in the following code:

```
CoffeeRecord {
    String: Name
    String: Brand
    Integer: Rating
    FloatingPoint: Cost_Per_Pound
    Boolean: Is_Dark_Roast
    String: Other_Notes
    Image: Barcode
}
```

We could still place all our items in a single massive array with one bin for every *possible* entry. In this case, the bin contains not just a single value but a pointer to a more complex data structure, as in the array of pointers in Figure 10-2.

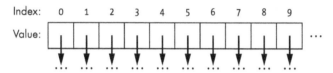

Figure 10-2: An array of pointers

However, this still leaves the question of how to do the actual lookup. If we want to find the rating we gave for "Jeremy's Gourmet High-Caffeine Experience: Medium Roast," one of the coffees introduced in Chapter 6, we cannot use the entire composite data structure as the value. We do not have all this information on hand. Even if we did have the full information on hand, it is not clear how we would use a composite data structure or even a string as an index.

Computer programs often use keys to identify records. A *key* is a single value stored with or derived from the data itself that can be used to identify a record. In the case of an RSVP list, the key might be the string containing the invitee's name; in the case of our coffee records, the key could be the name or barcode of the coffee. In many data structures, from sorted arrays to tries, we use the key to organize the data. For the numerical examples earlier in this book, the key is just the value itself. Each search of a sorted array or binary search tree for a specific numeric value corresponded to retrieving a record by looking for a matching numeric key. Similarly, the tries introduced in Chapter 6 use a string for the key.

This does not solve the indexing problem though. Unless we have an integer key, we still cannot index the array bin. Arrays do not have a bin with index "Jeremy's Gourmet High-Caffeine Experience: Medium Roast." We can search over our data structure, looking for a record with a matching key. Linear scan and binary search both work this way, using a target value as the key. However, we've lost the magic of our idealized data structure. We are back to searching for a matching key.

In some cases, we might be able to find a natural numeric key for our records. In the coffee example, we could list every coffee we've ever tasted in order of when we first tasted it and use the corresponding date as a key. If "Jeremy's Gourmet High-Caffeine Experience: Medium Roast" was first sampled on January 1, 2020 (and we magically remember that), we could retrieve the record with a binary search. Alternatively, we could use the coffee's barcode or its page number in the *Compendium of World Coffees, Brands, and Manufacturers*.

More generally, we want a function that generates an index from our key. In the next section, we introduce hash functions, which solve exactly this problem.

Hash Tables

Hash tables use mathematical mappings to compress the key space. They squish large key spaces into a small domain by using a *hash function* to map the raw key into the location in the table (also called the *hash value*). We denote the hash function that maps key k into a table with b bins as a function $f(k)$ with range $[0, b - 1]$. This mapping solves both problems from the previous section. We no longer require an infinite number of bins. We just need b of them. As we will see, functions can also map non-integers onto a numerical range, solving the problem of non-integer keys.

A simple example hash function for integer keys is to use the division method to compute the hash value from the numeric key. We divide the key by the number of bins and take the remainder:

$$f(k) = k \mathbin{\%} b$$

where % is the modulo operation. Every possible (integer) key is mapped to a single bin within the correct range $[0, b - 1]$. For example, for a 20-bin hash table, this function would produce the mappings shown in Table 10-1.

Table 10-1: Example Mappings for the Division Method of Hashing with 20 Bins

k	f(k)
5	5
20	0
21	1
34	14
41	1

Consider the problem of mapping the space of all credit card numbers into 100 bins. The division method compresses the key space from 16 digits to 2 digits using the last 2 digits of the card's number. Of course, this simplistic mapping might not produce the best results for some key distributions. If we have many credit cards ending in 10, they will all map to the same bin. However, it solves one of our core problems: with a single (and efficient) mathematical computation, we've compressed a large range of keys to a limited number of indices.

The skeptical reader might balk at the description above: "We can't store two different items in the same element of the array. You told us so in Chapter 1. And hash functions can clearly map two different values to the same bin. Just look at Table 10-1. Both 21 and 41 map to bin 1." This is the aforementioned caveat. Unfortunately, hash functions are not truly magical. As we will see in the next section, this complexity is where the rest of the hash table's structure comes in—to handle collisions. For now, we can note that the hash function partitions our keys into disjoint sets and we only need to worry about collisions within a set.

Hash functions are not limited to numbers. We can similarly define a hash function that maps a coffee's name to a bin. This allows us to directly access the coffee record for any entry in two steps, as shown in Figure 10-3. First, we use the coffee's name to compute its hash value. The key "House Blend" is mapped to a value of 6; we will describe a simple method for hashing strings later the chapter. Second, we look up the hash value in our table by using the hash value as an index into our array. We could even use this scheme to map our extensive real-world coffee collection to a fixed number of shelves in our coffee pantry.

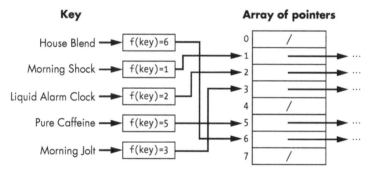

Figure 10-3: Hash functions mapping strings to indices within an array

One real-world example of hash tables is the registration tables we see throughout our lives, whether at the first day of summer camp, the morning of a race, or the beginning of an academic conference. The items to be stored (registration packets) are partitioned into unique bins based on their key (the name). People can find their correct bin by applying a hash function that is usually as simple as a sign mapping a range of the alphabet to a given line. Names starting with A–D go to line 1, names with E–G go to line 2, and so forth.

Collisions

Even the best hash functions in the world won't provide perfect one-to-one mappings of keys to bins. To do that, we'd need to return to our ginormous array and its excessive use of memory. Any mathematical function that maps a large set of keys to a much smaller set of values will encounter occasional *collisions*—instances where two keys map to the same hash value. Imagine applying this approach to mapping license plates to 10 parking spaces by taking the first number on the license plate. We don't need our coworker's license plate to exactly match our own in order to start a fight over a parking space. Imagine you go to register your car, with the plate "Binary Search Trees Are #1," only to find that your coworker has already claimed the spot with the plate "100,000 Data Structures and Counting." Both plates may happen to hash to 1, so they would be assigned the same spot.

We have lines at a conference's registration table because of collisions. Consider a conference registration that hashes into eight lines based on the first letter of your last name. Everyone with a name starting with A–D goes to table 1, everyone with a name starting with E–G goes to table 2, and so forth. If we have more than a handful of attendees, we're almost guaranteed to see a collision. If there were no collisions, everyone would have their own place to check in. Instead, attendees with surnames A–D wait in the same line because their keys (last names) collide.

We can alleviate some of the collisions by increasing the size of our hash table or by choosing a better hash function. However, as long as our key space is larger than the number of bins, it's not possible to eliminate collisions altogether. We need a way to gracefully handle two pieces of data fighting to sit in the same place. If this were a kindergarten class, we might be able to employ such strategies as "Ann was sitting there first," or "You need to learn to share." None of these approaches work in data structure context. We can't ignore new keys or overwrite the older data. The point of a data structure is to store all the requisite data. In the next two sections, we consider chaining and linear probing, two common approaches for handling collisions in a hash table.

Chaining

Chaining is an approach for handling collisions within a hash table by employing additional structure *within* the bins. Instead of storing a fixed piece of data (or a pointer to a single piece of data) in each bin, we can store the pointer to the head of a linked list:

```
HashTable {
    Integer: size
    Array of ListNodes: bins
}
```

where

```
ListNode {
    Type: key
```

```
    Type: value
    ListNode: next
}
```

These lists are like our line of conference attendees. Each person in line is a unique individual, but maps to the same registration table.

As shown in Figure 10-4, each bin's list contains all the data that mapped to that bin. This allows us to store multiple elements in each bin. Each item in our linked list corresponds to one of the elements inserted into the bin.

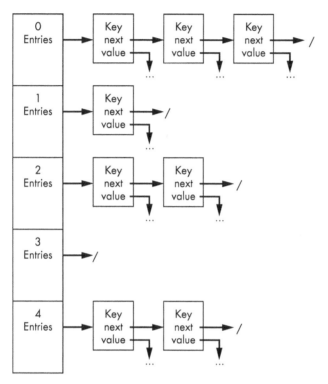

Figure 10-4: A hash table using a linked list to store entries within the same bin

The code for inserting a new item into a hash table with chaining is relatively simple:

```
HashTableInsert(HashTable: ht, Type: key, Type: value):
❶ Integer: hash_value = HashFunction(key, ht.size)

    # If the bin is empty, create a new linked list.
❷ IF ht.bins[hash_value] == null:
        ht.bins[hash_value] = ListNode(key, value)
        return

    # Check if the key already exists in the table.
❸ ListNode: current = ht.bins[hash_value]
```

```
WHILE current.key != key AND current.next != null:
    current = current.next
IF current.key == key:
  ❹ current.value = value
ELSE:
  ❺ current.next = ListNode(key, value)
return
```

We start by computing the hash value for the key ❶ and checking the corresponding bin. If the bin is empty (the pointer is null), we create a new linked list node holding the key and value inserted ❷. Otherwise, we need to scan through the bin's linked list and check each element for a matching key ❸. The WHILE loop checks that we have neither found the correct key (current.key != key) nor run off the end of the list (current.next != null). If the list already contains a matching key, we update the value associated with the key ❹. Otherwise, we append the new key and its corresponding value to the end of the list ❺.

Search follows a similar approach. However, the logic is simpler because we no longer need to insert new nodes:

```
HashTableLookup(HashTable: ht, Type: key):
 ❶ Integer: hash_value = HashFunction(key, ht.size)
 ❷ IF ht.bins[hash_value] == null:
       return null

    ListNode: current = ht.bins[hash_value]
 ❸ WHILE current.key != key AND current.next != null:
       current = current.next
    IF current.key == key:
      ❹ return current.value
 ❺ return null
```

The code for search starts by computing the hash value for the key ❶, checking the corresponding bin, and returning null if the bin is empty ❷. Otherwise, it scans over each element of the linked list using a WHILE loop ❸ and returns the value for the matching key ❹. If we make it to the end of the list without finding a matching key, the code returns null to indicate that the key is not present in the table ❺.

Finally, when removing an item, we need to find it in the list and, if it is present, splice it out. The following code both removes and returns the linked list node matching the target key:

```
HashTableRemove(HashTable: ht, Type: key):
 ❶ Integer: hash_value = HashFunction(key, ht.size)
    IF ht.bins[hash_value] == null:
       return null

    ListNode: current = ht.bins[hash_value]
    ListNode: last = null
 ❷ WHILE current.key != key AND current.next != null:
```

```
      last = current
      current = current.next
❸ IF current.key == key:
      IF last != null:
        ❹ last.next = current.next
      ELSE:
        ❺ ht.bins[hash_value] = current.next
      return current
  return null
```

The code again starts by computing the hash value for the key, checking the corresponding bin, and returning null if it is empty ❶. If the bin is not empty, we scan through it using a WHILE loop and look for a matching key ❷. In order to splice out the correct element, we need to track one additional piece of information: the final linked list node before the current node. If we find a match ❸, we need to check whether we are removing the first element in the list (last is null). If not, we can modify the last node's next pointer to skip the node we are removing ❹. Otherwise, we need to modify the pointer from the start of the hash bin to skip the node ❺. Finally, we return null if we do not find a matching node.

The skeptical reader might pause here and ask, "How does this help? We still must scan through a bunch of elements of a linked list. We have lost the ability to directly map to a single entry. We're back where we started." However, the primary advantage to this new approach is that we are no longer scanning through a linked list of *all* the entries. We only scan through those entries whose hash values match. Instead of searching through a giant list, we search through a single tiny list for this bin. In our coffee pantry, where our hash function maps the coffee's name to its corresponding shelf, we might be able to cull our search from 1,000 varieties to the 20 varieties on that one shelf. Back in the computational realm, if we maintain enough bins in our hash table, we can keep the size of these lists small, perhaps with only one or two elements.

Of course, the worst-case time for a lookup can be linear in the number of elements. If we choose a terrible hash function, such as $f(k) = 1$, we're basically implementing a single linked list with extra overhead. It's vital to be careful when selecting a hash function and sizing the hash table, as we'll discuss later.

Linear Probing

An alternate approach to handling collisions is to make use of adjacent bins. If we are trying to insert data into a bin that already contains another key, we simply move on and check the next bin. If that neighbor is also full, we move onto the next. We keep going until we find an empty bin or a bin containing data with the same key. Linear probing extends this basic idea to the hash table's operations. We start at the index corresponding to the key's hash value and progress until we find what we are looking for or can conclude it is not in the hash table.

Hash tables using linear probing need a slightly different structure. Because we are not using a linked list of nodes, we use a wrapper data structure to store the combination of keys and values:

```
HashTableEntry {
    Type: key
    Type: value
}
```

We also include an additional piece of data in the hash table itself, the number of keys currently stored in the table:

```
HashTable {
    Integer: size
    Integer: num_keys
    Array of HashTableEntry: bins
}
```

This information is critical, because when the number of keys reaches the size of the hash table, there are no available bins left. Often hash tables will increase the array size when they start to get too full, although care must be taken here. Because we are using a hash function that maps keys onto the range of the current array, keys may map to different locations in a larger array. In this section, we will only consider a simplified implementation of a fixed size table for illustration purposes.

Consider a hash table with linear probing where we have inserted a few of our favorite coffees, as shown in Figure 10-5.

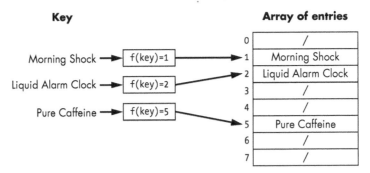

Figure 10-5: A hash table with three entries

After we have inserted these initial three entries, we try to insert "Morning Zap" as shown in Figure 10-6. The insertion function finds another key, Morning Shock, in bin 1. It proceeds to bin 2, where it finds Liquid Alarm Clock. The insertion function finally finds an opening at bin 3.

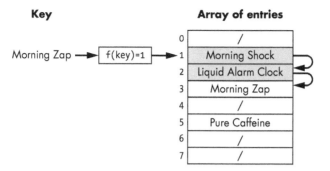

Key   **Array of entries**

Figure 10-6: Inserting the entry "Morning Zap" requires scanning through several bins in the hash table.

The code for inserting items into a fixed-size hash table is shown below. As noted previously, it is possible to increase the size of the array when the hash table is full, but this adds complexity to ensure the items are mapped correctly to new bins. For now, we will return a Boolean to indicate whether the item could be inserted.

```
HashTableInsert(HashTable: ht, Type: key, Type: value):
❶ Integer: index = HashFunction(key, ht.size)
❷ Integer: count = 0

  HashTableEntry: current = ht.bins[index]
❸ WHILE current != null AND current.key != key AND count != ht.size:
      index = index + 1
    ❹ IF index >= ht.size:
          index = 0
      current = ht.bins[index]
      count = count + 1

❺ IF count == ht.size:
      return False

❻ IF current == null:
      ht.bins[index] = HashTableEntry(key, value)
      ht.num_keys = ht.num_keys + 1
  ELSE:
    ❼ ht.bins[index].value = value
  return True
```

The code starts the search at the new key's hash value ❶. The code also maintains a count of bins it has checked to prevent infinite loops if the table is full ❷. This count is not needed if we use resizing or otherwise ensure there is always at least one empty bin. The code then loops through each bin using a WHILE loop ❸. The loop tests three conditions: (1) whether it found an empty bin, (2) whether it found the target key, and (3) whether it has searched all the bins. The first and third conditions test whether the key is not in the table. After incrementing the index, the code checks whether the index should wrap back to the beginning of the table ❹, which allows the code to search the entire table.

After the loop completes, the code first checks whether it has examined every bin in the table without finding the key. If so, the table is full and does not contain the key ❺, so the code returns False. The code then checks whether it has found an empty bin or matching key. If the bin is empty ❻, a new HashTableEntry is created and stored. Otherwise, the value of the entry with the matching key is updated ❼. The code returns True to indicate that it successfully inserted the key and value.

Search follows the same pattern. We start at the index of the key's hash value and iterate over bins from there. At each step, we check whether the current entry is empty (null), in which case the key is not in the table, or whether the current entry matches the target key.

```
HashTableLookup(HashTable: ht, Type: key):
  ❶ Integer: index = HashFunction(key, ht.size)
  ❷ Integer: count = 0

    HashTableEntry: current = ht.bins[index]
  ❸ WHILE current != null AND current.key != key AND count != ht.size:
        index = index + 1
      ❹ IF index >= ht.size:
            index = 0
        current = ht.bins[index]
        count = count + 1

    # Return the value if we found a match.
  ❺ IF current != null AND current.key == key:
        return current.value
  ❻ return null
```

The code starts by computing the hash value for the key to get the starting location of the search ❶. As with insertion, the code also maintains a count of bins it has checked to prevent infinite loops if the table is full ❷. The code then loops through each bin using a WHILE loop ❸. The loop tests three conditions: (1) whether it found an empty bin, (2) whether it found the target key, and (3) whether it has searched all the bins. After incrementing index, the code tests whether the search has run off the end of the table and, if so, wraps the search back to the start ❹. Once the loop terminates, the code checks whether it has found the matching key ❺. If so, it returns the corresponding value. Otherwise, the key is not in the table, and the code returns null ❻.

In contrast to search and insertion, deletion with linear probing requires more than a simple scan. If we remove an arbitrary element such as "Liquid Alarm Clock," shown in Figure 10-6, we might break the chain of comparisons needed for other elements. If we replace "Liquid Alarm Clock" with null in Figure 10-6, we can no longer find "Morning Zap." Different implementations use different solutions to this problem, from scanning through the table and fixing later entries to inserting dummy values into the bin.

The advantage of linear probing over chaining is that we make fuller use of the initial array bins and do not add the overhead of linked lists within the bins. The downside is that, as our table gets full, we might iterate over many entries during a search, and, unlike with chaining, these entries are not restricted to ones with matching keys.

Hash Functions

The difference between a good and bad hash function is effectively the difference between a hash table and a linked list. We'd want our hash function to map keys uniformly throughout the space of bins, rather than pile them into a few overloaded bins. A good hash function is like a well-run conference registration. Any clumping of attendees will lead to collisions, and collisions lead to more linear scanning (more time waiting in line). Similarly, in our conference registration example, bad hash functions, such as dividing the table into two lines for names starting with A–Y and names starting with Z, leads to long waits and annoyed attendees.

In addition, any hash function must be meet a couple of key criteria. It must:

Be deterministic   The hash function needs to map the same key to the same hash bin every time. Without this attribute, we might insert items into a hash table only to lose the ability to retrieve them.

Have a predefined range for a given size   The hash function needs to map any key into a limited range, corresponding to the number of hash buckets. For a table with b buckets, we need the function to map onto the range $[0, b - 1]$. We'd also like to be able to vary the hash function's range with the size of our hash table. If we need a larger table, we need a correspondingly larger range to address all the buckets. Without this ability to adjust the range, we may be stuck with a limited number of viable hash table sizes.

In our conference registration example, these criteria correspond to people being able to find their packets (deterministic for all users) and having everyone map to a line (correct range). It would be wasteful to set up a conference check-in with lines for empty parts of the range (all names starting with Zzza through Zzzb), and it would be rude to map some people's names to no line at all (no line for names starting with K). The best hash functions are like in-person organizers, holding clipboards and directing people to the correct lines.

Handling Non-numeric Keys

For numeric keys, we can often use a range of mathematical functions, such as the division method above. However, we may often need to handle non-numeric keys as well. Most importantly, we need to be able to compute the hash of a string containing the coffee name. The general approach to handling non-numeric keys is to use a function that first transforms the non-numeric input into a numeric value. For example, we could map each character to a numeric value (such as the ASCII value), compute the sum of values in a word, and modulo the resulting sum into the correct number of buckets. This approach, while straightforward and easy to implement, may not provide a good distribution of hash values due to how letters occur. For example, the hash function does not take into account the order of the letters, so words with the same letters, such as *act* and *cat*, will always be mapped to the same bin.

A better approach to hashing strings is an approach often called *Horner's method*. Instead of directly adding the letters' values, we multiply the running sum of letters by a constant after each addition:

```
StringHash(String: key, Integer: size):
    Integer: total = 0
    FOR EACH character in key:
        total = CONST * total + CharacterToNumber(character)
    return total % size
```

where CONST is our multiplier, typically a prime number that is larger than the largest value for any character. Of course, by multiplying our running sum, we greatly increase the size of the value, so we need to be careful to handle overflow.

There are a wide variety of hash functions, each with their own trade-offs. A full survey of the potential hash functions and their relative merits is a topic worthy of its own book; this chapter presents just a few simple functions for the point of illustration. The key takeaway is that we can use these mathematical functions to reduce the range of our key space.

An Example Use Case

Hash tables are particularly useful when tracking a set of items, which is why Python uses them to implement data structures such as dictionary and set. We can use them to aid in tracking metadata for the searches such as those seen in Chapter 4.

In both the depth-first and breadth-first search, we maintained a list of future options to explore. We used a queue for breadth-first search and a stack for depth-first. However, there is an additional set of information we need to track: the set of items we have already visited. In both searches, we avoid adding items to the list that we have already seen, allowing us to avoid loops or, at least, wasted effort. Hash tables provide an excellent mechanism for storing this set.

Consider the sixth step of our example breadth-first search from Chapter 4, as shown on the left side of Figure 10-7. The search has already visited the gray nodes (A, B, F, G, H, and I), and the circled node (G) is our current node. We do not want to re-add either of G's two neighbors to our list of items to explore; we have already visited both F and I.

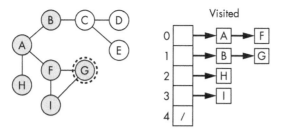

Figure 10-7: The visited nodes of a breadth-first search tracked in a hash table

We could store the visited items in a hash table as shown on the right of Figure 10-7. This hash table uses a simple function: the division function maps the letter's index in the alphabet into 5 bins. The letter *A* has index 0 and maps to bin 0. The letter *G* has index 6 and maps to bin 1. We insert a key for each item when we visit it. Before adding new items to our list of future topics, we check whether their key is in the hash table. If so, we skip the addition. Hash tables are particularly well suited to tracking this type of data because they are optimized for fast insertions and lookups.

Why This Matters

Hash tables provide a new way of organizing data by using a mathematical function. As opposed to tree-based structures, which structure the data around the keys themselves, hash tables introduce the intermediate step of mapping the keys to a reduced range. As with all things in computer science, this mapping comes with tradeoffs. Collisions mean that we can't always access the desired data directly. We must add another level of indirection, such as a linked list, to store items that map to the same location. As such, hash tables provide another example of how we can creatively combine data structures (in this case, an array and linked lists).

Understanding hash functions and how they map keys to bins provides a side benefit. We can use these types of mappings to partition items or spread out work, such as the lines at a conference registration or the coffees on our shelves; in the computational domain, we might use hashing to assign tasks to servers in a simple load balancer. In the next chapter, we see how hash tables can be used to create caches. Hash tables are used throughout computer science, since they provide a handy data structure with (on average) fast access time and reasonable memory tradeoffs. They are a vital tool for every computer scientist's toolbox.

11

CACHES

This chapter introduces *caches*, data structures that seek to alleviate high data access costs by storing some data closer to the computation. As we have seen throughout the previous chapters, the cost of data access is a critical factor in the efficiency of our algorithms. This is important not just to how we organize the data in storage but also to the type of storage we use. We say data is *local* when it is stored closer to the processor and thus quickly available for processing. If we copy some of the data from more expensive, distant locations to local storage, we can read the data significantly faster.

For example, we might use caches to accelerate access to web pages. Loading a web page consists of querying a server for the information contained on the page, transferring that data to your local computer, and rendering this information visually. If the web page contains large elements, such as images or videos, we may need to transfer a lot of data. To reduce this cost, browsers cache commonly accessed data. Instead of redownloading the logo of our favorite site every time we access the page, the browser keeps this image in a local cache on the computer's hard drive so that it can quickly read it from disk.

How should we choose which data to load into our cache? Obviously, we can't store everything. If we could, we wouldn't need the cache in the first place—we'd just copy the entire data set into the closest memory. There are a range of caching strategies whose effectiveness depends, as always, on the use case. In this chapter, we combine data structures we've previously explored to build one such strategy, the least recently used (LRU) cache, which can greatly facilitate the operations of our favorite coffee shop. We also briefly discuss a few other caching strategies for comparison.

Introducing Caches

Up to this point, we've treated all of the computer's storage equally, a single bookshelf from which we can grab any item we need with approximately the same amount of effort. However, data storage is not this straightforward. We can think of the storage as being like a large, multistory library. We have shelves of popular books arranged near the entrance to satisfy the majority of patrons, while we relegate the musty stacks of old computer science journals to the basement. We might even have a warehouse offsite where rarely used books are stored until a patron specifically requests them. Want that resource on the PILOT programming language? Odds are, it won't be in the popular picks section.

In addition to paying attention to how we organize data within our program, we need to consider *where* the data is stored. Not all data storage is equal. In fact, for different mediums, there is often a tradeoff among the size of storage available, its speed, and its cost. Memory on the CPU itself (registers or local caches) is incredibly fast but can only hold a very limited amount of data. A computer's random-access memory (RAM) provides a larger space at slower speeds. Hard drives are significantly larger, but also slower than RAM. Calling out to a network allows access to a huge range of storage, such as the whole internet, but incurs corresponding overhead. When dealing with very large data sets, it might not be possible to load the entirety of the data into memory, which can have dramatic impact on the algorithms' performance. It's important to understand how these tradeoffs impact the performance of algorithms.

Compare this to our own morning coffee-making routine. While it would be ideal to have thousands of varieties at our fingertips, our apartment can store only a limited amount of coffee. Down the street is a coffee distributor stocked with hundreds of varieties, but do we really want to walk there every time we want to make a new cup of coffee? Instead, we store small quantities of our preferred coffees in our apartment. This local storage speeds up the production of our morning brew and lets us enjoy our first cup before venturing out into the world.

Caches are a step before accessing expensive data, as shown in Figure 11-1. Before calling out to a remote server or even accessing our local hard drive, we check whether we already have the data stored locally in the cache. If we do, we access the data directly, and cheaply, from the cache. When we find the data in the cache, that's a *cache hit*. We can stop the lookup and avoid calling out to the more expensive storage. If the data isn't in the cache, we have a *cache miss*. We give a defeated sigh and proceed with the more expensive access.

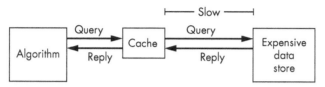

Figure 11-1: A cache sits between the algorithm and a slow, expensive data store.

Picture this in the context of a busy coffee counter. The daily menu contains 10 coffees ranging in popularity from the mega-popular house brew to the rarely purchased mint-cinnamon-pumpkin explosion. At the far end of the counter sits a coffee station with 10 pots of coffee, each on its own heater. Upon receiving an order, the barista walks to the coffee station and fills a cup with the appropriate coffee. After miles of walking each day, the barista asks the owner to install another heater right beside the register so they can give their tired feet a rest. The owner agrees but asks, "Which coffee will you keep near the register?" This question weighs on the barista's mind and they try a few strategies.

The barista quickly realizes that it isn't just a question of which coffee, but also when they should change it. They can store different coffees locally at different points of the day. They try keeping the house brew in the cache all day, moving the decaf closer at night, and swapping out the current selection for the house brew when there hasn't been a customer in the last 10 minutes. Some strategies work and others, especially anything involving caching mint-cinnamon-pumpkin explosion, fail miserably. If the barista chooses correctly, most orders result in a cache hit, and they can avoid the long walk. If they choose incorrectly, the local coffee is useless for most orders.

The barista could further improve the situation by installing a second heater by the register. Instead of storing a single flavor nearby, they can now store two. The cost, however, is that this second heater uses up precious counter real estate. Both computers and coffee shops have a limited amount of local space. We cannot store every coffee next to the register, and we cannot store the entire internet in our computer's RAM. If we make the cache too large, we will need to use slower storage for it. This is the fundamental tradeoff with a cache—memory used versus the speedup provided.

When the cache fills up, we determine which data to keep and which data to replace. We say the replaced data is *evicted* from the cache. Perhaps the triple-caffeinated blend replaces the decaf during a fall morning rush. By evicting the decaf from the nearby heater, the barista saves hours of walking to retrieve the trendier blend. Different caching approaches use different eviction strategies to determine which data to replace, from counting how often the data has been accessed thus far to making predictions about whether the data will be used again in the near future.

LRU Eviction and Caches

The *least recently used (LRU) cache* stores recently used information. LRU caches are a simple and common approach that provide a good illustration of the types of tradeoffs we face in using caches. The intuition behind this caching strategy is that we are likely to re-access information that we recently needed, which fits well with our web-browsing example above. If we commonly access the same sets of pages over and over, it pays to store some of the (unchanging) elements of these pages locally. We don't need to re-request the site's logo with each visit. LRU caches consist of a set amount of storage filled with the most recently accessed items. The cache starts evicting older items—those least recently used—when the cache is full.

If our barista decides to treat the heater closest to the register as an LRU cache, they keep the last ordered coffee on that heater. When they receive an order for something different, they take the current cached coffee back to the coffee station, place it on the heater there, and retrieve the new coffee. They bring this new coffee back to the register, use it to fulfill the order, and leave it there.

If every customer orders something different, this strategy just adds overhead. Instead of walking to the end of the counter with a cup, the barista is now making the same journey with a pot of coffee—probably complaining under their breadth about the length of the counter or resentfully judging customers' tastes: "Who orders mint-cinnamon-pumpkin explosion?" However, if most customers order in clumps of similar coffees, this strategy can be hugely effective. Three customers ordering regular coffee in a row means two round trips saved. The advantage can compound with the effect of customer interaction. After seeing the person in front of them order the pumpkin concoction, the next customer makes the (questionable) decision to copy their predecessor, saying, "I'll have the same."

This is exactly the scenario we can run into when browsing our favorite website. We move from one page of the site to another page of the same site. Certain elements, such as logos, will reappear on subsequent pages, leading to a significant savings from keeping those items in the cache.

Building an LRU Cache

Caching with the LRU eviction policy requires us to support two operations: looking up an arbitrary element and finding the least recently used element (for eviction). We must be able to perform both operations quickly.

After all, the purpose of a cache is to accelerate lookups. If we have to scan through an entire unstructured data set to check for a cache hit, we are more likely to add overhead than to save time.

We can construct an LRU cache using two previously explored components: a hash table and a queue. The hash table allows us to perform fast lookups, efficiently retrieving any items that are in the cache. The queue is a FIFO data structure that allows us to track which item hasn't been used recently. Instead of scanning through each item and checking the timestamp, we can dequeue the *earliest* item in the queue, as shown in the following code. This provides an efficient way to determine which data to remove.

```
LRUCache {
    HashTable: ht
    Queue: q
    Integer: max_size
    Integer: current_size
}
```

Each entry in the hash table stores a composite data structure containing at least three entries: the key, the corresponding value (or data for that entry), and a pointer to the corresponding node in the cache's queue. This last piece of information is essential, because we need a way to look up and modify entries in the queue. As in Listing 11-1, we store those pieces of information directly in the value entry of the hash table's nodes.

```
CacheEntry {
    Type: key
    Type: value
    QueueListNode: node
}
```

Listing 11-1: The data structure for a cache entry containing the data's key, value, and a link to its node in the queue

Figure 11-2 shows the resulting diagram of how these pieces fit together. The diagram looks a bit complex but becomes easier to understand when we break it down into two parts. On the left is the hash table. As in Chapter 10, each hash value corresponds to a linked list of entries. The value for these entries is the CacheEntry data structure in Listing 11-1. On the right-hand side is the queue data structure, which stores the entry's keys. A single pointer links across these data structures, pointing from the CacheEntry data structure to the queue node with the corresponding key.

Of course, the real-world layout of the components in Figure 11-2 throughout the computer's memory is even messier than it appears in the diagram, because the nodes do not actually reside next to each other.

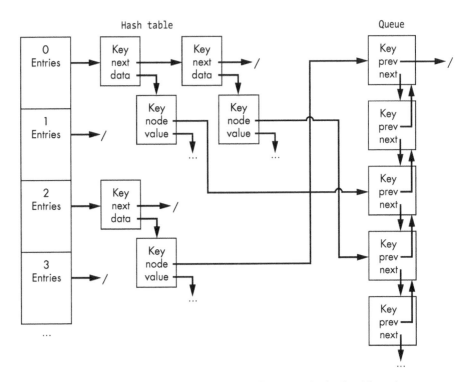

Figure 11-2: An LRU cache implemented as a combination of a hash table and queue

In Listing 11-2, we define a single lookup function, CacheLookup, that returns the value for a given lookup key. If there is a cache hit, the lookup function returns the value directly and updates how recently that data was accessed. If there is a cache miss, the function fetches the data via the expensive lookup, inserts it into the cache, and, if necessary, removes the oldest piece of data.

```
CacheLookup(LRUCache: cache, Type: key):
❶ CacheEntry: entry = HashTableLookup(cache.ht, key)

    IF entry == null:
      ❷ IF cache.current_size >= cache.max_size:
            Type: key_to_remove = Dequeue(cache.q)
            HashTableRemove(cache.ht, key_to_remove)
            cache.current_size = cache.current_size - 1

      ❸ Type: data = retrieve data for the key from
                      the slow data source.

      ❹ Enqueue(cache.q, key)
        entry = CacheEntry(key, data, cache.q.back)
      ❺ HashTableInsert(cache.ht, key, entry)
        cache.current_size = cache.current_size + 1
    ELSE:
        # Reset this key's location in the queue.
```

```
❻ RemoveNode(cache.q, entry.node)
❼ Enqueue(cache.q, key)

    # Update the CacheEntry's pointer.
❽ entry.node = cache.q.back
return entry.value
```

Listing 11-2: Code for looking up an item by its key

This code starts by checking whether key occurs in our cache table ❶. If so, we have a cache hit. Otherwise, we have a cache miss.

We deal with the case of a cache miss first. If the hash table returns null, we need to fetch the data from the more expensive data store. We store this newly retrieved value in the cache, evicting the (oldest) item from the front of the queue. We do this in three steps. First, if the cache is full ❷, we dequeue the key of the oldest item from the queue and use it to remove the corresponding entry in the hash table. This completes the eviction of the oldest item. Second, we retrieve the new data ❸. Third, we insert the (key, data) pair into the cache. We enqueue key into the back of the queue ❹. Then we create a new hash table entry with the new key, data, and pointer to the key's corresponding location in the queue (using the queue's back pointer). We store this entry in the hash table ❺.

The final block of code handles the case of a cache hit. When we see a cache hit, we want to move the element for this key from its current position to the back of the queue. After all, we've just seen it. It should now be the last element we want to discard. We move this element in two steps. First, we remove it from the queue with the RemoveNode function, using the pointer to the node ❻. Second, we re-enqueue the key at the back of the queue ❼ and update the pointer to that queue node ❽.

We can picture this update operation in the context of a line of customers in a coffee shop. If a customer leaves the line, they lose their position. When they rejoin the line in the future, they do so at the back.

Updating an Element's Recency

In order to support the RemoveNode operation in Listing 11-2, we need to change our queue to support *updating* an element's position. We need to move recently accessed items from their current position in the queue to the back in order to indicate that they were the most recently accessed. First, we modify our queue implementation from Chapter 4 to use a doubly linked list, which will allow us to efficiently remove items from the middle of the queue:

```
QueueListNode {
    Type: value
    QueueListNode: next
    QueueListNode: prev
}
```

As illustrated in Figure 11-3, the next field refers to the node directly behind the current node (the next node after this one to be dequeued), where the prev field refers to the node preceding this one.

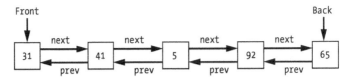

Figure 11-3: A queue implemented as a doubly linked list

Second, we modify the enqueue and dequeue operations accordingly. For both enqueue and dequeue, we add extra logic to update the previous pointers. The primary change from Chapter 4 is in how we set the prev pointer:

```
Enqueue(Queue: q, Type: value):
    QueueListNode: node = QueueListNode(value)
    IF q.back == null:
        q.front = node
        q.back = node
    ELSE:
        q.back.next = node
    ❶ node.prev = q.back
        q.back = node
```

In the enqueue operation, the code needs to set the new node's prev pointer to the previous last element q.back ❶.

```
Dequeue(Queue: q):
    IF q.front == null:
        return null

    Type: value = q.front.value
    q.front = q.front.next
    IF q.front == null:
        q.back = null
    ELSE:
    ❶ q.front.prev = null
    return value
```

The dequeue operation sets the prev pointer of the new front node to null to indicate that there is no node in front of it ❶.

Finally, we add the RemoveNode operation, which provides the ability to remove a node from the middle of our queue. This is where the use of a doubly linked list helps. By keeping pointers in both directions, we do not need to scan the entire queue to find the entry before the current one. The code for RemoveNode adjusts the pointers into the node from the adjacent nodes in the linked list (node.prev and node.next), the front of the queue (q.front), and the back of the queue (q.back).

```
RemoveNode(Queue: q, QueueListNode: node):
    IF node.prev != null:
        node.prev.next = node.next
    IF node.next != null:
        node.next.prev = node.prev
    IF node == q.front:
        q.front = q.front.next
    IF node == q.back:
        q.back = q.back.prev
```

This code contains multiple IF statements to handle the special cases of adding or removing from either end of the queue.

One question remains: How can we efficiently find the element we want to remove and reinsert? We can't afford to scan through the entire queue while searching for the node to update. Supporting a cache hit requires speedy lookups. In the case of our cache above, we maintain a pointer directly from the cache's entry to the element in the queue. This allows us to access, remove, and reinsert the element in constant time by following the pointers.

Other Eviction Strategies

Let's consider how three of the many alternate eviction strategies—most recently used, least frequently used, and predictive eviction—compare to LRU eviction. The goal isn't to provide an in-depth analysis of these methods but rather to help develop your intuition about the types of tradeoffs that arise when picking a caching strategy. The optimal caching strategy for a particular scenario will depend on the specifics of that scenario. Understanding the tradeoffs will help you pick the best strategy for your use case.

LRU is a good eviction strategy when we see bursts of common usage among certain cache items but expect the distribution of cached items to change over time. The local pot of coffee near the register described earlier is an excellent example. When someone orders a new type of coffee, the barista walks to the end of the counter, returns the old blend, retrieves the new blend, and leaves that carafe by the register.

Let's contrast that with evicting the *most recently used (MRU)* element. You can picture this in the context of an ebook reader that prefetches and caches books that you might enjoy. Since it is unlikely that we will read a book twice in a row, it might make sense to discard the recently completed book from our cache in order to free up space for a new one. While MRU can be a good approach for items with infrequent repetition, the same eviction would create constant tragedy in our coffee pantry. Imagine if we were forced to evict our favorite, go-to blend anytime we brewed a cup.

Instead of considering *when* the item was last accessed, we could also track how many times it has been accessed in total. The *least frequently used (LFU)* eviction strategy discards the element with the smallest count. This approach is advantageous when our cached population remains stable, such as with the tried-and-true coffee varieties we keep at home. We don't evict one of our three go-to varieties simply because we recently tried the seasonal blend at our local coffeehouse. The items in the cache have a proven track record and are there to stay—at least, until we find a new favorite. Unfortunately, when preferences change, it can take a while for newly popular items to accumulate enough counts to make it into our cache. If we encounter a new brew that is better than anything in our home collection, we'd need to sample individual cups of the coffee many times, making numerous trips to the coffee shop, before finally buying beans for our own pantry.

The *predictive eviction* strategy provides a forward-looking approach that tries to predict what elements will be needed in the future. Instead of relying on simple counts or timestamps, we can build a model to predict what cache entries are most likely to be accessed in the future. The effectiveness of this cache depends on the accuracy of the model. If we have a highly accurate model, such as predicting that we will switch from our go-to java blends to a seasonal fall blend only in October and November, we greatly improve the hit rate. However, if the model is inaccurate, perhaps associating each month with the first coffee we consumed that month last year, we can find ourselves reliving that onetime mistake of drinking mint-cinnamon-pumpkin lattes in August. Another downside of predictive eviction is that it adds complexity to the cache itself. It is no longer sufficient to track simple counts or timestamps; instead, the cache must learn a model.

Why This Matters

Caches can alleviate some of the access cost when dealing with expensive storage mediums. Instead of calling out to the expensive storage, caches store a portion of this data in a closer and faster location. If we choose the correct caching strategy, we can save significant amounts of time by pulling data from the cache instead of the slower locations. This makes caches a common and powerful tool in our computational toolbox. They are used throughout the real world, from web browsers to library shelves to coffee shops.

Caches also illustrate several key concepts. First, they highlight the potential tradeoffs to consider when accessing data from different mediums. If we could store everything in the fastest memory, we wouldn't need caches. Unfortunately, this usually isn't possible; our algorithms will need to access larger, slower data stores, and it's worth understanding the potential cost this adds. In the next chapter, we introduce the B-tree, a tree-based data structure that reduces the number of data accesses needed. This optimization helps reduce the overall cost when we cannot fit our data in nearby, fast memory.

Second, caches revisit the data structure–tuning question that we saw in previous chapters. Both the size of the cache and the eviction strategy are parameters that can have massive impact on your cache's performance.

Consider the problem of selecting the size of the cache. If the cache is too small, it might not store enough to provide a benefit. The single nearby pot of coffee in our café only helps so much. On the other hand, too large a cache will take important memory resources that might be needed for other parts of our algorithm.

Finally, and most importantly for this book's purposes, caches illustrate how we can combine basic data structures, such as the hash table and the queue, to provide more complex and impactful behaviors. In this case, by using pointers to tie hash table entries to nodes in a queue, we can efficiently track which entry in our cache should be removed next.

12

B-TREES

Chapter 11 showed how the cost of memory access can vary across mediums. In this chapter, we'll discuss how this problem extends beyond accessing individual values to the cost of accessing new blocks of data, introducing a new data structure to handle this situation.

Computer science is full of instances where accessing data within a block is cheap, but retrieving a new block is comparatively expensive. A computer might read an entire block of information, known as a *page*, from the hard drive and store it in memory. In the days of floppy disk–based video games, you might see a message directing you to "Insert disk 5 of 7" or wait while the game loaded the next chunk of data from a CD. Similarly, online applications might download coherent blocks of data from a server across the internet, allowing you to start watching a video before you've downloaded the entire thing.

This chapter covers the *B-tree*, a self-balancing tree-based data structure that computer scientists Rudolf Bayer and Edward McCreight designed to account for the cost of retrieving new blocks of data. B-trees store multiple pieces of data in a single node, allowing us to pay the expensive retrieval cost exactly once to extract all those values. Once the node is in local memory, we can quickly access the values within it. The tradeoff is additional complexity when dealing with the nodes.

In the computational domain, we may run into this problem when trying to index a massive data set. Consider the index for a literally astronomical data set that contains pointers to images of every star, galaxy, nebula, comet, asteroid, and other celestial body ever observed. The data set is still larger than the index, but the index itself might need to reside across many blocks of slow storage. B-trees provide an inventive way of combining the indexing and keys while minimizing retrieval costs.

B-trees are also one example of how to define trees' operations in such a way that they don't become horribly imbalanced. As we will see later in the chapter, the B-tree always remains perfectly balanced with all the leaf nodes at exactly the same depth.

B-tree Structure

B-trees apply the multi-way branching structure that we saw in tries or quadtrees to storing individual keys. Practically, this means that they allow internal nodes many more than two branches, so they're practically bristling with pointers. They also need to store more than a single key in each node. B-tree nodes are packed with keys, allowing them to both track multiway partitions and, more importantly, maximize the amount of data we can retrieve by fetching a single node.

We see the benefit of packing multiple items into a node in the everyday context of online shipping. We pay a cost for every box shipped, and these costs can add up quickly if we are shipping many small boxes. This is the equivalent of retrieving many small tree nodes from expensive storage. If we pack several items into the same box, however, we can reduce the cost by shipping them together. Similarly, B-trees reduce the cost of retrieving multiple keys by retrieving a block of them together.

Formally, we define the size of B-tree node with a size parameter k, which provides bounds on how many elements a non-root node can store. All non-root nodes store between k and $2k$ keys in sorted order. The root node is more flexible and is allowed to contain between 0 and $2k$ keys. Like a binary search tree, internal nodes use the values of these keys to define the ranges for the branches. Internal nodes store pointers for each possible split point, before and after each key in the node, allowing for between $k + 1$ and $2k + 1$ children for all internal nodes except the root node, which can have between 0 to $2k + 1$ children. These split points are conceptually the same as what we do in a binary search tree—they divide the space into keys that come before the split and keys that come after.

Figure 12-1 shows an example of this structure. The node with keys 12, 31, and 45 defines four separate partitions: keys that come before 12, keys after 12 but before 31, keys after 31 but before 45, and keys after 45. The subtree containing 13, 17, and 26 is defined by two split points in the parent node. All the keys in that node must be greater than 12 since their node's child pointer is to the right of key 12. Similarly, the keys must all be less than 31 since the pointer is to the left of key 31.

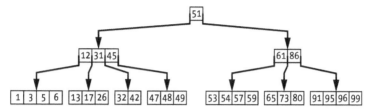

Figure 12-1: An example B-tree

NOTE *The notation used to describe the parameters of a B-tree varies from reference to reference, such as defining the size parameter as the maximum number of keys (or children) per node or varying how the children are indexed relative to the keys. When comparing implementations, it is important to account for these differences.*

Picture this structure in the context of indexing the vast collection at the Comprehensive Museum of Fun and Informative Collectibles. In an attempt to allow a dynamic collection, we store the index entry to each item on a small paper card with the name, a brief description, and the location in our massive collectibles warehouse. We can fit nine hundred cards into a single binder, so, for our collection of a hundred million items, we need over a hundred thousand binders to store the entire index.

While we would like to store the entire index locally, we simply lack enough space in our office. Once we have requisitioned and retrieved a binder containing a slice of the index, we can browse through its entries relatively easily. However, asking for each new volume involves a trip to the archives and a requisition form.

In this organization scheme, each index card corresponds to a single entry in the B-tree where the name string is the key. The binders correspond to B-tree nodes, each with 900 pockets and thus holding a maximum of 900 keys. The entries within the binder are in sorted order, allowing us to search for a key with a linear scan or binary search. In addition, we keep one more piece of data in each of the binder's pockets, a pointer to the binder containing entries between the current index card's key and the key of the previous index card. As shown in Figure 12-2, if we are looking for the target "Caffeine Unlimited Coffee Mug," we would first scan past "Caffeine Ten Coffee Mug," which comes before our target in alphabetical order, and then hit "Jeremy's Gourmet High-Caffeine Experience," which comes after the target. At this point, we have passed the potential location for our target key and know that we need to search the binder before the current entry.

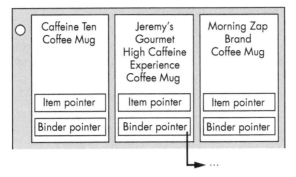

Figure 12-2: The binder pointer in our index cards indicates
which binder to use to continue our search.

We store a single additional pointer at the very back of the binder that
points to another binder containing only keys that come after the last key
in the current binder. In total, our binder can contain up to 900 keys (with
their pointers to the associated collectibles) and 901 pointers to other
binders.

As with the other tree-based data structures, we define B-tree structure
using both a top-level composite data structure and a node-specific data
structure:

```
BTree {
    BTreeNode: root
    Integer: k
}

BTreeNode {
    Integer: k
    Integer: size
    Boolean: is_leaf
    Array of Type: keys
    Array of BTreeNodes: children
}
```

In this data structure and the examples below, we store and retrieve individual keys to keep the code simple. As with the other data structures we
have introduced, in most cases it will be useful to store a composite data
structure with both the key and a pointer to the key's data, such as with the
item pointers in Figure 12-2.

One complication of the B-tree structure is that we store the keys and
children in two differently sized arrays. This means that we need to define
how a key at index i maps to its adjacent child pointers. For any given index
i, we can access the key at $keys[i]$, but we also need to be able to access the
node pointers before and after that key. We define the pointers such that
the value of all keys in or below $children[i]$ are less than $keys[i]$ and greater
than $keys[i-1]$ (if $i > 0$), as shown in Figure 12-3.

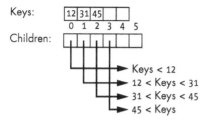

Figure 12-3: A mapping from the entries in the keys array to the corresponding elements in the children array

By definition, B-trees are balanced data structures. Every leaf node is exactly the same depth from the root. In a later section, we'll show how this structure is maintained by updating nodes as we insert and delete new keys.

Searching B-trees

We search the B-tree using the same general procedure that we use for all tree-based data structures: we start at the top of the tree and work our way down until we find the key of interest. The main difference between the B-tree and a binary search tree is that we might need to check more than one key per node. We scan along the keys in each node until we either find the target key or find a key with a value larger than our target. In the latter case, if we are at an internal node, we drop down to the appropriate child and continue the search, as follows:

```
BTreeSearch(BTree: tree, Type: target):
    return BTreeNodeSearch(tree.root, target)

BTreeNodeSearch(BTreeNode: node, Type: target):
    # Search the node's key list for the target.
    Integer: i = 0
❶ WHILE i < node.size AND target >= node.keys[i]:
        ❷ IF target == node.keys[i]:
            return node.keys[i]
        i = i + 1

    # Descend to the correct child.
❸ IF node.is_leaf:
        return null
❹ return BTreeNodeSearch(node.children[i], target)
```

The code for this search starts by scanning through the keys stored at the current node using a WHILE loop ❶. The loop continues until it hits the end of the key list (i == node.size) or hits a key larger than the target (target < node.keys[i]). The code checks whether it has found a matching key in the current node, and, if so, returns that key ❷. While the example code uses a linear scan to search the node for the purpose of simplicity in this example, we could also use binary search for better efficiency.

If the code does not find a match in the current node and the current node is a leaf, there is no match in the tree, and the code returns null ❸. Otherwise, the code recursively explores the correct child node. It can access the correct child directly with the loop iterator i ❹, because the loop stops when either i represents the last child or key[i] > target.

Consider the example of searching the B-tree shown earlier in Figure 12-1 for key 17. In the root node, we check the first key (51) and see that it is greater than 17, so we drop down a level using the first child pointer. At the next level, we check two keys: 12 is less than our target, so we proceed past it; 31 is greater than our target, so we drop down to the child node whose keys come before 31 using the second child pointer. This process continues at the leaf node. Figure 12-4 illustrates this search, indicating with gray the array bins we have accessed and compared.

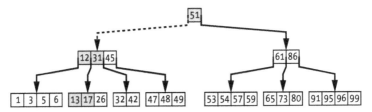

Figure 12-4: An example search of a B-tree. The shaded cells are the ones checked by the algorithm.

We should consider how searching the keys within a node impacts the runtime: instead of dropping down to the next level after a single comparison, we might now have to perform multiple comparisons per node. This is an acceptable tradeoff for two reasons. First, remember the B-tree is optimized to reduce the number of nodes fetched. In comparison, the data accesses within a node are expected to be relatively cheap because they are happening in local memory and do not require us to fetch another block of data from the expensive storage. Second, and equally important, the branching structure of the B-tree still provides ample opportunities for pruning. Each comparison still eliminates entire subtrees. And, like the current node, each skipped node may contain up to $2k$ keys and $2k + 1$ children.

Returning to our collectibles example, consider a search for a particular collectible. We start at the root binder. Since the keys are stored in alphabetical order, we can rapidly skim down the rows until we find our desired key or pass where it should be. If we don't see our desired key, we know it isn't in this binder. We mumble a few choice words about the unfairness of finite storage space and note the first key we encounter that comes after our target key has an item pointer reading "Binder #300." We mumble a few more complaints and ask the archivist for binder #300.

Let's contrast this storage approach with what happens if we instead store all our index cards in sorted order. Binder #1 contains the first set of cards *Aa* through *Ab*, binder #2 contains *Ac* through *Ad*, and so forth. This could work well for a static data set. We could perform a binary search over the binders, requesting the middle binder in our current range each time and limiting ourselves to a logarithmic number of requests. However, this approach begins to break down as we add or remove cards. Binders become overfull, requiring us to shift cards from one binder to the next. Updates to our collection might require cascading updates to many binders as cards must be shifted over. In the worst case, if we pack our binders full, we could end up needing to access every binder in our index. As we will see next, B-trees structures facilitate dynamic changes to the data set.

Adding Keys

Adding keys to a B-tree is more complex than adding to the tree-based data structures we've previously considered. In this case, we need to keep the structure balanced and limit the number of keys stored in each node (between k and $2k$). There are two approaches for handling full nodes. First, we could split as we proceed down the tree, making sure we never call insertion on a full node. Second, we can temporarily insert into a full node (allowing it to be overfull) and then split it on the way back up. We'll explore the later approach, which results in a two-stage algorithm for inserting new keys.

To perform insertions, we first proceed down the tree, searching for the position to insert the new key. Second, we return back up the tree, splitting nodes that have become overfull. Each split increases the branching factor of a node, but not necessarily the height. In fact, the only time we increase the height of the tree is when we split the root node itself. Because we only increase the height by splitting the root node (adding a depth of 1 to every leaf simultaneously), we can guarantee that the tree always remains balanced.

The Addition Algorithm

During the first stage of the algorithm, we recursively descend the tree, searching for the correct location to insert the new key. If we find a matching key along the way, we can update that key's data. Otherwise, we proceed down to a leaf node, where we insert the key into our array.

We start off by defining a simple helper function BTreeNodeAddKey to insert a key into a non-full node. For convenience, we also take a pointer to a child node (representing the child *after* the new key) so that we can reuse this function when splitting nodes. If we are at a leaf node, which doesn't store pointers to children, this next_child pointer is ignored.

```
BTreeNodeAddKey(BTreeNode: node, Type: key,
              BTreeNode: next_child):
❶ Integer: i = node.size - 1
   WHILE i >= 0 AND key < node.keys[i]:
       node.keys[i+1] = node.keys[i]
       IF NOT node.is_leaf:
           node.children[i+2] = node.children[i+1]
       i = i - 1
```

```
    # Insert both the key and the pointer to the child node.
❷ node.keys[i+1] = key
    IF NOT node.is_leaf:
        node.children[i+2] = next_child
❸ node.size = node.size + 1
```

The code starts at the *end* of the keys array (index node.size - 1) and proceeds toward index 0 using a WHILE loop ❶. At each step, it checks whether
the new key should be inserted here and, if not, shifts the current element of
both keys and children back one space. The loop terminates when it has gone
one step past the correct location, which might be the start of the array.
Once we have found the correct location for the new key, we have already
moved that and the following elements out of the way. We can directly insert
the new key and child ❷. The code finishes by adjusting the size of the node
to account for the insertion ❸.

Here we may gasp in dismay at the cost of linearly shifting down items
in the array to make room for our new element, as shown in Figure 12-5.
This is everything we warned about in Chapter 3. But remember, we are
trading off these (bounded) linear costs to minimize node accesses. We
are willing to put up with the hassle of moving down the cards within our
binder to minimize future requisitions to other binders.

*Figure 12-5: Shifting the elements
over to insert 26 in BTreeNodeAddKey*

We require a few more helper functions to handle the case where a
node fills up. Remember that we are restricted to at most $2k$ elements per
node—any more than that means we need to split the node. First, we start
with a simple accessor function BTreeNodeIsOverFull, which returns a Boolean
indicating whether the node contains more than $2k$ items:

```
BTreeNodeIsOverFull(BTreeNode: node):
    return node.size == (2 * node.k + 1)
```

This is equivalent to checking if we have used up all the pockets in our
binder.

We also add a second helper BTreeNodeSplit, which takes a node and
the index of a child and splits that child. Everything before that index is
retained in the original child. Everything after that index is cleared from
the child and added to a newly created sibling node. The key at the index
itself is cleared from the child and added to the current (parent) node.

```
BTreeNodeSplit(BTreeNode: node, Integer: child_index):
❶ BTreeNode: old_child = node.children[child_index]
  BTreeNode: new_child = BTreeNode(node.k)
  new_child.is_leaf = old_child.is_leaf

  # Get the index and key used for the split.
❷ Integer: split_index = Floor(old_child.size / 2.0)
  Type: split_key = old_child.keys[split_index]

  # Copy the larger half of the keys (and their children) to
  # new_child and erase them from old_child.
  Integer: new_index = 0
  Integer: old_index = split_index + 1
❸ WHILE old_index < old_child.size:
      new_child.keys[new_index] = old_child.keys[old_index]
      old_child.keys[old_index] = null

      IF NOT old_child.is_leaf:
          new_child.children[new_index] = old_child.children[old_index]
          old_child.children[old_index] = null
      new_index = new_index + 1
      old_index = old_index + 1

  # Copy the remaining child (after the last key).
❹ IF NOT old_child.is_leaf:
      new_child.children[new_index] = old_child.children[old_child.size]
      old_child.children[old_child.size] = null

  # Remove the key at index and add it to the current node.
❺ old_child.keys[split_index] = null
❻ BTreeNodeAddKey(node, split_key, new_child)

  # Update the sizes of the nodes.
❼ new_child.size = old_child.size - split_index - 1
  old_child.size = split_index
```

The code for BTreeNodeSplit starts by looking up the node to split (old
_child) and creating a new (empty) sibling node (new_child) ❶. This node
will be at the same level as the child to split, so we copy over the value of
is_leaf. Next the code determines what index and key to use as a split point
for old_child ❷. The code then uses a WHILE loop to copy everything after
split_index from both the keys and children in old_child to the corresponding
arrays in new_child ❸. The code uses a pair of indices to capture the index of
the old location (old_index) and the corresponding new location (new_index).
At the same time, the code removes the elements from old_child's arrays by
setting the entries to null. Because the children array is one element longer,
we need to copy that last element separately ❹. Finally, we remove the key
at split_index ❺, add both split_key and the new child pointer to the current
node ❻, and set both the children's sizes ❼.

Let's view this operation in the context of our collectibles storage index as shown in Figure 12-6. When a binder reaches capacity, we repartition its contents into two binders. First, we buy a new empty binder. This sibling will store approximately half the contents of the overfull binder. Second, we carefully relocate the back half of the overfull binder's contents into the new binder, preserving the sorted ordering. Third, we remove the single index card whose key lies between the keys in each binder and insert it in the parent binder in order to indicate the divide between the two child binders. The previously overfull child binder will contain cards whose keys come before this split, and the new binder will contain cards whose keys come after this split.

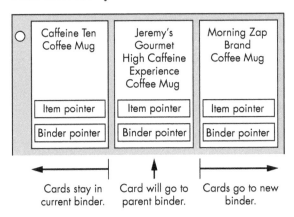

Figure 12-6: We repartition the binder by splitting it on the key of the middle card.

Given these helpers, we can now define an insertion function that performs the recursive search and the subsequent addition. We perform the addition at the leaf node. As the recursion returns up the tree, we check whether the recently accessed child node is full and thus needs to be split.

```
BTreeNodeInsert(BTreeNode: node, Type: key):
    Integer: i = 0
❶ WHILE i < node.size AND key >= node.keys[i]:
    ❷ IF key == node.keys[i]:
            Update data.
            return
        i = i + 1

    IF node.is_leaf:
        ❸ BTreeNodeAddKey(node, key, null)
    ELSE:
        ❹ BTreeNodeInsert(node.children[i], key)
        ❺ IF BTreeNodeIsOverFull(node.children[i]):
            ❻ BTreeNodeSplit(node, i)
```

The code starts by finding the correct location for key in the keys array ❶. The WHILE loop iterates through the array until it hits the end of the key

list (i == node.size) or hits a key that is larger than the target (key < node
.keys[i]). If the code finds an exact match, it updates any data for this key
and returns ❷. Otherwise, it needs to insert new data.

If the key is being inserted into a leaf, the code uses the BTreeNodeAddKey
function ❸, which shifts the array elements over and adds the new key to
the correct location. If the key is being inserted into an internal node, the
index i provides the pointer of the correct child for insertion. The code
recursively inserts into that child ❹, then checks whether it broke the properties of a B-tree (specifically the size of nodes falling between k and $2k$)
with the insertion ❺.

The code breaks the B-tree property if it inserts too many elements
into a node. We can use our helper function BTreeNodeIsOverFull to check if
the recently modified node has too many elements. The code conducts this
check from the parent node, so we can keep the logic of repairing the B-tree
simple. It uses BTreeNodeSplit to split the overfull child into two nodes ❻. In
the process of this insertion, we might break the current node when inserting the new separating key, but that's okay; we'll take care of it when we
return to this node's parent.

We use a little extra storage in order to simplify the code. The code
allows a node to temporarily overfill, storing $2k + 1$ keys and $2k + 2$ children
while waiting for its parent node to call BTreeNodeSplit. We can create this
buffer by simply allocating large enough arrays for the keys and children.

We can think of the first phase of the code as receiving a new coffee
mug for our collection. We create an index card for the mug and insert it
into our indexing binders. We start at the root binder and search for the
location to put the card. During our search, we follow the appropriate
pointers to child binders. Once we end up at a leaf binder, with no children
indicated on the index cards, we add the new card there. We check whether
the binder is now (over)full and, if it is, start repartitioning its contents.
Afterward, we return the binders to storage in the reverse order that we
requisitioned them. If we just split a binder and thus transferred a new card
to its parent, we also check whether we need to split the parent binder. This
process continues until we've returned to the root binder.

We need to define one additional special case for the root node. Remember that splitting the root node is the only way we are allowed to increase the
height of the tree. We need to define a wrapper function to do exactly that.
Luckily, we can reuse our previous helper functions:

```
BTreeInsert(BTree: tree, Type: key):
  ❶ BTreeNodeInsert(tree.root, key)

  ❷ IF BTreeNodeIsOverFull(tree.root):
      ❸ BTreeNode: new_root = BTreeNode(tree.k)
        new_root.is_leaf = False
        new_root.size = 0

      ❹ new_root.children[0] = tree.root
      ❺ BTreeNodeSplit(new_root, 0)
      ❻ tree.root = new_root
```

The code starts by inserting the key into the root node using BTree NodeInsert ❶. This function recursively descends the tree, finds the correct location to insert the new key, and returns through the levels fixing the broken B-tree property at all but the root node. Then the code checks if the root node has too many elements by using BTreeNodeIsOverFull on the root node ❷. If the root node has too many elements, the code adds a level to the tree by creating a new empty root node ❸, assigning the old root to be the first child of the new root ❹, splitting this (overfull) child ❺, and updating the tree's root ❻. After a split, the new root node will contain exactly one key and two children.

In the process of inserting a key, we complete a single round trip from the root node to a leaf node and back. The number of nodes we need to access (and modify) is thus proportional to the depth of the tree. Since our B-tree always remains balanced, with all leaf nodes at the same depth, and the branching factor of all non-root, internal nodes is at least $k + 1$, the node retrievals scales logarithmically in N. The total work also includes linear operations within the node, such as copying or shifting keys, so the total work required scales proportional to $k \times \log_k(N)$.

Examples of Adding Keys

Let's consider a few examples to better understand the functions we just covered. First, take the simplest case, shown in Figure 12-7, of adding a key to leaf node that will not be overfull. Suppose $k = 2$, where our non-root nodes can contain between 2 and $2k = 4$ items. If we add the key 30 to the subtree in Figure 12-7(a), we simply proceed down to the leaf node and add the new key in the correct part of the array with the BTreeNodeAddKey helper function. Since the leaf has four elements, we do not need to split it. We get the subtree shown in Figure 12-7(b).

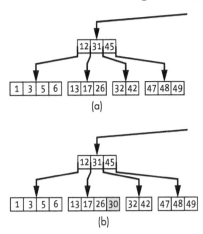

Figure 12-7: Inserting the key 30 into a non-full B-tree leaf (a) results in a leaf node with four elements (b).

The logic becomes more complex as we fill up nodes. Consider the example shown in Figure 12-8(a) of adding the key 29 to the same tree. After inserting the new key in Figure 12-8(b), the leaf node is overfull. We handle this by identifying the split point of the overfull node (key = 26) and promoting that to the parent node. We then use the helper function BTreeNodeSplit to divide the leaf into two siblings as shown in Figure 12-8(c). If the promotion of the middle element fills up the internal node, we need to split that as well.

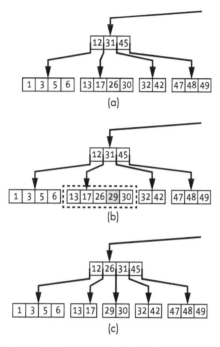

(a)

(b)

(c)

Figure 12-8: Inserting the key 29 into an already-full leaf node (a) gives the leaf too many elements (b). We must split the overfull leaf to restore the B-tree conditions (c).

Finally, consider what happens if our splits propagate all the way back to the root node. Suppose that, after an insertion, the root node itself overfills as shown in Figure 12-9(a). We solve this problem in Figure 12-9(b) by splitting the root node and creating a new level for the tree. The new root node contains exactly one element, the middle key of the previous root node. Note that, unlike all the other nodes, the root node is allowed to have less than k items. In fact, every time we split the root node, we create a new root with exactly one item.

As the examples in this section show, the modifications to the B-tree are limited to only those nodes explored during the initial search for the insertion location. Since we do not need to update or repair other branches, the total number of modified nodes is limited by the depth of the tree and thus scales proportional to $\log_k(N)$.

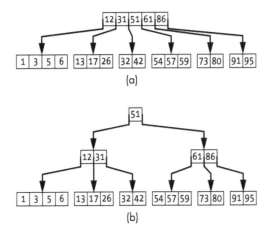

Figure 12-9: When the root node of a B-tree becomes overfull (a), we split it into two siblings and promote the middle element to the new root node (b).

Removing Keys

Removing keys follows a similar approach to adding keys. We again need to keep the structure balanced and limit the number of keys stored in each node (between k and $2k$). This results in a multi-stage algorithm for deleting keys. First, we proceed down the tree as though we were searching for the key. Once we find it, we delete the key. Finally, we return back up the tree checking for and fixing nodes with too few keys. Since we never remove a node except an empty root node (decreasing the depth of all the leaves by one), we again guarantee that the tree always remains balanced.

Fixing Under-full Nodes

When we remove keys from a B-tree, we run the risk of nodes dropping below the minimum of k keys. We can check this condition with a simple helper function:

```
BTreeNodeIsUnderFull(BTreeNode: node):
    return node.size < node.k
```

Depending on the structure of the B-tree, there are two different approaches we may need to use to fix an under-full node, both of which I'll discuss in this section. Each approach relies on augmenting the node's keys with keys from an adjacent sibling. In the first case, we directly merge two small sibling nodes into a single node. In the second case, we transfer a key from a larger sibling to the under-full node. Which function we use depends on how many keys in total the two siblings have. Both of these helper functions are called from the parent node with the index for the key that separates the adjacent sibling nodes.

The merge operation takes two adjacent sibling nodes, along with the key separating them, and concatenates them into a single large child node. As such, it requires that the combined number of keys in the two siblings be *less* than 2*k* so that the new child is guaranteed to be valid. Figure 12-10 shows this procedure, with Figure 12-10(a) depicting a subtree before the merge operation, where the middle child has a single key. Figure 12-10(b) shows the same subtree after the merge.

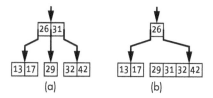

Figure 12-10: The merge operation on B-tree nodes

Listing 12-1 shows the code for merging two adjacent siblings.

```
BTreeNodeMerge(BTreeNode: node, Integer: index):
❶ BTreeNode: childL = node.children[index]
   BTreeNode: childR = node.children[index + 1]

   # Copy over the parent's key and the right child's first child pointer.
❷ Integer: loc = childL.size
   childL.keys[loc] = node.keys[index]
   IF NOT childL.is_leaf:
       childL.children[loc + 1] = childR.children[0]
   loc = loc + 1

❸ # Copy over the right child's keys and children.
   Integer: i = 0
   WHILE i < childR.size:
       childL.keys[loc + i] = childR.keys[i]
       IF NOT childL.is_leaf:
           childL.children[loc + i + 1] = childR.children[i + 1]
       i = i + 1
   childL.size = childL.size + childR.size + 1

   # Remove the key from the current node.
   i = index
❹ WHILE i < node.size - 1:
       node.keys[i] = node.keys[i + 1]
       node.children[i + 1] = node.children[i + 2]
       i = i + 1
   node.keys[i] = null
   node.children[i + 1] = null
   node.size = node.size - 1
```

Listing 12-1: Code for merging two child nodes

The code appends the keys from the right child and the separating key from the parent onto the left child. It starts by retrieving both child nodes, which we call childL and childR for left and right respectively ❶. By definition, any key in `childL` is less than the separating key, and any key in `childR` is greater than the separating key. The code then appends the separating key from the parent and the first child pointer from the right child to the end of the left child ❷. It uses a `WHILE` loop to copy the remaining keys and pointers from the right child ❸. It also updates the left child's size. At this point, it has successfully created the merged node out of the two children. The merged child's pointer is stored in `node.children[index]`.

The code finishes by cleaning up the parent node ❹. It removes the previous separating key and the pointer to the right child by shifting the subsequent keys and pointers over, setting the final bins to `null`, and updating the current node's size.

In the process of merging two nodes, we are taking a key from their parent. This could leave the parent node with less than *k* keys, and our repairs would need to continue at the next higher level of the tree.

This process is directly analogous to merging binders in our storage indexing example. If an index binder contains too few keys, it is a waste of space and requisition time. We wouldn't want to requisition a binder with a single index card. Merging binders consists of taking the cards from one child binder, along with the separating card from the parent binder, and putting them in the other child binder in the correct order. Since we have already requisitioned the parent and one child (and thus have them in local memory), we can do this merge quickly with only a single additional requisition for the other child.

The second approach to fixing an under-full node is to shift one of the keys (and potentially children) from its adjacent sibling. This works only when the sibling can afford to lose a key and thus applies to cases where the combined number of keys of the siblings must be at least 2*k*. While we could merge and optimally resplit the adjacent siblings, for illustrative purposes we use a simpler approach of transferring only one key. Since we only ever remove a single key from a node during deletion or the merge operation, transferring a single key is sufficient to fix our under-full node.

However, as shown in Figure 12-11, we can't just take a key from one child and give it to the other. The separating key in the parent node enforces the bounds of the split. Instead, we do a two-stage transfer. First, we transfer the current separating key from the parent to the under-full node. Second, we replace the separating key in the parent node with a key from the other sibling.

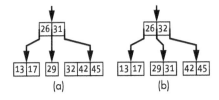

Figure 12-11: The transfer left operation on B-tree nodes

As shown in Listing 12-2, we break the code into two helper functions, one to transfer a key from the right child to the left child and one to transfer the other way. The code to transfer a key from the right child to the left child transfers two keys: one from the right child to the parent and one from the parent to the left child.

```
BTreeNodeTransferLeft(BTreeNode: node, Integer: index):
❶ BTreeNode: childL = node.children[index]
  BTreeNode: childR = node.children[index + 1]
  Type: middle_key = node.keys[index]

❷ node.keys[index] = childR.keys[0]
❸ childL.keys[childL.size] = middle_key
  IF NOT childR.is_leaf:
      childL.children[childL.size + 1] = childR.children[0]
  childL.size = childL.size + 1

❹ Integer: i = 0
  WHILE i < childR.size - 1:
      childR.keys[i] = childR.keys[i + 1]
      IF NOT childR.is_leaf:
          childR.children[i] = childR.children[i + 1]
      i = i + 1

❺ childR.keys[i] = null
  IF NOT childR.is_leaf:
      childR.children[i] = childR.children[i + 1]
      childR.children[i + 1] = null
❻ childR.size = childR.size - 1
```

Listing 12-2: Code for transferring a key and child pointer to an under-full node from its right-hand sibling

The code starts by retrieving the two adjacent siblings and the separating key ❶. It moves the first key from the right-hand child to replace the previous separating key ❷. It adds the previous separating key from the parent (middle_key) and the first child pointer from the right-hand child to the end of the arrays in the left-hand child ❸. Both the left-hand child and parent are now updated. The code then cleans up the right-hand child. It uses a WHILE loop to shift over the remaining elements ❹, marks the now empty spots as null ❺, and adjusts the size ❻.

The code for transferring a key from the left child to the right child is similar to that shown in Listing 12-3. The two-key transfer works in the opposite direction: one from the left child to the parent and one from the parent to the right child.

```
BTreeNodeTransferRight(BTreeNode: node, Integer: index):
❶ BTreeNode: childL = node.children[index]
  BTreeNode: childR = node.children[index + 1]
  Type: middle_key = node.keys[index]

  # Make space in childR for the new key and pointer.
❷ Integer: i = childR.size - 1
  WHILE i >= 0:
      childR.keys[i+1] = childR.keys[i]
```

```
        IF NOT childR.is_leaf:
            childR.children[i+2] = childR.children[i+1]
        i = i - 1
    IF NOT childR.is_leaf:
        childR.children[1] = childR.children[0]

❸ childR.keys[0] = middle_key
    IF NOT childR.is_leaf:
        childR.children[0] = childL.children[childL.size]
    childR.size = childR.size + 1

❹ node.keys[index] = childL.keys[childL.size - 1]

❺ childL.keys[childL.size - 1] = null
    IF NOT childL.is_leaf:
        childL.children[childL.size] = null
    childL.size = childL.size - 1
```

Listing 12-3: Code for transferring a key and child pointer to an under-full node from its left-hand sibling

The code again starts by retrieving the two adjacent siblings and the separating key ❶. The code then shifts over the keys and children in the right-hand node to make room for the new addition ❷. It appends the previous separating key from the parent (middle_key) and the last child pointer from the left child to the *beginning* of the right-hand node ❸, increasing its size by 1. The code then moves the last key in the left-hand child to replace the separating key in the parent ❹. The code completes by cleaning up the left-hand child by marking the now empty entries null and updating the size ❺.

Unlike the merge operation, neither transfer operation reduces the number of keys in the parent. Thus, we do not need to perform repairs at higher levels of the tree. The physical corollary of these transfer operations is requesting a sibling storage binder and shifting two index cards between the two children and the parent. We take the intermediate card (that falls between the range of the two binders) from the parent and add it to the less full child binder. We replace this card in the parent with the appropriate one from the child that has more cards.

We can encapsulate all three of these repair functions as well as the logic to choose them into a helper function that takes in the current node and the index of the under-full child:

```
BTreeNodeRepairUnderFull(BTreeNode: node, Integer: child):
  ❶ IF child == node.size:
        child = child - 1
  ❷ Integer: total = (node.children[child].size +
                      node.children[child + 1].size)

    IF total < 2 * node.k:
      ❸ BTreeNodeMerge(node, child)
        return
```

```
❹ IF node.children[child].size < node.children[child + 1].size:
       BTreeNodeTransferLeft(node, child)
   ELSE:
       BTreeNodeTransferRight(node, child)
```

To know which repair strategy to employ, the code needs to find an adjacent sibling and check the two children's total number of keys. Here, for illustrative purposes, we use a simplistic strategy of always using the next child (child + 1) as the sibling unless we are repairing the last child in the array ❶. If we are repairing the last child in the array, we use the previous child for its sibling. The code checks the total count of keys in these two child nodes ❷. If the number of keys is small enough (under $2k$), it merges those nodes with the BTreeNodeMerge function ❸. Otherwise, if the nodes have $2k$ or more keys, the code uses either BTreeNodeTransferLeft or BTreeNodeTransferRight to move a single key to the smaller node ❹.

Finding the Minimum Value Key

We use one more helper function as part of the deletion operation—code to find and return the minimum key at or below a given node. This code, in Listing 12-4, can also be useful in its own right, such as for computing the bounds of the keys in the B-tree.

```
BTreeNodeFindMin(BTreeNode: node):
❶ IF node.size == 0:
       return null
❷ IF node.is_leaf:
       return node.keys[0]
   ELSE:
       ❸ return BTreeNodeFindMin(node.children[0])
```

Listing 12-4: Code to find the minimum key at or below a given node

The code consists of three possible conditions. If the node is empty, the code returns null to indicate that there is no minimum key there ❶. This should occur only in an empty root node, as all other nodes will have at least k keys. If the node is a non-empty leaf, the code returns the first (and thus minimum) key in the node's array ❷. Finally, if the node is internal, the code recursively checks the first child ❸.

The Removal Algorithm

We start the description of the deletion algorithm with the top-level wrapper function. This function is relatively simple. It calls the recursive deletion function using the tree's root node.

```
BTreeDelete(BTree: tree, Type: key):
   BTreeNodeDelete(tree.root, key)

   IF tree.root.size == 0 AND NOT tree.root.is_leaf:
       tree.root = tree.root.children[0]
```

Just as we added a level only when we split the node, we remove a level from the tree only when the root node becomes empty. If the B-tree is not completely empty, the empty root node will still have a single valid child in array position 0. We use this child to replace the former root node.

The core deletion algorithm recursively descends the tree, searching for the key to delete. Since we might reduce the number of keys below the required k, we need to know check whether the modified child is now under-full and, if so, repair it.

```
BTreeNodeDelete(BTreeNode: node, Type: key):
❶ Integer: i = 0
   WHILE i < node.size AND key > node.keys[i]:
       i = i + 1

   # Deletion from a leaf node.
   IF node.is_leaf:
       IF i < node.size AND key == node.keys[i]:
         ❷ WHILE i < node.size - 1:
               node.keys[i] = node.keys[i + 1]
               i = i + 1
           node.keys[i] = null
           node.size = node.size - 1
       return

   # Deletion at an internal node.
   IF i < node.size AND key == node.keys[i]:
     ❸ Type: min_key = BTreeNodeFindMin(node.children[i+1])
       node.keys[i] = min_key

     ❹ BTreeNodeDelete(node.children[i+1], min_key)
       IF BTreeNodeIsUnderFull(node.children[i+1]):
           BTreeNodeRepairUnderFull(node, i+1)
   ELSE:
     ❺ BTreeNodeDelete(node.children[i], key)
       IF BTreeNodeIsUnderFull(node.children[i]):
           BTreeNodeRepairUnderFull(node, i)
```

The code starts by searching for the key to delete in the current node by scanning across the array of keys ❶. If there is a matching key in this node, the WHILE loop terminates such that i is the index matching the key.

The code then considers the leaf case. If the node is a leaf and the key is found, the code deletes it by shifting over the keys ❷. The code also sets the last element to null and updates the size. The code doesn't need to change the child pointers because they are not set for leaf nodes. If the node is a leaf and the key is not found, then the code simply returns.

The code next handles the case of internal nodes. There are two cases to consider: the key is in the node, or it is not. If the code finds the key in the internal node, it replaces the key with the key that immediately *follows* the target key in sorted order ❸. The code finds this subsequent key using BTreeNodeFindMin from Listing 12-4, called on the child node immediately after the target key. The code deletes this following key from the child's subtree by calling BTreeNodeDelete ❹. The code then checks whether the child node is under-full and, if so, fixes it.

If the target key is not in an internal node, then the code recursively calls BTreeNodeDelete on the appropriate child ❺. Again, it needs to check whether that child node is now under-full and, if so, fix it.

As with insertion, our goal is to limit the number of nodes retrieved during this operation. Deletion will make at most a single pass from the root node to a leaf. Even if we delete from an internal node, the subsequent replacement and deletion operations still only continue the trek to a single leaf. We pay one additional requisition whenever we repair a node to retrieve the under-full node's sibling.

Examples of Removing Keys

Let's look at a few examples of the removals that we just covered. First, take the simplest case, shown in Figure 12-12, of removing a key from a leaf node with more than $k + 1$ keys. Suppose $k = 2$, where our non-root nodes can contain between 2 and $2k = 4$ items. If we remove key 5 from the subtree in Figure 12-12(a), we simply proceed down to the leaf node and remove the key in the array. Since the resulting leaf has three elements, we do not need to repair it. We get the subtree shown in Figure 12-12(b).

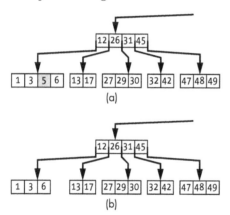

Figure 12-12: Deleting the key 5 from a B-tree leaf (a) results in a leaf node with three elements (b).

Next, we consider the case of removing a key from an internal node without needing repairs as shown in Figure 12-13. If we remove key 45 from the subtree in Figure 12-13(a), we find that key in an internal node. To remove it, we replace it with the next key in order, which is 47. Since the resulting nodes all have at least two elements, we do not need to perform any repairs. We get the subtree shown in Figure 12-13(b).

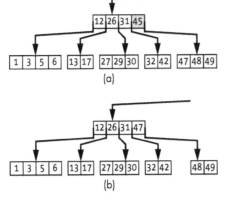

Figure 12-13: Deleting the key 45 from an internal B-tree node (a)
results in taking a key from one of the children (b).

Finally, we consider the different cases where removing a key requires us
to repair an under-full node. Figure 12-14 shows a case where we can merge
two nodes. We start by deleting the key 32 in Figure 12-14(a). Figure 12-14(b)
shows the keys that we use for the merge operation: the keys in the under-full
node, the keys in its right-hand adjacent sibling, and the key in the parent
separating the two. Figure 12-14(c) shows the repaired tree. The new child
node has four keys, and the previous parent has three.

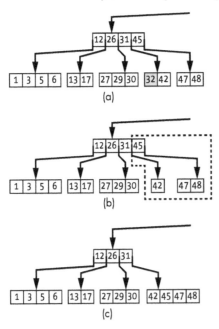

Figure 12-14: Deleting the key 32 from an almost empty node (a)
gives the leaf too few elements (b). We must merge with an
adjacent sibling to restore the B-tree conditions (c).

Figure 12-15 shows a case where we can transfer a key from a larger sibling node. We start by deleting the key 32 in Figure 12-15(a). Figure 12-15(b) shows the keys that we use to restore balance: the keys in the under-full node, the keys in its right-hand adjacent sibling, and the key in the parent separating the two. Figure 12-15(c) shows which keys will move and where. The repaired tree is shown in Figure 12-15(d).

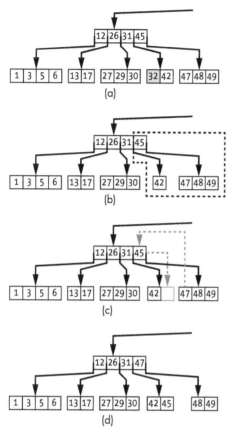

Figure 12-15: Deleting the key 32 from an almost empty node (a) gives the leaf too few elements (b). We can repair this by taking a key from an adjacent sibling (c) to restore the B-tree conditions (d).

Finally, Figure 12-16 shows a case where we remove a level from the tree by merging the only two children below the root. Figure 12-16(b) shows that after the merge, we are left with an empty root node. Its one key has been moved to the merged node. We repair this in Figure 12-16(c) by removing the old root node and promoting that node's single child to be the new root node.

Unlike addition, where the modifications to the B-tree are limited to only those nodes explored during the initial search for the insertion location, deletion can modify nodes in other branches. Both merging nodes and transferring keys use a sibling node at the same level. However, the total number of nodes modified is still limited by the depth of the tree. At most, we access one sibling node per level, and the number of nodes accessed scales logarithmically with N.

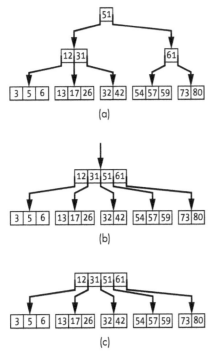

Figure 12-16: Merging the only two children under the root node (a) results in an empty root (b). We repair this by promoting the root node's only child to be the new root (c).

Why This Matters

B-trees illustrate a few important concepts. First, they show how we can adapt the behavior of previous data structures to handle cases where memory accesses between nodes are more expensive than accesses within a node. B-trees combine indexing and storage in such a way as minimize the number of accesses we need. This is critical for large data sets that might keep information on a disk or an external server. By enforcing a minimum of k keys for each non-root node, we ensure a branching factor of at least $k + 1$ at each node and thus flatten out the overall data structure. This helps limit the overall depth of the tree and thus the number of retrievals needed for search, insertion, or deletion. We also guarantee that each non-root node always remains at least half-full, meaning that we do not waste time retrieving nodes with only a few elements (except possibly the root).

It is useful to contrast the B-tree's approach with a more specialized indexing scheme for our collectibles. We could develop a data structure that initially splits on category. The top-level index maps the collectible's category, such as coffee-related collectibles, to a binder for that specific category. Each category's binder then maps to all the subcategories, such as coffee mugs or coffee posters. And so forth. This is also a valid approach that builds off the branching structures we have seen throughout this book. The tradeoff becomes one of generalizability versus efficiency. In many cases, we can further optimize a data structure to a particular task at hand but lose the ability to apply it to other problems. In some cases, this tradeoff might be worth it. In others, it might not. Compared to a categorical focused indexing scheme, B-trees provide a more general approach that can work for any sortable set of keys.

The second concept B-trees illustrate is a second level of dynamism within the data structure itself. The B-tree constantly rearranges its structure to adapt to the distribution of data it stores and thus remain balanced. As we saw in Chapter 5, we lose the advantages of the tree-based structure if our tree becomes highly unbalanced. B-trees programmatically prevent this through a combination of bounds on the number of keys in each node (k to $2k$) and a guarantee that all leaf nodes have exactly the same depth. They adapt to "bad" distributions of input data by rebalancing—fixing nodes with too many or too few items. While there are a wide range of other balancing strategies for trees, B-trees provide a simple and clear example of how we can use additional structure (in this case, multiple keys per node) to avoid worst-case scenarios.

13

BLOOM FILTERS

As we saw in the previous chapter, we often need to be cognizant of how our data structures fit into local memory and how to limit retrievals from slower memory. As a data structure grows, it can store more data but might not be able to fit into the fastest memory. This chapter introduces the *Bloom filter*, a data structure that extends the core concepts behind a hash table to limit the amount of memory needed to filter over a large key space.

Bloom filters were invented in 1970 by computer scientist Burton Bloom. A Bloom filter tracks which keys have been inserted while ruthlessly optimizing for both memory usage and execution time. It tries to answer one very simple yes/no question: have we previously seen this key? For example, we might use a Bloom filter to check if a password is on a list of known weak passwords. Alternatively, we can use Bloom filters as prefiltering step before accessing a larger and more comprehensive, but slower, data structure.

In its quest for ultimate efficiency, the Bloom filter uses an approach that can result in false positives. This means that with some non-zero probability, the Bloom filter will indicate that a key has been inserted when it, in fact, has not. In other words, a Bloom filter of bad passwords might occasionally reject a good one.

As we will see, the combination of low memory overhead, fast execution time, and a guaranteed lack of false negatives—cases that indicate a key has not occurred when it actually has—make Bloom filters useful for prefiltering tasks and early checks before accessing a more expensive data structure. This leads to a two-stage lookup similar to the approach for caches in Chapter 11. To check whether a record is in our data set, we first check whether it has been inserted into the Bloom filter. Since the Bloom filter is a compact data structure in fast memory, we can perform this check quickly. If the Bloom filter returns false, we know the record is not in our data set, and we can skip the expensive lookup in the comprehensive data structure. If the Bloom filter returns true, then either we have received a false positive or the record is in our larger data structure, and we perform the full search.

Imagine we'd like to determine whether a given record exists in a large database of medical records before we do a more computationally expensive search. The medical database is huge, includes images and videos, and must be stored across a multitude of large hard drives. Further, given the many millions of records, even the index is too large to fit into local memory. While it will occasionally return a false positive and send us searching for a record that does not exist, the Bloom filter will also help us avoid many pointless searches. Whenever the Bloom filter indicates that a record is not in the data set, we can stop the search immediately!

Introducing Bloom Filters

At its heart, a Bloom filter is an array of binary values. Each bin tracks whether or not we have ever seen anything mapping to that hash value before. A value of 1 indicates that a given bin has been seen before. A value of 0 indicates that it has not.

Bloom filters can be incredibly useful when we want to easily search for a single value within a large number of values. Imagine this filtering in the context of searching a large, crowded ballroom for a friend. We could spend hours wandering the floor and peering at faces before concluding that our friend is not in attendance. It's much simpler to ask a knowledge-able event organizer first. We describe our friend to the organizer, who has an excellent memory and can confirm whether anyone matching the description is there. Our description, and the organizer's mental map, consists of a series of basic attributes. Our friend is tall, wears sneakers, and has glasses.

The event organizer's answer may still not be 100 percent accurate—we are using general attributes, and multiple people will share those individual descriptors. Sometimes the organizer will give us a false positive, saying, "I saw someone with those characteristics" when our friend isn't there. But they will never make a false negative statement and tell us our friend isn't there when they really are. If the organizer has not seen someone with the three characteristics we list, then we can guarantee our friend is not at the event. The response doesn't need to have zero false positives to help us on average. If the organizer can save us 9 out of every 10 searches, it would be a tremendous win.

Let's examine how we can extend the hashing techniques we learned Chapter 10 to this prefiltering question. We start with a simple indicator array and examine where it falls short. Then we show how the use of multiple hash functions can provide a more robust filtering scheme.

Hash Tables of Indicators

Consider the simplest filter, a binary indicator array mapped to by a single hash function. When we insert a key, we compute the hash value and mark the appropriate bin with a 1. When we look up a key, we compute the hash value and check the corresponding bin. It's simple. It's elegant. And, unfortunately, it breaks at the slightest hash collision.

Imagine we implement this simple single-hash-function filter for our thousand-page coffee log. Whenever we want to look up a type of coffee in our log, we first ask the filter the simple question, "Have I tried this type of coffee before?" This filter often allows us to avoid binary searching through a thousand pages if we know that we have never tried the coffee before.

For the first month it works perfectly. Every time we sample a new coffee, we add it to the log and flip the appropriate bit in our filter from 0 to 1, as shown in Figure 13-1. We use the coffee name as the input to our hash function, allowing us to check future coffees by name.

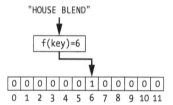

Figure 13-1: A single hash function can map a string to the index of an array.

For the first few entries, the single-hash-function Bloom filter acts similarly to a regular hash table (without collision resolution) that stores binary values for each entry. We insert a 1 into the appropriate bin for each key seen, and a value of 0 indicates we have not seen any entry hashing to that value. When we ask whether we've tried the House Blend variety, we receive a simple "yes" when our lookup returns a 1.

However, problems emerge as we add more and more values to our filter. After a day of coffee drinking, our binary array begins to fill up. As shown in Figure 13-2, even if we're only consuming a few varieties of coffee a day, we start to fill the array with 1s.

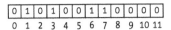

0	1	0	1	0	0	1	1	0	0	0	0
0	1	2	3	4	5	6	7	8	9	10	11

Figure 13-2: A binary array that is starting to fill up

Since Bloom filters, unlike hash tables, don't use chaining or any other mechanism to resolve collisions, two different coffees will occasionally map to the same entry. Soon we don't know whether we really sampled the Burnt-Bean Dark Roast or whether the corresponding 1 is due to our previous tasting of Raw Bean, Uncooked, Bitter Blast, which happens to map to the same entry. Remember from Chapter 10 that whenever we are mapping from a large key space (the set of coffee names) to a smaller key space (the entries in an array), we will see collisions. This problem grows worse and worse as we add more entries to our log.

Within a year, our initial filter is effectively useless. Our varied coffee experiences, while enjoyable, have packed the array with 1s. We now have something like the array shown in Figure 13-3. Well over half of our queries result in hash collisions and thus false positives. The filter is no longer an efficient prefilter. Rather, it almost always adds the overhead of a useless check before the real search. In our party example, this correlates to using a single attribute to describe our friend. If we provide only our friend's hair color, the event organizer will almost always have seen someone matching that description.

0	1	0	1	1	0	1	1	1	1	0	1
0	1	2	3	4	5	6	7	8	9	10	11

Figure 13-3: A binary array that is too full to be a useful coffee tracker

The simplest fix to our mounting collisions would be to increase the space of hash values. We could make our binary array larger. Instead of using 100 indicator values, we could try 1,000. This reduces the likelihood of collisions, but does not remove it entirely. A single collision will still result in a false positive, and, as we saw in Chapter 10, some collisions are unavoidable. Our hashing approach isn't doomed yet, though. We can do even better by adopting a strategy that also reduces the *impact* of each collision.

The Bloom Filter

A Bloom filter solves the problem of collisions by taking the idea of hash functions to the extreme. Instead of using a single hash function for each key, it employs *k* independent hash functions, all mapping the key onto the same range of hash values. For example, as shown in Figure 13-4, we might use three hash functions for our coffee list. The hash function *f1* maps this key to index 2; the second function, *f2*, maps it to index 6; and the third, *f3*, maps it to index 9.

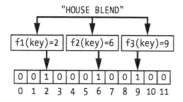

Figure 13-4: Inserting the string HOUSE BLEND into a Bloom filter using three hash functions

Formally, we define the Bloom filter's operations as follows:

Insert key   For each of our k hash functions, map the key to an index and set the value at that index to 1.

Lookup key   For each of our k hash functions, map the key to an index and check whether the value at that index is 1. Return true if and only if all k array values are 1.

At first glance, all we have done is make matters worse. Instead of filling up one bin per sample, we're filling three. Our array is practically guaranteed to fill up faster and see collisions earlier. If we add a second entry, as shown in Figure 13-5, we add more 1s to our array.

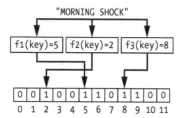

Figure 13-5: Inserting the string MORNING SHOCK into a Bloom filter using three hash functions

On the contrary, we've actually improved things. The power of the Bloom filter enables us to look up entries efficiently. Instead of succumbing to a single collision, producing a false positive if we see a see a single 1, we require *all* the bins for our target string to contain a 1, as shown in Figure 13-6.

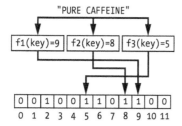

Figure 13-6: Looking up the string PURE CAFFEINE in a Bloom filter with three hash functions

If we see a single 0, we know that this entry has not been inserted into the array. In Figure 13-7, we can see we've never sampled the Caffeine +10 roast. In the ballroom, the event organizer only needs to know that our friend is wearing a bowler hat to categorically answer that they've seen no one of that description. They've seen someone of the correct height and someone with the correct hair color, but no one wearing that hat. We can safely avoid a full search.

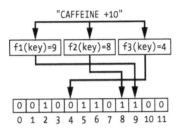

Figure 13-7: Looking up the string CAFFEINE +10 in a Bloom filter with three hash functions

To register a false positive, *each* of our hash values must collide with a previous entry. If we balance the size of our array with the number of hash functions, we can reduce the probability for a false positive.

We can visualize a Bloom filter's treatment of collisions via a conversation with a knowledgeable barista. Imagine that, on a recent trip, a friend hands us an incredible cup of coffee. After basking in the joy of the rich flavors and potent caffeine content, we ask our friend about this new discovery. To our dismay, our soon to be former friend shrugs, points in a general direction, and claims that they purchased it at a shop "that way." They can't remember the name of the barista, the shop, or even the coffee brand. Unfortunately, we don't have time to find the shop and interrogate the owner ourselves. We need to get on our flight home. Holding back tears at the lost knowledge, we jot a few attributes on a piece of paper and resolve to track down the mystery coffee.

Upon returning home, we visit the most knowledgeable barista we know and show them our notes. We have managed to capture five key traits about our coffee, such as "primary smell is chocolate." This clearly isn't enough information to identify the coffee uniquely, but we can ask our barista if they know of anything matching this description. Before paging through their own 10,000-page coffee log to look for a coffee matching all five attributes, the barista considers them independently and rules out a match. Despite our arguments that the flavors worked surprisingly well, our expert has never heard of any coffee that includes an "extra-sweet bubblegum flavor." They give us a funny look and mumble something about having standards.

In this case, our five attributes are effectively hash functions, projecting the complex coffee experience into a lower-dimensional space—an array of descriptor words. The barista uses each of these attributes individually to check whether they know of any coffee that could match, using the index of their very own coffee log. An entry in the index means at least one match. The per-attribute test might run into false positives, but that's okay. In the worst case, we waste some time looking through old coffee log entries before determining that nothing perfectly matches. At least we know we will never see a false negative. If even one of the characteristics is unique, the barista can confidently say no, and we can leave confident in the knowledge that no coffee in our barista's extensive catalog could be our mystery blend.

We can use just the Bloom filter step to make fast, in-the-moment decisions without subsequently searching a larger data structure. Imagine that our trusted barista maintains a secret list of coffees to avoid, 500 coffees around the world that are so vomit-inducingly terrible they will make us stop drinking coffee for a full month. For various liability reasons, they don't publish the list. But if we ask our barista friend about a specific coffee on the list, they will give a polite warning that maybe we'd prefer decaf instead. Before sampling any new coffee, we'd do well to check it isn't on their list.

Of course, we won't be able to call the barista each time we get the opportunity to try a new coffee, so we need a quick way of making the decision. Using five informative attributes, including primary smell and viscosity, the barista constructs a Bloom filter for those coffees, marking 1 for each of the five attributes for each coffee on the list. When we have an opportunity to sample a new coffee, we check the five attributes against the list. If any of them map to 0, we can safely drink the new coffee. It is guaranteed to not be on the barista's list. However, if all the attributes are 1, maybe we should order something else. As a bonus, the barista never has to distribute their secret list.

We can apply Bloom filters to computer science applications in a similar fashion. Consider the problem of checking a password against a list of known weak passwords. We could systematically search the full list every time someone proposes a new password. Alternatively, we could create a Bloom filter to quickly check if we should reject the password. Occasionally we might reject a reasonable password, but we can guarantee we'll never let a bad one through.

Bloom Filter Code

In its simplest form, a Bloom filter can be stored as just an array of binary values. To make the code clearer, we wrap the Bloom filter in a simple composite data structure containing the parameters, such as the size and the number of hash functions:

```
BloomFilter {
    Integer: size
    Integer: k
    Array of bits: bins
    Array of hash functions: h
}
```

Given this wrapper, the code for both the insertion and lookup functions can be implemented with a single WHILE loop:

```
BloomFilterInsertKey(BloomFilter: filter, Type: key):
    Integer: i = 0
```

```
        WHILE i < filter.k:
            Integer: index = filter.h[i](key)
            filter.bins[index] = 1
            i = i + 1

BloomFilterLookup(BloomFilter: filter, Type: key):
    Integer: i = 0
    WHILE i < filter.k:
        Integer: index = filter.h[i](key)
        IF filter.bins[index] == 0:
            return False
        i = i + 1
    return True
```

In this code, filter.h[i](key) denotes the Bloom filter's ith hash function
applied to key. Both functions use a loop to iterate over the *k* hash functions,
computing key's hash value and accessing the corresponding bin in the Bloom
filter's array. In the case of insertion, the code sets the value of the bin to 1. In
the case of lookup, the code checks whether the bin contains a 0 and returns
False if so.

In the worst case, the functions cost scales linearly with *k* as we need
to iterate over each hash function for each operation. The structure of
lookup provides an additional potential advantage. The lookup can terminate immediately after finding the first 0, skipping any further hash
functions. Importantly, the runtime of both insertion and lookup is independent of both the size of the Bloom filter (number of bins) and the number of items inserted.

Tuning Bloom Filter Parameters

There are multiple parameters that impact the Bloom filter's false positive
rate, including the size of the array and the number of hash functions used.
By tuning these parameters to the problem at hand, we can often keep the
false positive rate very low while minimizing the amount of memory used.
We can do this empirically with real data, through simulation, or with a
variety of mathematical approximations of the false positive rate.

One common and simple approximation is:

$$FalsePositiveRate = (1 - (1 - 1/m)^{nk})^k$$

where *n* is the number of items inserted into the Bloom filter, *m* is the size
of the array, and *k* is the number of hash functions used. This approximation uses simplified assumptions, but it gives a good view into how the various parameters interact:

- Increasing the size of the array (*m*) always decreases the false positive
  rate, because there are more bins to store information.

- Increasing the number of items inserted (*n*) always increases the false
  positive rate, because we set more of those bins to 1.

- Increasing the number of hash functions (k) can increase or decrease the false positive rate depending on the other parameters. If we use too many hash functions, we are going to fill up large quantities of the array with each insertion. If we use too few, a small number of collisions could produce a false positive.

Table 13-1 provides insight into how the Bloom filter sizes (m) and number of hash functions (k) impact the false positive rate for a fixed number of items inserted ($n = 100$).

Table 13-1: Example False Positive Rates for Different Parameterizations (m, k) with $n = 100$

m	$k = 1$	$k = 3$	$k = 5$
200	0.3942	0.4704	0.6535
400	0.2214	0.1473	0.1855
600	0.1536	0.0610	0.0579
800	0.1176	0.0306	0.0217
1000	0.0952	0.0174	0.0094

Ultimately the optimal parameter setting will depend on the specific problem. We need to choose a tradeoff among false positive rate, computational cost, and memory cost that best suits our application.

Bloom Filters vs. Hash Tables

At this point, the skeptical reader may again fling their hands in the air in protest: "Why not just use a hash table? Whenever a key occurs, we can add it along with some trivial data, such as a Boolean value of True, to the hash table. Then we can search this table for exact match keys. Sure, we might have to do some chaining due to collisions, but we'd get exact answers. Why do you always make things so complicated?"

It's a fair point. Hash tables do allow us to answer the same question that Bloom filters answer, and more exactly. But, as our skeptical reader noted, they do so at the cost of additional space and potentially runtime. In order for a hash table to fully resolve collisions, we need to store enough information to deterministically say that we have seen this exact key before, and that means storing the key itself. Add to that the overhead of pointers in a chained hash table, as shown in Figure 13-8, and we could be using significantly more memory.

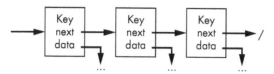

Figure 13-8: A hash table with chaining requires memory for each key and at least one pointer.

In contrast, the Bloom filter doesn't bother storing the keys or pointers to subsequent nodes. It only keeps around a single binary value for each bucket. We can store m bins using exactly m bits. This extreme space efficiency proves valuable for multiple reasons. First, it allows us to vastly increase the number of bins (the size of our filter) while keeping the memory manageable. We can store 32 individual bins for the price of a single 32-bit integer.

Second, and more importantly for computationally sensitive applications, it often allows us to keep the Bloom filter in memory, or even in the memory's cache, for fast access. Consider the tradeoffs we explored in the previous chapter of structuring B-tree nodes to reduce the number of retrievals from slower memory. Bloom filters work to maximize the amount of the data structure that directly helps with filtering with the goal of keeping the whole data structure in very fast memory.

Why This Matters

Bloom filters can be powerful tools when we need to hyper-optimize the tradeoff between memory usage and accuracy. They combine the mathematical mappings introduced in Chapter 10 with the focus on fitting data into a compact form that can be stored in local memory that we saw in Chapter 12. Like caches, they provide an intermediate step to an expensive lookup that can help reduce the cost on average.

More important, however, is that Bloom filters provide a glimpse into a new type of data structure—one that can occasionally return a false positive. The accuracy of a lookup operation is not guaranteed but rather probabilistically depends on the data. If we're lucky, we could insert a large number of elements before seeing any false positives. If we're not, though, we could see collisions early on. This type of data structure provides a different approach to thinking about how we organize data and the relevant tradeoffs. If we are willing to accept some (hopefully small) number of errors, how far can we push the efficiency?

In the next chapter, we consider a data structure that relies on a different type of randomness. Instead of providing a probabilistically correct answer, skip lists use randomness to avoid bad worst-case behavior and provide efficient operations on average.

14

SKIP LISTS

This chapter introduces the *skip list*, a sorted linked list with multiple pointers that allow us to occasionally jump forward to an element further ahead in the list during operations like search, insertion, or deletion. This potential to jump mitigates one of the major concerns with linked lists—that we have to scan through all the elements to find a single target. Skipping some elements saves precious time.

To envision how skip lists work, consider the strategy I employ every time I lose my place in a book. Determined to avoid spoilers, I do not use binary search, which may jump to parts of the text I haven't read yet. Instead, I start at the beginning of the book and skip forward multiple pages at a time—in sections large enough that I'm not scanning every page, but small enough that, if I overshoot, it won't ruin the story. I use larger jumps in the beginning of my search but shift to smaller and smaller jumps as I near where I left off. Skip lists use a similar approach to dramatically change the behavior of the linked list, enabling it to take on problems that we'd previously reserved for tree-based data structures.

Skip lists, proposed by computer scientist William Pugh, are probabilistic data structures that make operations such as insertion, deletion, and searching significantly more efficient in the *average* case. Instead of storing a single linked list, skip lists effectively create a layer of linked lists, each with only a subset of the nodes at the layer below. This means we start our search at higher levels of the skip list, where there are fewer nodes, and take large steps across the list to *skip* unnecessary nodes. As we get closer to our target and refine our search, we drop down in the multilevel hierarchy. In the case of searching for our place in a book, this corresponds to using smaller and smaller jumps as we near our most recent location.

I've included skip lists in this book for two reasons. First, in keeping with almost every other data structure presented here, they demonstrate how additional information or structure can provide significant algorithmic advantages. In this case, multiple levels of links decrease the cost of a search. Second, and perhaps more exciting, skip lists are randomized data structures. Unlike Bloom filters, which are deterministic given the data, skip lists push the use of randomness a step further: their very structure is probabilistically determined in order to balance out performance in the average case. We use a random number generator to choose the level of each node and thus how far ahead it will let us skip.

Randomized vs. Deterministic Structures

The change from a deterministically generated data structure to a randomized one introduces both complexities and benefits. The structure of every data structure we have examined so far is fully determined by the data we insert. For example, if we insert the same data in the same order into a binary search tree, we always get the same structure. The same applies for heaps, tries, grids, quadtrees, and so forth. Even two hash tables or Bloom filters will be identical if we use the same hash functions and insert the same set of items.

This determinism can lead to problems in the face of worst-case data. As we saw in Chapter 5, if we start with an empty binary search tree and insert elements in sorted order, our tree effectively becomes a sorted linked list. Each node will have a single child node in the same direction. One potential way to mitigate this problem is to insert the data in random order. While we still might happen to choose a bad ordering, the probability is significantly lower.

We can extend this randomized approach to constructing the data structures themselves by randomly choosing parameters during each insertion. Instead of varying the order of the data, we are varying how we link that data into our structure.

At first, the randomized approach can seem unintuitive. If we don't know our input distribution, we may easily end up making bad structural choices for that distribution. We might worry that we will always choose the worst-case parameter. However, if we use a good randomization strategy, this level of failure will be exceedingly rare. On the other hand, the randomized design prevents us from making consistently suboptimal choices.

While it might not lead to an optimal solution, it will often produce a reasonable one. The randomness can provide good average case performance. The randomness also helps smooth out cases where the data arrives in a pathologically bad ordering.

Introducing Skip Lists

As we saw in Chapter 3, certain operations on linked lists are inherently limited by the list's structure. We can't efficiently search a linked list because we can't randomly access elements. This has tragic consequences; even when we know the nodes are sorted, we can't use binary search. We're forced to crawl along the pointers from one node to another until we reach the target node. This frustrating limitation has caused many new computer scientists to tear out their hair, muttering unkind things.

Skip lists help alleviate this inefficiency by providing the ability to jump ahead multiple entries. At its heart, a skip list is simply a sorted linked list with multi-height nodes:

```
SkipList {
    Integer: top_level
    Integer: max_level
    SkipListNode: front
}
```

The field top_level represents the highest level currently in use, while the field max_level represents the highest allowable level. For simplicity, we specify max_level independently so we can preallocate an array of pointers at the start of our list.

Skip lists' complexity, and thus their power, arises from the pointer structure within the nodes. Instead of storing a single pointer to the next node in the list, each node has a predefined level, or *height*, in which it stores pointers to the next node. Nodes of level L maintain $L + 1$ different forward pointers, one for each level $[0, L]$. Critically, the pointer at level L links the current node to the next node *at the same height*, meaning that the pointers in next will often point to different skip list nodes.

```
SkipListNode {
    Type: key
    Type: value
    Integer: height
    Array of SkipListNodes: next
}
```

Since the higher levels of a skip list contain fewer nodes than the layers below them, nodes at these higher levels can link further than would have been possible at the lower layers. This allows algorithms to take larger steps at the higher layers and skip many intervening nodes. As the levels progress higher and higher, the number of nodes decreases, and these linkings jump further and further ahead.

Imagine the process of searching a skip list in terms of passing messages between buildings by signaling with flashlights. How far you can pass a message depends on what floor you are on and the heights of the buildings in your path. If you are stuck on the first floor, you can only pass messages to the adjacent building. Any building beyond that is blocked by the adjacent building itself. However, if you are lucky enough to be in a tall building, you can pass messages over the heads of closer, but shorter, buildings, as shown in Figure 14-1. Alternatively, if you need to send a message to your immediate neighbor, you can simply move down to the lowest floor.

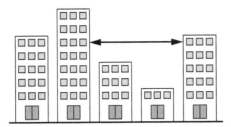

Figure 14-1: Moving between nodes in a skip list is like passing messages by flashlight between buildings in a city.

Skip lists create these linkings probabilistically. The program gives each node a random height, independent of the key stored in the node, and inserts the new node into its corresponding list for each level. Thus, a node with height 0 will only appear in the bottommost list, while a node with height 2 will appear in the lists for levels 0, 1, and 2. Figure 14-2 shows an example of this. In the message-passing example above, this would be equivalent to a building with only a single floor compared to a building with three floors. The building with three floors is able to pass messages at three different heights, potentially accessing up to three neighbors.

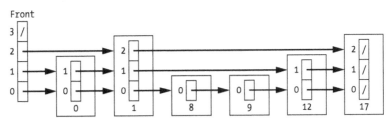

Figure 14-2: An example skip list

Since higher nodes provide the ability to skip further ahead, over the tops of the lower nodes, we ideally want to use them sparsely and sprinkle them throughout the list. In the message-passing example, we do not want our cityscape to include only buildings of the same height. We want a lot of single-story buildings with some medium buildings and a few taller buildings that allow us to jump our messages down the street. By choosing heights with the correct probability distribution, we can, on average, balance out the density at each level. Nodes of level $L + 1$ are less numerous than nodes at level L. This leads to good average case performance and can help avoid the worst-case scenarios that can occur in other data structures.

As shown in Figure 14-2, this skip list implementation uses a dummy node front to store the pointers at the front of each level. The node front is a SkipListNode but contains no key or value. Tracking the front of the list in a SkipListNode makes the code for insertion and deletion significantly simpler, as we'll see later in the chapter.

Searching Skip Lists

To search a skip list, we start at the front of the top-most level and iterate through the list nodes. Speaking more informally based on the illustration in Figure 14-2, we start at the top left corner and proceed downward and to the right. At each iteration, we check whether there is another node along this level and, if so, whether its key is less than our target. If both those conditions are met, we move along to the next node at that level. If either of these conditions is false (we have hit the end of the level or found a node whose key is larger than or equal to our target), we drop down a level and continue our search from there. Our search terminates when we try to drop below the bottom level.

```
SkipListSearch(SkipList: list, Type: target):
    Integer: level = list.top_level
❶ SkipListNode: current = list.front

❷ WHILE level >= 0:
        WHILE (current.next[level] != null AND
                current.next[level].key < target):
            current = current.next[level]
        level = level - 1

❸ SkipListNode: result = current.next[0]
❹ IF result != null AND result.key == target:
        return result.value
    ELSE:
        return null
```

The code for a skip list search starts with the current node at the front of the topmost list ❶. Two nested WHILE loops handle the traversal. The inner loop iterates through the current linked list until it hits the end of the list (current.next[level] == null) or a node with a key larger than or equal to target (current.next[level].key >= target). The outer loop drops down a single level each iteration until we hit the bottom of the list ❷. If the target is in the list, it will be at the next node in the list ❸. However, we must check that that node both exists and has the correct key ❹. When the search loop terminates, we are guaranteed to be at the last node in the list with a key *less* than the target. The target is either the next node in the list or does not exist.

Consider searching for a target of 14 in the list shown in Figure 14-3. We start at the front of level 3. The first node at this level has a key of 13, which is less than our target, so we progress to that node. At this point we've reached the end of the list for level 3. We can't progress any further at this height. The next node pointer is null.

The search then drops down a level and continues on level 2. Here we find the next key in the list (14) is *not* less than our target, so we drop down to level 1. The same condition holds true on level 1 and level 0—the next key in the list is not less than our target. Our search terminates once we have completed level 0. At this point, our current node's (key = 13) next pointer leads to the target node.

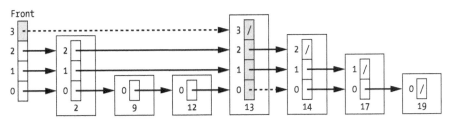

Figure 14-3: Searching a skip list for the target of 14. The shaded entries and dashed pointers represent the ones traversed during the search.

Note that although we pointed to the target node for several iterations (at levels 2, 1, and 0), we continued the search until we passed the bottom level. This is due to our termination criteria in the code. We could add additional logic to halt the search earlier, but we keep the logic simpler here to match the logic used later for insertion.

In contrast, if we were searching the same list for a target of 12, as shown in Figure 14-4, we'd drop down to the bottom level significantly earlier in our search and progress along the bottom level.

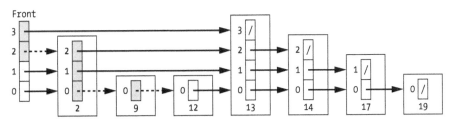

Figure 14-4: Searching a skip list for the target of 12. The shaded entries and dashed pointers represent the ones traversed during the search.

We can picture this traversal as a squirrel's navigation along a row of trees. Enjoying the views from higher branches, the squirrel jumps from tree to tree until there are no more trees of that height before its destination. Whenever possible it jumps between tall, old oak trees and sails over the shorter saplings in between. Since the taller trees are rarer, and thus further apart, the squirrel also covers more distance per jump. Moving from the wide branches of a tall tree to those of its tall neighbor requires fewer jumps than traversing all the small saplings in between.

However, the squirrel is unwilling to waste time backtracking and thus never overshoots its destination. Eventually the squirrel reaches a point where it will pass its destination if it jumps to the next tree at this level. Or perhaps there are no more trees of this height. Either way, the squirrel sighs and reluctantly descends to the lower level of branches before continuing forward. It progresses at the next level, taking jumps as large as possible and enjoying the scenic route, until it again hits a point where it needs to descend.

Adding Nodes

The distribution we use to select the height of a new node can have a significant impact on the structure and performance of the skip list. If everything is the same level, whether minimum or maximum, our skip list devolves into nothing more than a sorted linked list with additional memory overhead. Worse, if we set all the heights to the maximum, we create multiple parallel lists without adding any search efficiencies. Ideally, we'd like fewer tall nodes with increasing numbers at each level below.

William Pugh's original approach to selecting heights is to continually use a constant probability p of adding another level. All nodes start at level 0. We keep flipping a weighted coin—choosing a random number from 0 to 1 and checking if it is less than p—until we either get a number greater than p or hit the maximum allowable height. We count the number of flips less than p and set that as our new level. For example, we could use $p = 0.5$, in which case we'd expect approximately half the nodes at level L to be promoted to level $L + 1$. We can use the value of p to balance search efficiency with memory usage. A smaller value of p will mean fewer tall nodes and thus fewer pointers per node. We cap a node's height at max_level to stay consistent with the preallocated array in the front node.

You can visualize this approach in terms of an inconsistent parent responding to a child's request for more candy. When the child gets candy, they always gets a single piece, and then they always want more. Every time the child asks for candy, the parent randomly (with probability p) decides whether to grant the request. If so, they give the child another piece. This corresponds to increasing the height of the node by one. Naturally the child, seeing their victory, asks again immediately. The process continues until the parent finally gets annoyed, with probability $(1 - p)$, and shouts a definitive "No more candy!" Similarly, we continue to increase the height of the node until either our random number generator or our max threshold tells us to stop altogether.

Adding nodes to a skip list follows the same flow as searching for a target node: we progress downward and to the right, looking for a place to insert the new node. In fact, we can reuse the basic structure of the search for our insertion. We just need to track one additional piece of data: the last node at each level that could point to our new node.

```
SkipListInsert(SkipList: list, Type: key, Type: value):
    Integer: level = list.top_level
❶ SkipListNode: current = list.front
❷ Array: last = a size list.max_level + 1 array of SkipListNode pointers
                initially set to list.front for all levels.

❸ WHILE level >= 0:
    ❹ WHILE (current.next[level] != null AND
            current.next[level].key < key):
        current = current.next[level]
    ❺ last[level] = current
      level = level - 1

    SkipListNode: result = current.next[0]
❻ IF result != null AND result.key == key:
      result.value = value
      return

❼ Integer: new_level = pick a random level
❽ IF new_level > list.top_level:
      list.top_level = new_level
    SkipListNode: new_node = SkipListNode(key, value, new_level)

    Integer: j = 0
❾ WHILE j <= new_level:
        new_node.next[j] = last[j].next[j]
        last[j].next[j] = new_node
        j = j + 1
```

We begin at the top left corner of the list (list.top_level of list.front) ❶.
With a pair of nested WHILE loops, we progress downward and to the right as
we search for the correct place to insert the node. The outer WHILE loop ❸
iterates through the list's levels, saving the last node seen at each level and
then dropping down to the next level. The inner WHILE loop ❹ traverses the
skip list, moving forward whenever another node along this level has a key
less than our target.

Every entry in the array last starts off at list.front, indicating that the
node is inserted in the front of the list ❷. We update last for each level each
time we drop down from that level ❺, because we have seen that the key of
the next node at this level is greater than or equal to the key to be inserted
(or the next node is null) and therefore we will need to insert before that
node. If we happen to find a matching key while traversing the skip list, we
simply update the data for that key ❻. This means that, like our other data
structures, our skip list implementation treats each key as unique.

When we find the correct point to insert the new node, we pick a random level for this node ❼. As we discussed previously, the probability distribution we use to select this height will have a significant impact on the
structure and performance of the skip list. Since we cap the new level to
be less than list.max_level, we avoid an invalid access to the last array. We
check whether the selected level represents a new top level for the list and,
if so, update list.top_level ❽.

Finally, the code inserts the new element by using a WHILE loop to update the pointers from the new node to point to the correct following node ❾. Then it updates each of the nodes listed in last to point to our new node. Here we can see the benefit of using the dummy node front (with the maximum height) to store the pointers to the beginning of the list. We can track and update this "front of list" position as we would any other node. This greatly simplifies the code.

Figure 14-5 shows how we would insert the key of 10 into an example skip list. The shaded nodes indicate which entries we traverse during the search.

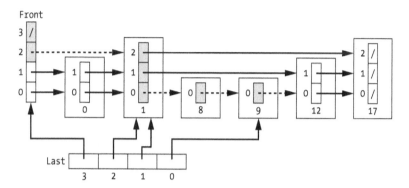

Figure 14-5: Inserting the key of 10 into a skip list. The array last tracks which node comes before the inserted node.

By tracking the last node at each level *before* the target, we are effectively tracking which node needs to point to the new node. As we traverse the list, we are noting down the locations where we will need to insert new links. At each level, we reach a point where the next key is larger than or equal to our new key, and we can exclaim, "I see where we need to insert the new node. It's right after this one!" We then descend a level to continue our work. By the time the search phase reaches the bottom layer, we already have a full list of all the nodes whose forward pointers we need to adjust.

Deleting Nodes

Deleting nodes from a skip list follows almost the same algorithm as inserting nodes. We first search the skip list for the deletion target while tracking the last node at each level that comes *before* the target node. Once the search phase completes, we update this list of previous nodes to remove the node we are deleting.

```
SkipListDelete(SkipList: list, Type: target):
    Integer: level = list.top_level
  ❶ SkipListNode: current = list.front
    Array: last = a size list.max_level + 1 array of SkipListNode pointers
                  initially set to list.front for all levels.

  ❷ WHILE level >= 0:
        WHILE (current.next[level] != null AND
```

```
                            current.next[level].key < target):
                        current = current.next[level]
                last[level] = current
                level = level - 1

    ❸ SkipListNode: result = current.next[0]
      IF result == null OR result.key != target:
          return

      level = result.height
      Integer: j = 0
    ❹ WHILE j <= level:
            last[j].next[j] = result.next[j]
            result.next[j] = null
            j = j + 1

    ❺ IF level == list.top_level:
          Integer: top = list.top_level
          WHILE top > 0 AND list.front.next[top] == null:
                top = top - 1
          list.top_level = top
```

The initial block of deletion code is identical to the code for insertion. We start at the top left of the list ❶. A pair of nested WHILE loops ❷ searches across each level until we hit a node with a key greater than or equal to target or the end of the list (null). At this point, we record the last node visited and drop down to the next level to continue our search. At the end of the search, we check that we've found a node whose key matches target ❸. Otherwise, there is no match in the skip list and thus nothing to delete.

To remove the identified node, we use a WHILE loop ❹ to simply link the next pointers for each node in the skip list's last to point past the current node: last[j].next[j] = result.next[j] for all levels j. This splices our node out of the list. We also set result.next[j] to null because result is no longer in the list.

Finally, we need to check whether the skip list's top level is still valid ❺. If we deleted the sole node with height of top_level, then top_level should be decreased to reflect the current maximum height. We can update top_level by proceeding down the front node and checking the next pointers until we find one that is not null. The last block of code in our deletion function updates the list's top level if needed. It finds the first level where our dummy front node points to a valid data node. If the list is empty, we simply default to a top level of zero.

Again, we can visualize the initial search required for deletion in terms of how we are viewing the next node and maintaining the list of nodes to update. At each level, we identify the node to delete (if it exists) while still at the node immediately preceding it at that level. The next node's key is greater or equal to the key we need to delete. We pause: "I'd better mark down this current node, because I will need to change its pointers to skip the deleted node." We record the pointer to the current node in last and proceed to the next level. At the end of our journey, we have collected a full list of the nodes whose pointers need to be updated.

Runtimes

The cost of search, insertion, and deletion operations will all depend on the nodes' locations and distributions of heights. In an ideal case, the nodes at level L would include every other node from level $L - 1$. We drop half the nodes at each level and space them evenly apart. In this case, the behavior of a skip list mirrors that of binary search. We can prune half the search space by looking at the single node in the top layer. We then drop down a layer and cut the space in half again. Thus, in the best case, our performance will be logarithmic in terms of the number of entries.

The worst-case performance of a skip list is equivalent to that of a standard linked list—it is linearly proportional to the number of nodes. If every node in the list is the same height, our skip list is nothing more than a sorted linked list. We're forced to scan through each node in sequence to find a given target.

Assuming that we use a good probability distribution of heights, such as that provided by the previously described Pugh's original technique (with $p = 0.5$), the *expected* costs of insertions, deletions, and searches all scale logarithmically with the number of entries. Unlike worst-case cost, expected cost provides an estimate of how the data structure will perform on average. This puts the average performance of skip lists on par with binary search trees.

Why This Matters

Skip lists are intended to be a simpler alternative to balanced search trees, as yet another dynamic data structure that enables efficient search. However, unlike the other algorithms we've applied to this task, including sorted arrays and binary search trees, skip lists rely on randomized structure to provide good performance. The *expected* computational cost of our common operations—search, insertion, and deletion—is logarithmic in the size of the list.

This naturally poses a question: why should we trust the performance of our algorithm to randomized behavior? We could easily run into cases where the tall nodes are clustered, or the distribution of heights is too flat. Yet the same is true of binary search trees. If we insert and remove nodes in a suboptimal order, we can end up with a linked list of tree nodes. Where more sophisticated extensions of binary search trees can be employed to avoid this worst-case behavior, skip lists rely on randomization to avoid terrible behavior. In exchange, they use much simpler code. Thus, skip lists demonstrate how randomization can provide both a robust defense against bad data and simplicity in a data structure's implementation.

15

GRAPHS

Graphs are one of the fundamental data structures in computer science. They arise throughout numerous problems and programming tasks. Unlike the other data structures in this book, designed to optimize certain computations, the structure of *graphs* arises naturally from the data itself. In other words, graphs mirror the data they represent. Examining graph algorithms gives us insight into how we can define algorithms to utilize the inherent structure of the data.

Previous chapters focused on the problem of structuring the data to aid the algorithms; high-level problems, such as searching for a value, motivated and drove the design of the facilitating data structures. This chapter covers the opposite problem: graphs show us how the structure of the data can drive the development of new algorithms. In other words, given data in the form of a graph, we examine how to create algorithms that will use it. This chapter examines three graph algorithms that use different aspects of the graph's structure: Dijkstra's algorithm for shortest paths, Prim's algorithm for minimum-cost spanning trees, and Kahn's algorithm for topological sort.

Introducing Graphs

Graphs are composed of a set of *nodes* and a set of *edges*. As shown in Figure 15-1, each edge connects a pair of nodes. This structure is similar to a large number of real-world systems, including social networks (nodes are people and edges are their connections), transportation networks (nodes are cities and edges represent paths), and computer networks (nodes are computers and edges represent the connections between them). This variety of real-world analogs makes graph algorithms fun to visualize, as simple searches transform into careful exploration of castles or frantic sprints through a city's crowded alleys.

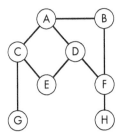

Figure 15-1: A graph with
undirected edges

A graph's edges can have additional properties to capture the real-world complexities of the data such as whether or not the edges are directional. *Undirected edges*, like those in the graph in Figure 15-1, represent two-way relationships such as most roads and happy friendships. *Directed edges*, as illustrated in Figure 15-2, are like one-way streets and indicate a flow in a single direction. To represent undirected access, we use a pair of directed edges—one in each direction—between nodes. In a social context, directed edges could represent romantic interest in a television teen drama: an edge from Alice to Bob indicates Alice likes Bob, while the lack of an edge from Bob to Alice illustrates the devastating lack of reciprocity.

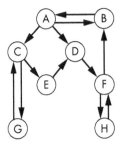

Figure 15-2: A graph with
directed edges

In addition to allowing us to model one-way streets or unrequited love, directed edges allow us to model more abstract problems, such as task dependence. We can specify a set of tasks as nodes and use directed edges to indicate the order dependency between tasks. In this way, we could create a graph to represent the tasks required for brewing the perfect cup of coffee, as shown in Figure 15-3. Nodes include such steps as heating the water, measuring out the beans, grinding the beans, and adding water to the grounds. The edges represent dependencies between these steps. We need to add a directed edge from the node for "grinding beans" to the node for "putting the grounds in the filter" to indicate that we must grind the beans first. The order of these two steps is critical, as anyone who has tried brewing unground beans can attest. However, we wouldn't need an edge between "heating the water" and "grinding the beans" in either direction. We can perform those tasks in parallel.

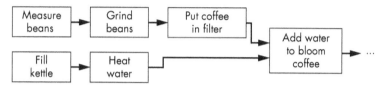

Figure 15-3: Using a graph to represent the order of operations for a task

Edge weights further increase the modeling power of graphs. *Weighted edges* capture not only the link between nodes but also the cost of that link. For example, we could weight the edges in a transportation graph by the distance between locations. We could augment our social network with a measure of closeness, such as a count of how many times two nodes have spoken in the last month. Figure 15-4 shows our example graph with weighted edges.

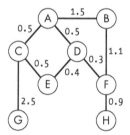

Figure 15-4: A graph with
weighted edges

Using a combination of weighted and directed edges allows us to capture complex interrelations among the nodes. Entire social dramas can be represented and played out through the nodes and edges of a well-constructed graph.

Representing Graphs

While the abstract structure of a graph is relatively simple, there are multiple ways to represent nodes and edges in the computer's memory. Two of the most common representations are *adjacency matrices* and *adjacency lists*. Both representations can handle directed, undirected, weighted, and unweighted edges. As with all the other data structures in this book, the difference between these structures lies in how the data is stored in memory and thus how different algorithms can access it.

The adjacency list formulation stores a separate list of neighbors for each node. We could use an array or linked list of neighbors within the node composite data structure:

```
Node {
    String: name
    Array of Nodes: neighbors
}
```

Or we could even create a separate edge data structure to store auxiliary information about the edges, such as their directionality or weights. For the examples below, we also provide a single numerical ID for each of the nodes, corresponding to the node's index in the parent graph data structure:

```
Edge {
    Integer: to_node
    Integer: from_node
    Float: weight
}

Node {
    String: name
    Integer: id
    Array of Edges: edges
}
```

In either case, the graph itself would contain an array of nodes:

```
Graph {
    Integer: num_nodes
    Array of Nodes: nodes
}
```

Regardless of the exact implementation, we can access the neighbors of any given node through a list linked from the node itself. Figure 15-5 shows an example of this structure.

In the case of directed edges, a node's list of edges or neighboring nodes contains only those that can be accessed when *leaving* the node. For example, node A may contain an edge to node B while B does not contain an edge to A.

Adjacency lists provide a localized view of neighbor relationships that mirrors real-world cases such as social networks. Each node tracks only the node to which it has connections. Similarly, in a social network, each person determines who qualifies as their friend, thus maintaining a list of their own connections. We don't need a separate central repository to tell us who our friends are, and we might not have a full view into anyone else's friends.

Arguably, we might not even know which of our friends (outgoing edge) actually consider us a friend in return (incoming edge). We know only about our own outgoing connections.

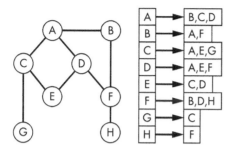

Figure 15-5: A graph (left) and its adjacency list representation (right). Each node stores a list of neighboring nodes.

In contrast, an adjacency matrix represents a graph as a matrix, as shown in Figure 15-6, with one row and one column for each node. The value in row i, column j represents the weight of the edge from node i to node j. A value of zero indicates that no such edge exists. This representation allows us to directly look up whether an edge exists between any two nodes from a single central data source.

	A	B	C	D	E	F	G	H
A	0	1	1	1	0	0	0	0
B	1	0	0	0	0	1	0	0
C	1	0	0	0	1	0	1	0
D	1	0	0	0	1	1	0	0
E	0	0	1	1	0	0	0	0
F	0	1	0	1	0	0	0	1
G	0	0	1	0	0	0	0	0
H	0	0	0	0	0	1	0	0

Figure 15-6: The adjacency matrix representation of a graph

This global view of the graph arises in real-world situations where a single planner is viewing the entire network. For instance, an airline company may use a global view of flight routes, where nodes are airports and edges indicate flights between them, to plan new service.

While the adjacency graph representation is useful in some cases, we will focus on the adjacency list representation for the remainder of this chapter. The list representation fits naturally with the pointer-based approach we've been using for other data structures. Further, the use of individual node data structures allows additional flexibility in terms of storing auxiliary data.

Searching Graphs

If we look back to our web-crawling example from Chapter 4, where we explored our favorite online encyclopedia for information related to coffee grinders, we can immediately see how the links in our favorite online encyclopedia form a graph of topics, with each page representing a node and each hyperlink representing a directed edge. We can progressively explore topics, diving deeper and deeper into the world of coffee grinders, by iteratively exploring each node and adding new nodes onto our list of topics to explore in the future. This type of exploration forms the basis of a graph search.

Imagine that we are interested in finding a specific node in the graph. Perhaps we are conducting online research and looking for a coffee brand whose name we have long forgotten. We explore the relevant web pages (graph nodes) one at a time, reading the information on one page before moving to another. As we saw in Chapter 4, the order in which we explore the nodes greatly influences our search pattern. By using a stack data structure to track our future exploration options, we conduct a depth-first search over the graph. We pursue individual paths deeper and deeper until we hit a dead end. Then we backtrack and try other options we skipped along the way. If we instead use a queue to track our future search states, we perform a breadth-first search over the nodes. We check the nodes closer to our starting location before venturing further and further into the graph. Of course, there are a variety of other ways we could order our search. For example, best-first search orders the future nodes according to a ranking function, focusing on exploring high-scoring nodes first. In our search for nearby coffee shops in a new city, this prioritization of nodes can keep us from wasting hours wandering through residential neighborhoods instead of focusing on commercial areas.

Regardless of the order, the concept of searching a graph by exploring one node at a time illustrates the impact of the data's structure on the algorithm. We use the links between nodes (edges) to constrain and guide the exploration. In the next few sections, we look at common useful algorithms that do exactly this.

Finding Shortest Paths with Dijkstra's Algorithm

Probably the single most common task when dealing with real-world graphs is to find the shortest distance between two nodes. Imagine we're visiting a new city for the first time. As morning dawns, we stumble out of our hotel room, jetlagged and in search of refreshment. As good travelers, we've done copious research on the city's coffee scene and created a list of four coffee shops to sample while in town. As the elevator reaches the lobby, we pull out a street map of the city, carefully marked with the location of the hotel and those coffee shops. It's time to determine how to get to the shops on our list.

Dijkstra's algorithm, invented by the computer scientist Edsger W. Dijkstra, finds the shortest path from any given starting node to all other nodes in the graph. It can work on directed, undirected, weighted, or unweighted graphs. The only constraint is that all the edge weights must be non-negative. You can never decrease the total path length by adding an edge. In our coffee-themed sightseeing example, we search for the shortest path from the hotel to each of the coffee shops. As shown in Figure 15-7, nodes represent either street intersections or shops along the street. Weighted, undirected edges represent the distance along the roads between these points.

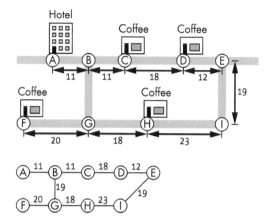

Figure 15-7: Points along a map with corresponding distances (top) can be represented as a weighted graph (bottom).

Our goal is to find the shortest path from the starting node to each of the coffee shop nodes. The intersection nodes aren't goals in their own right but allow our path to branch over different streets.

Dijkstra's algorithm operates by maintaining a set of unvisited nodes and continually updating the *tentative* distance to each unvisited node. At each iteration, we visit the closest unvisited node. Upon doing so, we remove this new node from our unvisited set and update the distances to each of its unvisited neighbors. Specifically, we examine the new node's neighbors and ask whether we have found a better path to each neighbor. We compute the length of the new proposed path by taking the distance to the current node and adding the distance (edge weight) to the neighbor. If this new distance is less than the best distance seen so far, we update the distance.

```
Dijkstras(Graph: G, Integer: from_node_index):
  ❶ Array: distance = inf for each node id in G
    Array: last = -1 for each node in G
    Set: unvisited = set of all node indices in G
    distance[from_node_index] = 0.0

  ❷ WHILE unvisited is NOT empty:
      ❸ Integer: next_index = the node index in unvisited
                              with the minimal distance
        Node: current = G.nodes[next_index]
        Remove next_index from unvisited

      ❹ FOR EACH edge IN current.edges:
          ❺ Float: new_dist = distance[edge.from_node] +
                              edge.weight
          ❻ IF new_dist < distance[edge.to_node]:
                distance[edge.to_node] = new_dist
                last[edge.to_node] = edge.from_node
```

The code starts by creating a series of helper data structures ❶, including an array of distances to each node (distance), an array indicating the last node visited before a given node (last), and a set of unvisited nodes (unvisited). The code then processes the unvisited nodes one by one. A WHILE loop iterates until the set of unvisited nodes is empty ❷. In each iteration, the code chooses the node with the minimal distance and removes it from the unvisited set ❸. A FOR loop iterates over each of the node's neighbors ❹, computing the distance to that neighbor through the current node ❺ and updating the distance and last arrays if the code has found a better path ❻.

NOTE *While both the pseudocode and illustrations use an explicit distance array and unvisited set for the sake of illustration, these can be combined into min-heap for efficiency. The min-heap functions as a priority queue that always returns the lowest-priority item. In this case, it stores the list of unvisited nodes, keyed by their current distance. Finding the closest node consists of returning the minimum key in the queue, and updating the best distance so far corresponds to updating a node's priority.*

Figure 15-8 shows an example shortest-path search from node A in Figure 15-4's weighted graph. The circled node is the one currently being examined. The grayed-out nodes and list entries represent nodes that have been removed from the unvisited list and thus are no longer available for consideration.

For the search in Figure 15-8, we start Dijkstra's algorithm with all distances at infinity except for node A, which is set to zero (Figure 15-8(1)). This starting configuration corresponds to our initial knowledge about the best paths. We are already at node A, so the best path there is trivial. Since we have not found paths to any of the other nodes, they could be any distance away. We also maintain information for each node of which node precedes it in our search. The last column indicates the preceding node. This information allows us to trace paths backward. While not all uses will need to reconstruct the path, our coffee search certainly does. It is pointless to find the shortest distance to coffee if we don't also find the actual path. To construct the path to node F, we follow the last pointers back until we reach node A.

Our search starts, as shown in Figure 15-8(2), by selecting the node with the smallest distance (node A), removing it from the unvisited list, and examining its neighbors. For each of A's neighbors, we test whether traveling to that neighbor through A is shorter than any path seen so far. Since the distance to Node A is zero, the distance through A to each of its neighbors will be equal to the corresponding edge weights. Each time we update the distance to an unvisited node, we also update the back pointer to reflect the best path so far. Three nodes now point to A (Figure 15-8(2)).

The search progresses, choosing the next closest, unvisited node. In this case, it could be either C or D. We break the tie using the node's order in our list: node C wins! Again, we consider C's neighbors and update their best distances (Figure 15-8(3)). Remember the distances represent the best total distance from our starting node. The new distances are the sum of the distance to C and the distance from C to each neighbor.

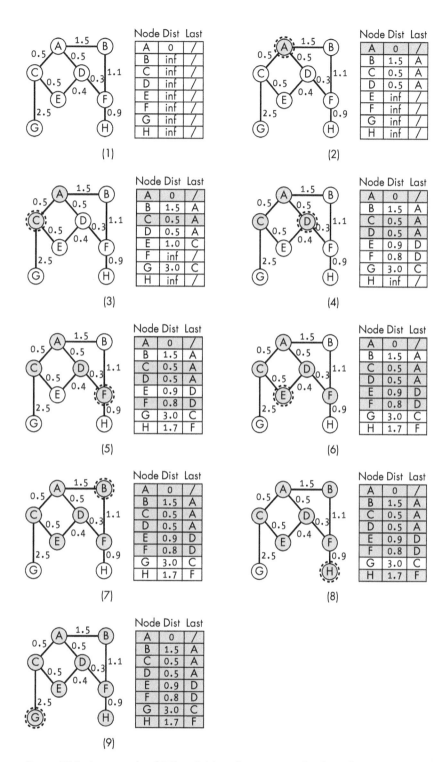

Figure 15-8: An example of Dijkstra's algorithm on a weighted graph

The search progresses to node D—the new unvisited node with the minimum distance (Figure 15-8(4)). While examining node D's neighbors, we find new shortest distances to both nodes E and F. Node E is particularly interesting, as we already had a candidate path to E through C. We can travel from A to C to E with a distance of 1.0. However, this is not the best possible path. Our search revealed a new path, through D, that is slightly shorter with a total distance of 0.9. We update both the potential distance and the backward pointer. Our best path to E now goes through D. On to the next closest node in our unvisited set, node F!

The search continues through the remaining nodes, but nothing else interesting occurs. The remaining nodes are all at the end of the shortest paths and don't offer opportunities for shorter paths. For example, when considering node E's neighbors (Figure 15-8(6)), we examine both nodes C and D. The distance to either node when traveling through E would be 1.4, longer than the paths we've already discovered. In fact, both C and D have already been visited, so we wouldn't even consider them. Similar logic applies when considering nodes B, H, and G as shown in Figure 15-8(7), 15-8(8), and 15-8(9). Since those nodes' neighbors have all been visited, we do not consider them.

In examining how Dijkstra's algorithm traverses a graph while finding the shortest path, we can see the clear interrelation between the structure of the data and the algorithm itself. Shortest-path algorithms like Dijkstra's are only necessary because of the structure of the problem. If we could effortlessly hop from any node to any other node, there would be no need to find a path along the edges. This is the real-world equivalent of teleporting from our hotel lobby to the target coffeeshop—convenient, but not allowed by the structure of the physical world. Thus, while searching for these shortest paths, we need to obey the structure of the graph itself.

Finding Minimum Spanning Trees with Prim's Algorithm

The problem of finding the *minimum spanning tree* of a graph provides another example of how the structure of graph data enables us to ask new questions and thus create new algorithms suited to answering these questions. The minimum spanning tree of an undirected graph is the smallest set of edges such that all of the nodes are connected (if possible). We can think of these trees in terms of a budget-conscious city planner, trying to determine which roads to pave. What is the absolute minimal set of roads needed in order to ensure that anyone can get from one place (node) to any other place (node) on a paved road? If the edges are weighted, such as by the distance or the cost of paving a road, we extend the concept to finding the set that minimizes the total weight: the *minimum-cost spanning tree* is the set of edges with the minimum total weight that connect all the nodes.

One method of finding the minimum spanning tree is *Prim's algorithm*, which was independently proposed by multiple people, including computer scientist R. C. Prim and mathematician Vojtěch Jarník. The algorithm operates very similarly to Dijkstra's algorithm in the previous section, working through an unvisited set and building up a minimum spanning tree one node at a time. We start with an unvisited set of all nodes and randomly choose one to visit. This visited node forms the start of our minimum spanning tree. Then, on each iteration, we find the unvisited node with the minimum edge weight when compared to *any* of the nodes that we've previously visited. We are asking, "Which node is closest to our set's periphery and thus can be added with the least cost?" We remove this new node from the unvisited set and add the corresponding edge to our minimum-cost spanning tree. We keep adding nodes and edges, one per iteration, until every node has been visited.

We can picture Prim's algorithm as a construction company hired to build bridges between islands in an archipelago. The builders start at a single island and work outward, connecting more and more islands. At each step, they choose the closest island to the ones in the currently connected set. One end of the bridge sits on an island in the connected set and one end sits on an island outside the connected set (bringing the new island into the connected set). By always starting new bridges from an island in the connected set, the builders are able to move their equipment to the starting island using the existing bridges. And by always ending bridges on islands outside the connected set, the builders increase the coverage of the connected set at every stage.

We can simplify the algorithm's code by tracking additional information. At each step, we maintain a list of the best edge (including weight) that we have encountered to each node. Every time we remove a new node from the unvisited set, we examine that node's unvisited neighbors and check whether there are better (i.e., lower-cost) edges to any of its neighbors. If there are, we update the neighbor's entry in the list with the new edge and weight.

```
Prims(Graph G):
 ❶ Array: distance = inf for each node in G
   Array: last = -1 for each node in G
   Set: unvisited = set of all node indices in G
   Set: mst_edges = empty set

 ❷ WHILE unvisited is NOT empty:
     ❸ Integer: next_id = the node index in unvisited with
                          the minimal distance
     ❹ IF last[next_id] != -1:
           Add the edge between last[next_id] and
           next_id to mst_edges
       Remove next_id from unvisited

       Node: current = G.nodes[next_id]
     ❺ FOR EACH edge IN current.edges:
           IF edge.to_node is in unvisited:
               IF edge.weight < distance[edge.to_node]:
                   distance[edge.to_node] = edge.weight
                   last[edge.to_node] = current.id
   return mst_edges
```

The code starts by creating a series of helper data structures ❶, including an array of distances to each node (distance), an array indicating the last node visited before a given node (last), a set of unvisited nodes (unvisited), and the final set of edges for the minimal spanning tree (mst_edges). As with Dijkstra's algorithm, the pseudocode (and the figures we'll discuss in a moment) use a combination of lists and sets for the sake of illustration. We can more efficiently implement the algorithm by storing the unvisited nodes in a min-heap keyed by the distance. For now, we will list all the values in order to explicitly illustrate what is happening.

The code then proceeds like Dijkstra's algorithm, processing the unvisited nodes one at a time. A WHILE loop iterates until the set of unvisited nodes is empty ❷. During each iteration, the node with the minimal distance to any of the visited nodes is chosen and removed from the unvisited set ❸. The code checks whether an incoming edge to the node exists, which is necessary because the first node visited will not have an incoming edge ❹, and adds the corresponding edges to the minimum spanning tree. After adding the new node, a FOR loop iterates over each of the node's neighbors ❺, checking whether the neighbor is unvisited and, if so, checking its distance to the current node. In this case, the distance is simply the weight of the edge. The code finishes by returning the set of edges making up the minimum spanning tree.

Consider what happens when we run Prim's algorithm on the weighted graph from Figure 15-4, as illustrated in Figure 15-9. We start with all last edges set to null (we have not found any yet) and all "best" distances to infinity. For simplicity's sake, we'll break ties in alphabetical order of the nodes.

To begin, we remove the first node A from our unvisited set. We then consider all of A's neighbors and check whether there is a lower-cost edge from A to that neighbor. Given that all our current best distances are infinity, this isn't difficult. We find lower-cost edges for all of A's neighbors: (A, B), (A, C), and (A, D). Figure 15-9(1) shows this new state.

During the second iteration, we find two potential nodes in our unvisited set to use: C and D. Using alphabetical order to break the tie, we select C. We remove C from the unvisited set and add the edge (A, C) to our minimum-cost spanning tree. Examining C's unvisited neighbors, we find better candidate edges to nodes E and G (Figure 15-9(2)).

The next closest node is D. We remove that from our unvisited set and add the edge (A, D) to the minimum-cost spanning tree. When we examine D's unvisited neighbors, we find new, lower-cost edges to both nodes E and F (Figure 15-9(3)). Our best candidate edge to node E now originates from node D instead of node C.

The algorithm progresses through the remaining nodes in our unvisited set. Next, we visit node F, adding the edge (D, F), as shown in Figure 15-9(4). Then, as shown in Figure 15-9(5), we add node E and edge (D, E). The algorithm completes by adding nodes H, B, and G in that order. At each step, we add the corresponding best edge seen so far: (F, H), (F, B), and (C, G). The final three steps are shown in Figure 15-9(6), Figure 15-9(7), and Figure 15-9(8), respectively.

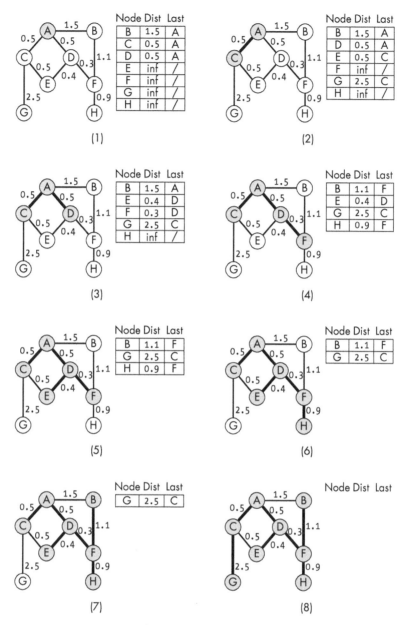

Figure 15-9: An example of Prim's algorithm on a weighted graph

Prim's algorithm doesn't care about the total path lengths from our starting node. We're only interested in the cost of adding the new node to our connected set—the edge weight that will link that node to any other node in the visited set. We are not optimizing for final drive times between nodes, just for minimizing the cost of paving roads or building new bridges.

What if we had broken ties randomly instead of by alphabetical order? When deciding between choosing nodes D or E from our unvisited set after Figure 15-9(2), we could have used either one. If we had chosen E instead of

D, we would have found a lower-cost edge weight linking D into our graph. The algorithm would link in node D through E rather than through A. This means that we can find different minimum-cost spanning trees for the same graph. Multiple different trees may have the same cost. Prim's algorithm only guarantees that we find one of the trees with the minimal cost.

Topological Sort with Kahn's Algorithm

Our final example of a graph algorithm uses the edges of a *directed acyclic graph (DAG)* to sort the nodes. A directed acyclic graph is a graph with directed edges arranged such that the graph contains no *cycles*, or paths that return to the same node, as shown in Figure 15-10. Cycles are critical in real-world road networks. It would be terrible if roads were constructed such that we could get from our apartment to our favorite coffee shop but could never navigate back. Yet this is exactly what happens in an acyclic graph—the path out of any node will never return to that same node.

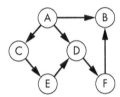

Figure 15-10: A directed acyclic graph

We can use directed edges to indicate an ordering of the nodes. If the graph has an edge from A to B, node A must come before node B. We ordered nodes in this way in our coffee-brewing example at the beginning of the chapter: each node represented a step in the process, and each edge indicated one step's dependency on the next. The person brewing the coffee has to perform a given step before they can perform any of the following steps. These types of dependencies arise throughout both computer science and the rest of life. An algorithm that sorts the nodes in order of their edges is called a *topological sort*.

Computer scientist Arthur B. Kahn developed one approach, now called *Kahn's algorithm*, to perform topological sort on a directed acyclic graph representing events. This algorithm operates by finding the nodes with no incoming edges, removing them from our list of pending nodes, adding them to our sorted list, and then removing the outbound edges from that node. The algorithm repeats until we have added every node to our sorted list. Intuitively, this sort mirrors how we might perform a complex task in the real world. We start with a subtask that we can accomplish—one with no dependencies. We perform that subtask and then chose another to do. Any subtask that requires us to have performed a yet uncompleted task needs to wait on our list until we have finished all its dependencies.

When implementing Kahn's algorithm, we don't need to actually remove edges from our graph. It's sufficient to keep an auxiliary array counting the number of incoming edges to each node and modifying those counts.

```
Kahns(Graph G):
  ❶ Array: sorted = empty array to store result
    Array: count = 0 for each node in G
    Stack: next = empty stack for the next nodes to add

    # Count the incoming edges.
  ❷ FOR EACH node IN G.nodes:
        FOR EACH edge IN node.edges:
            count[edge.to_node] = count[edge.to_node] + 1

    # Find the initial nodes without incoming edges.
  ❸ FOR EACH node IN G.nodes:
        IF count[node.id] == 0:
            next.Push(node)

    # Iteratively process the remaining nodes without
    # incoming connections.
  ❹ WHILE NOT next.IsEmpty():
        Node: current = next.Pop()
        Append current to the end of sorted
      ❺ FOR EACH edge IN current.edges:
            count[edge.to_node] = count[edge.to_node] - 1
          ❻ IF count[edge.to_node] == 0:
                next.Push(G.nodes[edge.to_node])

    return sorted
```

The code starts by creating several helper data structures ❶, including an array to hold the sorted list of nodes (sorted), an array storing the count of incoming edges for each node (count), and a stack of the next node to add to sorted (next). The code uses a pair of nested FOR loops over the nodes (outer loop) and each node's edges (inner loop) to count the number of incoming edges for each node ❷. Then a FOR loop over the count array finds nodes that have no incoming edges and inserts them into next ❸.

The code then uses a WHILE loop to process the next stack until it is empty ❹. During each iteration, the code pops a node off the stack and adds it to the end of the sorted array. A FOR loop iterates over the node's edges and reduces the count (effectively removing the incoming edge) for each neighbor ❺. Any neighbor with an incoming count of zero is added to next ❻. Finally, the code returns the array of sorted nodes.

If our graph does contain cycles, our sorted list will be incomplete. We may want to add an additional check at the end of the function to test that the number of elements in our sorted list equals the number of nodes in the graph.

Consider running this algorithm on the graph from Figure 15-10, as is illustrated in Figure 15-11. We start off by counting the number of incoming edges (shown as the number adjacent to each node) and determining that node A is the only node without any incoming edges (Figure 15-11(1)). Kahn's algorithm then adds A to the sorted list and removes its outgoing edges (by decreasing the corresponding counts), as shown in Figure 15-11(2).

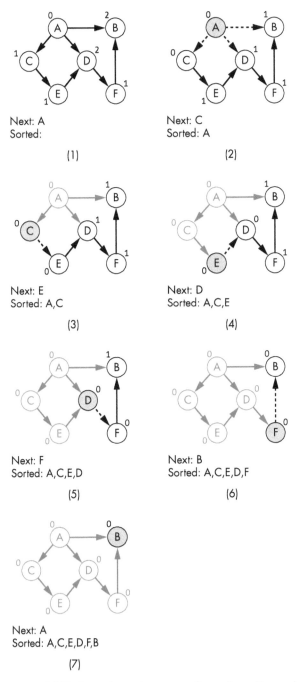

Figure 15-11: A topological sort on a directed acyclic graph

We continue the algorithm on node C (Figure 15-11(3)), which no longer has any incoming edges. We removed the only such edge when we processed node A. We remove C from our list of nodes under consideration (our stack next), remove its edges from the graph, and add it to the end of our sorted list. In the process, we've left node E without any incoming neighbors. E goes onto our stack.

The sort progresses through the remainder of the list. While processing node E, we remove the last incoming edges to node D, making it the next up for the algorithm (Figure 15-11(4)). The sort then adds D, then F, then B to our sorted list as shown in Figure 15-11(5), Figure 15-11(6), and Figure 15-11(7), respectively.

Kahn's algorithm presents an example of both the usefulness of directed edges in a graph and how we can design an algorithm to operate on them. The directionality of the edges further constrains how we explore nodes.

Why This Matters

Graphs are pervasive throughout computer science. Their structure allows them to mirror a large variety of real-world phenomena, from streets to social or computer networks to sets of complex tasks. Graphs are useful for tasks like path planning and determining the order in which to compile a program's source code. There are a myriad of algorithms designed to operate over these data structures, performing such tasks as searching the graph, determining the minimum spanning tree, or determining the maximum flow through a graph. We could devote an entire book to this single vastly impactful data structure.

For the purposes of this chapter, however, we focus on the tight coupling between the structure of the data and the algorithms that operate on it. The graph structure of data drives new problems, such as finding the minimum spanning tree, and thus new algorithms. In turn, the algorithms use the graph structure of the data, traversing the edges and exploring from node to node. This interplay demonstrates the importance of understanding the structure of data when defining both problems and new solutions.

CONCLUSION

Throughout this book, we examined a range of different data structures, how they impact the algorithms that use them, and whether they can aid us in our search for coffee. We showed how the organization of the data can lead to significant decreases in computational cost or changes to an algorithm's behavior. We looked at the tradeoffs between different representations and why they matter. In doing so, we tried to provide an intuitive foundation for how to think about data structures.

Understanding each data structure's motivation, construction, uses, and tradeoffs is critical in order to use them in the development of efficient solutions. If you randomly choose a data structure that looks "good enough," you can run into worst-case scenarios and terrible performance. Below we revisit some core themes from the preceding chapters in order to highlight some of the questions that every computer science practitioner should ask when selecting a data structure.

What Is the Impact of the Data's Structure?

Starting with binary search in Chapter 2, we saw how adding even a small amount of structure to the data can greatly impact the efficiency of algorithms. Structure within the data allows us to efficiently access values, aggregate computations, or prune out regions of the search space. As in the case of binary search, this structure can be as simple as putting the data in sorted order. This single change allows us to cut the worst-case runtime, changing its relationship to the number of values from linear to logarithmic. Similarly, organizing our coffee pantry can optimize our coffee making experience in different ways—most often in reducing the time needed to make our first cup.

Binary search trees, tries, quadtrees, and k-d trees showed us how to further facilitate pruning during a search. Tree-based data structures provide an explicit branching organization that allows us to prune out large regions of the search space with simple tests. We encode the bounds of the data into the structure of the trees and the nodes themselves. Further, the branching nature of the data allows us to clearly visualize the question we ask at each level: "Given bounds on the points lying below this node in a tree, could the point of interest be in this subtree?"

Even if we don't actively optimize the data's organization for the algorithm at hand, its arrangement can profoundly impact the behavior and efficiency of our algorithms, as stacks and queues demonstrate. Switching from a stack to a queue, for example, moves a search from depth-first to breadth-first. In the extreme case, the structure of the data requires the development of completely new algorithmic approaches: graphs' connection-based structure drives a range of new algorithms to search, sort, and perform other computations.

Do We Need Dynamic Data Structures?

Dynamic data structures dramatically increase the flexibility and adaptability of our approaches. Using these structures means we're no longer constrained to preallocating blocks of memory that may turn out to be too small for the task at hand. Instead, we can link locations throughout the memory with pointers, allowing our data structures to grow and shrink as necessary. Most importantly, dynamic data structures allow us to continually grow our coffee log and store multiple coffee shop locations in our geographic grid cells.

Dynamic data structures provide the foundation for some of the most exciting, interesting, and powerful algorithms in computer science. Almost every data structure described in this book takes advantage of pointers (or a related linkage) to organize the data across different blocks of memory. We used pointers to link the nodes in a binary search tree, create linked lists in both our grid cells and hash table bins, and represent the very structure of graphs.

The tradeoff for this power and flexibility is additional complexity when accessing the data. In an array, we can look up any item given its index. However, this direct approach doesn't work once pointers are involved. Our search for a particular piece of data must follow the chain of pointers through the memory, whether across the nodes of a linked list, down the nodes in a tree, or across the nodes in a graph. Depending on the arrangement of these pointers (linked list versus search tree), we may make the operations more or less efficient for the task at hand. We always need to understand how the algorithms will use the structure. It's not enough just to buy a piece of fancy coffee-making equipment; we need to understand how to use it.

What Is the Amortized Cost?

When considering whether to use any data structure, it's important to take into account both the cost of constructing the data structure and the savings it will enable. Sorting an array or constructing a binary search tree can be more expensive than scanning through the data to find a single value. It's almost always the case that searching once through each data point is more efficient than constructing an auxiliary data structure. Yet the math changes as soon as we move beyond a single search.

Sorted arrays, binary search trees, and other data structures are useful because they reduce the cost of *all* future searches. If we pay a one-time $N\log_2(N)$ cost to sort an array of integers, we can then perform as many $\log_2(N)$ binary searches as we want. We win because we amortize the cost of sorting the data over many future searches. In the same way, sorting cartons of milk in our refrigerator by expiration date can save us precious seconds during retrieval.

How Can We Adapt Data Structures to a Specific Problem?

Basic data structures provide not only a set of tools that are useful in their own right but also a foundation on which to build more adaptive and specialized approaches. With the trie, we examined how to extend the branching structure of the binary search tree to a higher branching factor that enables efficient search over strings. We saw how linked lists provide a second level of flexibility to handle collisions in a hash table or multiple items in a grid cell.

Spatial data structures provide an excellent example of our ability to adapt, combine, and refine data structures. Combining the spatial partitioning of grids with a tree-based structure gives us the adaptive structure of a quadtree. However, both grids and quadtrees break down in higher dimensions. We saw how k-d trees adapt spatial data structures to split along a single dimension at each branch, not only helping the structure scale to higher dimensions but also improving its pruning power. As we consider new coffee-related problems, such as matching logos or optimizing the parameters of our brewing equipment, we should reexamine and potentially adapt the approaches in our toolbox to the specifics of the problem.

What Are the Memory vs. Runtime Tradeoffs?

The tradeoff of memory and runtime is a classic consideration in computer science. We can often significantly decrease the cost of an algorithm by pre-computing and storing additional data. Heaps allow us to efficiently find and extract the minimal (or maximal) element in a list, either within search algorithms or as an auxiliary data structure. The tradeoff is the cost of the heap itself. We use extra memory in a linear relationship to the size of the data we want to store. Similarly, by using extra memory to build a quadtree or k-d tree, we can drastically decrease the runtime of future nearest-neighbor searches.

Even within data structures, this tradeoff holds. We can decrease the collision rate in a hash table by increasing its size. Storing additional information in a linked list allows us to implement a skip list and realize better average performance for searches. Similarly, precomputing the bounds of spatial tree nodes and storing them in the node may allow us to more efficiently test whether we can prune a node.

It is critical to understand these tradeoffs and adapt them to a given project's environment. Is the video game you are writing going to run on a personal computer, mobile device, or large server in a data center? Low memory environments might call for different approaches than high memory environments. The size of our coffee pantry will impact not only the total amount of coffee we can store but also whether adding brightly colored dividers is worth it. In a large pantry—such as a bedroom converted to a storage area, perhaps—the dividers might help us find coffee faster. In a small pantry, such as the kitchen cabinet, they might just cost us precious shelf space.

How Can We Tune Our Data Structure?

Some data structures have parameters that greatly impact the performance of operations. The performance of grids on a nearest-neighbor search is highly dependent on the number and granularity of the grid cells. Similarly, the size parameter k of B-trees allows us to adapt the size of each node to our local memory. These parameters almost always depend on the context in which we use the data structure. There is no one perfect setting.

It is important to understand how a data structure's parameters impact performance and how they depend on the specifics of the problem. In some cases, we can analytically determine what parameter to use. For example, we can choose the size parameter k for a B-tree using information about the size of memory blocks on the device where our code will run. We choose k so that a full B-tree node fits snuggly in the memory block, allowing us to retrieve the maximum amount of data with a single access.

Other times, we may need to empirically test different parameters on real data. One simple approach is to use the data with a range of parameter settings and see which one performs best.

How Does Randomization Impact Expected Behavior?

When examining binary search trees and hash tables, we noted that both data structures' worst-case performance could degrade to linear time. If we insert sorted items into a binary search tree or choose a bad hash function for the data, we effectively end up with linked lists. The performance of our data structures isn't guaranteed to be optimal under all conditions but depends on the data itself. Sometimes the best we can do is improve expected (or average case) runtime.

Understanding the possibility of extreme performance is critical to choosing and tuning the best data structure for your problem. When choosing the parameters of a hash table, we want to select a table size large enough to lower the probability of collisions while avoiding wasted memory. More critical is the choice of hash function, which, for hash tables, requires us to understand the distribution of keys. If the keys themselves have structure, such as consisting only of even numbers, we need to pick a hash function that is robust to that structure. Similarly, if we are organizing a conference for coffee lovers whose last name starts with K, the registration table shouldn't partition attendees by the first letter of their last name.

We can mitigate the impact of pathologically bad data somewhat by randomizing the data structure itself. If we are always adding data into a binary search tree in sorted order, we effectively end up with a linked list. Skip lists provide a technique for intentionally injecting randomness into the level of our list nodes to provide, on average, logarithmic running times. Randomization isn't a cure-all, though. Skip lists may choose bad heights by chance. In the worst case, like linked lists, skip lists' performance degrades to be linear in the size of the data. However, the odds that they do so are small, and we can expect them to perform well on average, even in the face of pathologically bad data.

Why This Matters

There is no one perfect data structure in computer science. It would be fantastic if we could point to a single data structure and say, "Always use X," but unfortunately, it's not that simple. All data structures come with their own tradeoffs of complexity, performance, memory usage, and accuracy.

Throughout this book, we examined a sampling of different data structures, their tradeoffs, and how they could impact algorithms. Our coverage was far from exhaustive; there's a wide range of data structures further optimized for individual algorithms, problems, or domains. For example, red-black trees provide a self-balancing extension of binary search trees, while metric trees provide a different approach to spatial partitioning for higher-dimensional data. Both these approaches, and the hundreds of other impressive data structures out there, come with their own sets of tradeoffs and optimal use cases. We barely scratched the surface of the rich and complex world of data structures.

This book aimed to encourage you to think carefully about how to store and organize your data. As much as specific programming languages or clever algorithms, data structures can have a material impact on the performance, accuracy, and complexity of your programs. It's important for all computer science practitioners to understand not only the specifics of individual data structures but also how those data structures function in the broader context of the problem they are trying to solve.

Especially if coffee is involved.

INDEX

floating-point, 2
Floor, 17
Fredkin, Edward, 78

G

graph, 50–54, 247–264
    adjacency lists, 250–251
        Edge, 250
        Graph, 250
        Node, 250
    adjacency matrix, 251
    best-first search, 252
    breadth-first search (*see* breadth-first search)
    cycle, 260
    DAG, 260
    directed acyclic graph, 260
    edge, 248–249
        directed, 248–249
        undirected, 248
        weighted, 249
    minimum-cost spanning tree, 256
    minimum spanning tree, 256
    node, 51, 248
    search, 251–252
    shortest distance path, 252–256
    topological sort, 260
    See also depth-first search;
        Dijkstra's algorithm; Kahn's
        algorithm; Prim's algorithm
grid, 119–138
    bin, 119
    bin width, 120, 134–135
    cell, 119
    deletion, 122–124
    Grid, 120
    GridDelete, 123
    GridInsert, 122
    GridPoint, 121
    insertion, 122
    MinDistToBin, 126
    search, 124–134
        expanding search, 128–134
        GridCheckBin, 131
        GridLinearScanNN, 127
        GridSearchExpanding, 132
        linear scan over bins, 127–128
        pruning, 124–127

tuning, 138
using linked lists, 121

H

hash function, 174–175, 183–184
    collision, 176
    division method, 174
    hash value, 174
    Horner's method, 184
    StringHash, 184
    use in a hash table (*see* hash table)
    use in Bloom filters (*see* Bloom
        filter: hash functions)
hash table, 174–185
    bin, 174
    chaining, 176–179
        HashTable, 176
        HashTableInsert, 177
        HashTableLookup, 178
        HashTableRemove, 178
        ListNode, 176
    collision, 176–183
    hash value, 174
    linear probing, 179–183
        HashTable, 180
        HashTableEntry, 180
        HashTableInsert, 181
        HashTableLookup, 182
    use in a cache. (*see* cache: LRU)
    use in search algorithms, 184–185
    using a linked list, 176–179
hash value, 174
heap, 96–112
    adding elements, 98–101
    Heap, 98
    HeapInsert, 99, 104
    heap property, 96
    HeapRemoveMax, 103
    max heap property, 96
    min heap, 106–108
    min heap property, 106
    removing max element, 101–104
    root, 97
    UpdateValue, 105
    updating priorities, 105
    use in heapsort, 108–111
    using an array, 97–108
    using a tree, 96–108

heap property, 96
heapsort, 108–111
    cost, 111
    HeapSort, 108
Horner's method, 184

I
index (array), 5
insertion sort, 8–10
    InsertionSort, 8
integer, 3

J
Jarník, Vojtěch, 256

K
Kahn, Arthur B., 260
Kahns, 261
Kahn's algorithm, 260–263
k-d tree, 159–169
    BuildKDTree, 166
    ComputeBoundingBox, 165
    construction, 165–168
    deletion, 168–169
    insertion, 168
    internal node, 160
    KDTree, 162
    KDTreeNode, 161
    KDTreeNodeMinDist, 169
    pruning, 169
    RecursiveBuildKDTree, 166
    search, 169
    tight spatial bounds, 163–165
key, 173–174

L
last-in, first-out (LIFO), 44
least recently used cache. See cache: LRU
linear cost, 23, 72
linear scan, 14–16, 114–116
    LinearScan, 14
linked list, 26, 30–39
    access, 32–33
    deletion, 37–39
    end of list, 31, 37
    head, 32, 36, 37, 38, 46
    insertion, 34–37
    LinkedListDelete, 38

LinkedListInsert, 36
LinkedListInsertAfter, 35
LinkedListLookUp, 32
LinkedListNode, 31
    next pointer, 31
    as a queue, 49–50
    as a stack, 46–47
    node, 31
    use in a priority queue, 95
    use in a skip list. See skip list
    use in grids, 121
    use in hash tables (see hash table:
        chaining)
local storage, 187
logarithmic cost, 23, 71, 101, 103, 210,
    222
LRU cache. See cache: LRU

M
Manhattan distance, 130
max heap. See heap
max heap property, 96
McCreight, Edward, 199
min heap, 106–108
    MinHeapInsert, 106
    min heap property, 106
    MinHeapRemoveMin, 107
min heap property, 106
minimum-cost spanning tree, 256
minimum spanning tree, 256

N
nearest neighbor search, 114–138
    candidate nearest neighbor, 115
    linear scan, 114–116
    LinearScanClosestNeighbor, 116
    non-spatial data, 136–138
    spatial data, 116–118
    using a grid (see grid)
    using a k-d tree, 169
    using a quadtree, 150–159
Nil, 30
None, 30
null, 30

O
object, 3–4
octtree, 159

RESOURCES

Visit *https://nostarch.com/data-structures-fun-way* for errata and more information.

More no-nonsense books from **NO STARCH PRESS**

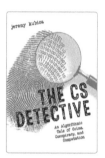

THE CS DETECTIVE
An Algorithmic Tale of Crime,
Conspiracy, and Computation
BY JEREMY KUBICA
256 PP., $17.95
ISBN 978-1-59327-749-9

LEARN TO CODE BY SOLVING
PROBLEMS
A Python Programming Primer
BY DANIEL ZINGARO
336 PP., $34.99
ISBN 978-1-7185-0132-4

THE MISSING README
A Guide for the New Software Engineer
BY CHRIS RICCOMINI
AND DMITRIY RYABOY
288 PP., $24.99
ISBN 978-1-7185-0183-6

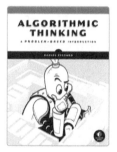

ALGORITHMIC THINKING
A Problem-Based Introduction
BY DANIEL ZINGARO
408 PP., $49.95
ISBN 978-1-7185-0080-8

THINK LIKE A PROGRAMMER
An Introduction to
Creative Problem Solving
BY V. ANTON SPRAUL
256 PP., $34.95
ISBN 978-1-59327-424-5

THE RECURSIVE BOOK OF
RECURSION
Ace the Coding Interview
with Python and JavaScript
BY AL SWEIGART
328 PP., $39.99
ISBN 978-1-7185-0202-4

PHONE:
800.420.7240 OR
415.863.9900

EMAIL:
SALES@NOSTARCH.COM
WEB:
WWW.NOSTARCH.COM

Never before has the world relied so heavily on the Internet to stay connected and informed. That makes the Electronic Frontier Foundation's mission—to ensure that technology supports freedom, justice, and innovation for all people—more urgent than ever.

For over 30 years, EFF has fought for tech users through activism, in the courts, and by developing software to overcome obstacles to your privacy, security, and free expression. This dedication empowers all of us through darkness. With your help we can navigate toward a brighter digital future.

LEARN MORE AND JOIN EFF AT EFF.ORG/NO-STARCH-PRESS